MW00757447

EMOTION AND TRAUMATIC CONFLICT

EMOTION AND TRAUMATIC CONFLICT

Reclaiming Healing in Education

Michalinos Zembylas

OXFORD
UNIVERSITY PRESS

OXFORD
UNIVERSITY PRESS

Oxford University Press is a department of the University of
Oxford. It furthers the University's objective of excellence in research,
scholarship, and education by publishing worldwide.

Oxford New York
Auckland Cape Town Dar es Salaam Hong Kong Karachi
Kuala Lumpur Madrid Melbourne Mexico City Nairobi
New Delhi Shanghai Taipei Toronto

With offices in
Argentina Austria Brazil Chile Czech Republic France Greece
Guatemala Hungary Italy Japan Poland Portugal Singapore
South Korea Switzerland Thailand Turkey Ukraine Vietnam

Published in the United States of America by
Oxford University Press
198 Madison Avenue, New York, NY 10016

Library of Congress Cataloging-in-Publication Data
Zembylas, Michalinos.
Emotion and traumatic conflict : reclaiming healing in education / Michalinos Zembylas.
pages cm
Includes bibliographical references and index.
ISBN 978-0-19-998276-9 (alk. paper)
1. Affective education. 2. Psychic trauma in children. 3. Emotional problems of
children. 4. Emotions—Study and teaching. 5. Conflict management—Study and
teaching. 6. Peace—Study and teaching. 7. Educational psychology. 8. Multicultural
education. 9. Education—Social aspects. 10. Education—Political aspects. I. Title.
LB1072.Z46 2015
370.15′34—dc23
2015002129

9 8 7 6 5 4 3 2 1
Printed in the United States of America
on acid-free paper

History, despite its wrenching pain
Cannot be unlived, but if faced
With courage, need not be lived again.

—MAYA ANGELOU, *"On the Pulse of Morning"*

Losing too is still ours; and even forgetting
still has a shape in the kingdom of transformation.
When something's let go of, it circles; and though we are
rarely the center
of the circle, it draws around us its unbroken, marvelous
curve.

—RAINER MARIA RILKE, *"Losing"*

One should neither laugh nor cry at the world, but understand it.

—SPINOZA

CONTENTS

ACKNOWLEDGMENTS

I am privileged to have many good friends and colleagues who have supported me in numerous ways while I was writing this book. I acknowledge the contributions of Zvi Bekerman, Monique Eckmann, Claire McGlynn, Rob Hattam, Phillip Hammack, Tony Gallagher, Constadina Charalambous, Panayiota Charalambous, Helena Flam, Andre Keet, Jochen Kleres, Vivienne Bozalek, Dorothee Holscher, Jonathan Jansen, Brenda Leibowitz, Ronelle Carolissen, Zeus Leonardo, Sharon Chubbuck, Lynn Fendler, J.C. van der Merwe, Maija Lanas, all of whom have been exceptional intellectual partners in discussing many of the issues raised in this book.

In addition I thank Petros Pashiardis, Athena Michaelidou, Panayiota Kendeou, Charalambos Vrasidas, Sotiris Themistocleous, Dimitris Hadjisofoklis, Stalo Lesta, Galatia Agathocleous, Elena Papamichael, Maria Hamali, Andreas Pavlakis, and Stavros Stavrou for their friendship and support. I have also benefited enormously from discussions with audiences at the Max Planck Institute for Human Development (Berlin), Stellenbosch University, University of the Western Cape, Queens University Belfast, Hebrew University Jerusalem, Marquette University, Oulu University, University of South Australia, and University of the Free State, where I was privileged to have been given the opportunity to present early versions of this work. I have also presented versions of this work at conferences and much of the material in this book took shape in various journals. I am thankful to have had the opportunity to re-work and enrich this material. Thanks to the Open University of Cyprus for its funding to conduct the research on which this book is based. I was also lucky to have expert editorial assistance from Abby Gross, who supported me from the very beginning of this endeavor.

My greatest debt is to my family—my wife Galatia and my children Orestis and Mariza—who are always patient and loving and who tolerate the (difficult) time I spend away from them.

PERMISSIONS

Portions of this volume have been adapted from other works by Michalinos Zembylas.

Chapter 3: Zembylas, M. (2011). Investigating the emotional geographies of exclusion in a multicultural school. *Emotion, Space and Society, 4*, 151–159.

Chapter 4: Zembylas, M. (2010). Racialization/ethnicization of school emotional spaces: The politics of resentment. *Race Ethnicity & Education, 13*(2), 253–270.

Chapter 5: Zembylas, M. (2010). Children's construction and experience of racism and nationalism in Greek-Cypriot primary schools. *Childhood, 17*(3), 312–328.

Chapter 6: Zembylas, M. (2010). Teachers' emotional experiences of growing diversity and multiculturalism in schools and the prospects of an ethic of discomfort. *Teaching and Teachers: Theory and Practice, 16*(6), 703–716; and Zembylas, M. (2010). Greek-Cypriot teachers' constructions of Turkish-speaking children's identities: critical race theory and education in a conflict-ridden society. *Ethnic and Racial Studies, 33*(8), 1372–1391.

Chapter 7: Zembylas, M. (2010). Negotiating co-existence in divided societies: Teachers' and students' perspectives at a shared school in Cyprus. *Research Papers in Education, 25*(4), 433–455.

Chapter 8: Zembylas, M. (2010). Pedagogic struggles to enhance inclusion and reconciliation in a divided community. *Ethnography and Education, 5*(3), 277–292.

Chapter 9: Zembylas, M. (2013). The emotional complexities of "our" and "their" loss: The vicissitudes of teaching about/for empathy in a conflicting society. *Anthropology & Education Quarterly, 44*(1), 19–37.

Chapter 10: Zembylas, M. (2012). The affective (re)production of refugee representations through educational policies and practices: Reconceptualizing the role of emotion for peace education in a divided country. *International Review of Education, 58*(4), 465–480.

Chapter 11: Zembylas, M. (2012). Citizenship education and human rights in sites of ethnic conflict: Toward critical pedagogies of compassion and shared fate. *Studies in Philosophy and Education, 31*, 553–567.

Chapter 12: Zembylas, M. (2011). Reclaiming nostalgia: Counter-memory, aporetic mourning, and critical pedagogy. *Discourse: Studies in the Cultural Politics of Education, 32*(5), 641–655.

INTRODUCTION AND THEORETICAL POSITIONING

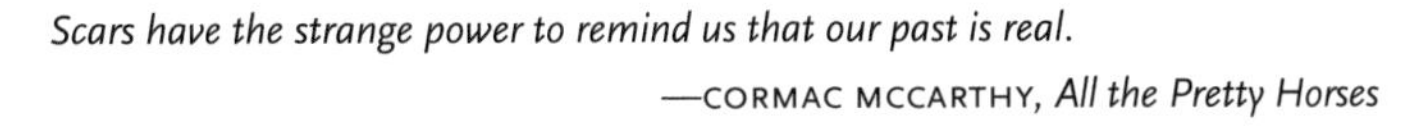

Scars have the strange power to remind us that our past is real.

—CORMAC MCCARTHY, *All the Pretty Horses*

As my sufferings mounted I soon realized that there were two ways in which I could respond to my situation—either to react with bitterness or seek to transform the suffering into a creative force. I decided to follow the latter course.

—MARTIN LUTHER KING, JR.

Healing is a matter of time, but it is sometimes also a matter of opportunity.

—HIPPOCRATES

1 INTRODUCTION

Traumatic events, such as wars, genocides, and terrorist attacks, generate powerful *emotions*—most notably, fear, grief, anger, shame, resentment, and hatred (Hutchison & Bleiker, 2008). These emotions fuel people's perceptions and actions and make conflicts, wars, and genocides imaginable (Des Forges, 1999). Emotions, in this manner, become important components of historical consciousness and ethnohistorical practices in conflicted societies, and they strongly shape collective narratives, identities, and memories. In fact, some theorists (e.g. Retzinger & Scheff, 2000) argue that it is often these powerful emotions, rather than material interests, that pose the most serious obstacles to peacebuilding, healing, and reconciliation efforts.

The focus on the role of emotion as a site of conflict and peace illuminates the ways in which the relation between collective narratives and individual experiences is fundamental to the formation of ethnicized and racialized groups and communities. Scholars in sociology, anthropology, history, and cultural studies have pointed to the lack of research on how emotions contribute to creating ethnicized and racialized identities and communities (Ahmed, 2004; Bennett, 2005; Scheff, 1994). There is strong evidence of the ways in which emotions accompany historical matters in societies (Svašek, 2008), but there have been few sustained investigations, especially in the field of education, concerning how and with what implications emotions are mobilized and performed in schools as a crucial site of power, control, belonging, and identification. In particular, there has been limited research on how emotions of trauma may be addressed through the body of work that is known as *peace education*,[1] and most notably how pedagogical tools, strategies, and practices that are conscious of the role of emotion make a constructive contribution to what has become known as "critical peace education" (Bajaj, 2008; Bajaj & Brantmeier, 2011; Brantmeier, 2011; Trifonas & Wright, 2012; Wulf, 1974). Briefly speaking (I will come back to this in chapter 2), critical peace education is understood here as the approach to peace education that pays attention to issues of structural inequalities and aims at cultivating a sense of transformative agency (both individual and collective) to advance peacebuilding. In general, the word *critical*—which is prominent in this book—denotes a sustained commitment to highlight issues of inequality, injustice, and the possibilities of personal and social transformation, and to interrogate assumptions about these issues that often are taken for granted.

As someone who has lived for most of his life in a conflicted and divided society that perpetuated animosity toward the "other," I was troubled for years in my attempts to explore how education—which seemed to have an important role in cultivating such negative emotions—might contribute to peacebuilding, healing, and reconciliation. I grew up in Cyprus in the 1970s, in the aftermath of the "Turkish invasion" (as known by Greek Cypriots; the "Peace Operation" as it is known among Turkish Cypriots) that took place in the summer of 1974 and divided my country and its population; Greek Cypriots were forced to move to the southern part of the country, while Turkish Cypriots found refuge to the north. These traumatic events resulted in many thousands of deaths, the creation of many more thousands of refugees, the loss or destruction of property, as well as newly enclaved communities, missing persons, and the ongoing division of my country. When I attended elementary school the theme of the *Den Xehno* (I don't forget) campaign became prominent in the public life of the Greek-Cypriot community. Pictures of the Greek-Cypriots' occupied places in the north decorated classrooms, homes, and public buildings. The goal of the campaign was to teach the young generations that the Turkish invasion should never be forgotten, and that Greek Cypriots should be ready, if necessary, to fight and liberate our occupied land. The depiction of the Turkish and Turkish-Cypriot communities as cruel, insensitive, and barbarian was total and overwhelming. The daily reminders in my world were powerful: *we* were the victims, who suffered tremendous trauma and loss; *they* were the perpetrators, who committed unspeakable atrocities and barbarisms against our community. The emotions associated with these representations have become important components of Greek-Cypriot historical consciousness and educational practice, and over the years they have strongly shaped collective narratives, identities, and memories about "us" (Greek Cypriots) and "them" (Turkish Cypriots).

A number of important questions can be raised in efforts to deepen the understanding of the entanglement of emotions, historical consciousness, and peace education: Do the emotional responses of students and teachers to traumatic conflict constitute insurmountable obstacles in peace education efforts? How do hegemonic narratives shape the emotions of ethnic identity and collective memory, and what can be done pedagogically to transform the powerful influence of such narratives and emotions? Can peace education efforts that foreground emotion in critical ways become a productive pedagogical intervention in conflicted societies? My ethnographic research in Cyprus over the last ten years has taught me how teachers and students remain firmly emotionally rooted in the hegemonic narratives of their own community, even when these emotional practices are challenged and clearer alternatives to the reigning ones are being considered. At the same time, however, I have witnessed inspiring examples of pedagogical practices through which small but powerful transformations have taken place.

At stake in these struggles and small transformations is a tense and open-ended process of *politicization* of emotions. More often than not, emotions of traumatic conflict are appropriated by social and political institutions, such as schools, to justify collective narratives and ideologies about the victims and perpetrators of a conflict (Bekerman & Zembylas, 2012; Zembylas, 2008a, 2010b). A classic example of how emotions of trauma can be politically appropriated, not only in society at large (Bourke, 2006; Furedi, 2006; Robin, 2004) but also in schools (Giroux, 2003), is the case of "fear." Schools seem to be particularly successful in passing down fear (Fisher, 2006). Fear—e.g. of the "evil other" who is deemed responsible for unspeakable trauma against "us"—works both at the psychic level and the sociopolitical level, and it structures how the "other" is viewed through unconscious feelings, expectations, anxieties, and defenses. The emotion of fear, just like hatred and resentment, *does* something extraordinary, as Ahmed (2004) explains; it establishes a distance between bodies that are read as "similar" and those that are considered to be "different." In other words, fear is politicized by establishing boundaries between "us" (the "good") and "them" (the "evil"); the others are fearsome—and thus it is easier to dehumanize them—because in our thinking they are constructed as a danger to our very existence.

In general, much research in conflicted societies provides evidence of how schools stimulate prejudices and stereotypes and contribute to the normalization of emotions of trauma for political purposes (Bekerman & McGlynn, 2007; McGlynn, Zembylas, Bekerman, & Gallagher, 2009). Educators in such societies must confront the following question: How can the ideological appropriation of emotions of conflict be critically challenged, when schools themselves often contribute to this appropriation? To put it another way: Which pedagogical theories and practices could be used to undermine the ideological appropriation of emotions in schools within conflicted societies? This challenge is at the heart of this book.

My goal is to create a space at the intersection of multiple discussions on emotion, conflict, and critical peace education. I draw on academic literature that has attempted to highlight the possibilities and the pitfalls of considering the role of peace education in healing and reconciliation. These multiple discussions do not in themselves render this book distinctive. What distinguishes this book is how it approaches emotion and the role of education in peacebuilding, healing, and reconciliation. Drawing from psychoanalytic and sociopolitical perspectives of trauma and emotion (Ahmed, 2004, 2005; Kristeva, 1993, 2000), my concern is to highlight the pedagogical practices with which emotions can be engaged as critical and transformative forces in peace education. While the emotions of trauma are a very real, and a very devastating feature of life in conflict and post-conflict societies, I argue that educators can work toward peacebuilding, healing, and reconciliation through devising critical pedagogies that do not remain stuck in trauma or stay too firmly grounded in such pairings as oppressor/oppressed, master/slave, and power/freedom (Jansen, 2009).

The overarching concept on which I build my theorization in this book, one that provides the common thread that connects the multiple discussions on emotion, conflict, and critical peace education, is the notion of *critical emotional praxis* (Zembylas, 2008a, 2012a). I have been working on this concept during the last few years as a theoretical and practical tool that identifies patterns in our emotional, historical, and material lives, and that helps us realize how these patterns are formed and what their consequences are for maintaining the status quo or motivating action for change. The concept of critical emotional praxis is further theorized in this book (see chapters 2 and 13, in particular) as a part of the process of developing and sustaining pedagogies of critical peace education in schools. In particular, this book examines how the notion of critical emotional praxis may serve as a construct for building critical insights into teaching and for learning about traumatic conflict, healing, and reconciliation in schools. The challenges and prospects of critical emotional praxis as such a tool in critical peace education are shown through detailed evidence from my ethnographic research in Cyprus conducted between 2007 and 2011. My purpose, then, is not simply to show the political appropriation of emotions of traumatic conflict in schools and its consequences within a particular setting (Cyprus) but also to suggest how critical emotional praxis and its related theorization may provide informed insight into efforts that deal constructively with emotional tensions, dilemmas, and difficulties and formulate critical responses to peace education efforts.

I begin with a brief presentation of the sociopolitical, historical, and educational realities of the setting in which I have conducted my research. This is helpful as a basis for understanding the wider context of the emotional complexities and dilemmas that are involved in the educational process. I then go on to say a few things about the role of education in situations of conflict in general and I describe my research methodology and the structure of the book. The next chapter (chapter 2), which completes Part I, delves deeper into the theoretical framework of the book. Parts II and III contain a number of empirical case studies; although these case studies come from a particular place, they raise issues that are believed to be relevant to other conflicted settings. Part IV concludes the study with more theoretical transversal discussions that emphasize what happens when we take seriously the role of emotions in educational settings in countries fraught with traumatic conflict.

My goal is to assess the prospects and challenges of pedagogies that take a critical stance toward the politicization of trauma in schools and to seek openings through which to promote peacebuilding, healing, and reconciliation. Now let's begin with the background of the conflict in Cyprus that would help readers who may be unfamiliar with its historical context.

The Cyprus Conflict

The "Cyprus Conflict" (also referred to as the "Cyprus Problem" or the "Cyprus Issue"), as it has become known in the international political arena, refers to the clash between Greek and Turkish Cypriots in the island. The question of who has the longer presence on the island is one of the most crucial issues in this dispute, because the Greek and Turkish communities in Cyprus make claims to ownership of the territory. Greek Cypriots trace their presence to the end of the second millennium BC with the Mycenaean colonization of the island; Turkish Cypriots base their claims on their centuries-long presence on the island, for which Turkish soldiers have shed their blood (Bryant, 2004). The Ottomans differed from previous rulers of Cyprus (e.g. the Venetians, the Franks, the Arabs) in that they brought with them large numbers of settlers. That strategy is thought to have been the first large-scale settlement of Cyprus since the influx of Greeks during Mycenaean times. As a result of the two periods of settlement, nearly all areas on the island came to have mixed Greco-Turkish populations (Morag, 2004). The Ottomans ruled Cyprus until 1878, when the island was leased to Britain. The Muslims who stayed on the island later formed what became known as the Turkish-Cypriot community.

In 1925, after the fall of the Ottoman Empire, Cyprus was annexed by the United Kingdom and was made a Crown Colony. During the period of Ottoman rule, the Greek Orthodox Church had acquired considerable administrative power; however, following annexation, the Church was stripped of that power, but it assumed the role of *Ethnarchy*—that is, the national and religious leadership of the Greek-Cypriot community. In the first half of the twentieth century, there was a gradual rise, first of Greek nationalism and later of Turkish nationalism; both communities in Cyprus began to form strong "motherland" feelings toward Greece and Turkey, respectively (Kizilyürek, 1999a). As Kizilyürek argues, under the influence of Greek and Turkish nationalism, as well as the historical burden of Greco-Turkish warfare, Greek and Turkish Cypriots became antagonistic about the political future of Cyprus. Gradually, there was also a movement of Cypriots away from mixed villages and toward segregated Greek or Turkish villages.

By the mid-1950s, Greek Cypriots (the majority, 80%) started a guerrilla struggle set up by EOKA (Εθνική Οργάνωση Κυπρίων Αγωνιστών—National Organization of Cypriot Fighters) against British colonial rule. This anti-colonial rebellion, however, did not aim toward independence but *enosis*, union with the motherland, Greece. During the same time, Turkish Cypriots (18%), set up TMT (Türk Mukavemet Teşkilati—Turkish Resistance Organization), in an effort to counteract EOKA; TMT aimed at *taksim*, ethnic partition, that is, union of part of the island with the motherland, Turkey. The 1950s was a period of intense interethnic mistrust and fears between Greek Cypriots and Turkish Cypriots. The Zurich-London Agreements of 1959 gave birth to the Republic of Cyprus, a sovereign and independent state. The independence document was drafted by Britain, Greece, and Turkey (who were to act as guarantors of the sovereignty of the new state), leaving both communities' political aspirations unfulfilled.

The two ethnic groups continued to pursue their separate objectives during the 1960s, a decade in which Cyprus witnessed interethnic violence, primarily in the years 1963–64 and 1967 (Attalides, 1979; Calotychos, 1998). By 1964, hundreds of Turkish Cypriots and Greek Cypriots were killed or went missing, presumed dead. These events resulted in the creation of a "Green Line," a dividing line in the capital, Nicosia, to keep the two factions apart; the line was patrolled by a United Nations Peace Keeping Force. During this period, the Turkish Cypriots suffered the greater losses (Kizilyürek, 1999a). Around one fifth of the Turkish-Cypriot population was displaced and moved to areas that gradually became armed enclaves under their control. The enclave period significantly contributed to the further deterioration of relations between the two communities (Morag, 2004). The Turkish Cypriots withdrew from the government and the Cyprus Republic was run exclusively by Greek Cypriots. The time between 1963 and 1974 was a period in which the two communities were drawn further apart; Greek Cypriots experienced economic prosperity and modernization, whereas Turkish Cypriots became completely dependent on Turkey, both economically and culturally.

After Turkey's bombardments of Cyprus in 1967 and the rise of a military junta in Greece during the same year, Greek-Cypriot leaders gradually began to separate their position from union with Greece; in the face of attempts by the Greek junta to dictate politics in Cyprus, the Greek Cypriots sought to preserve the independence of Cyprus (Papadakis, 1998). While armed confrontations between the two communities ceased after 1967, a new conflict, now among Greek Cypriots, began. On one side, there was a paramilitary right-wing organization, EOKA B, which had the support of the Greek junta and aimed for *enosis*; on the other side, there was the president of the Republic, Archbishop Makarios, and his supporters, who wanted to solve intercommunal problems within the framework of an independent Cyprus. With the support of the Greek junta, EOKA B staged a coup in 1974 against President Makarios. Turkey reacted by invading Cyprus, bringing heavy Greek-Cypriot casualties (thousands of dead and missing) and dividing the island, forcing 200,000 Greek Cypriots (one third of the total population) to be displaced from their homeland and move to the south (Hitchens, 1984; Mallinson, 2005). Also, 45,000 Turkish Cypriots (one fourth of the total population) were displaced to the northern side. After the declaration of the "Turkish Republic of Northern Cyprus" in 1983 (considered legally invalid by the U.N. and recognized only by Turkey), there are in effect two rival states in situ (Constantinou & Papadakis, 2001), and they lack any sort of substantial contact. The Turkish government also began a policy of settling Anatolian Turks in villages taken from the Greek Cypriots (Morag, 2004). Over the years the demographic composition in the north has changed, creating what has become known as "the settlers" problem.

After the events of 1974, there have been, on and off, a series of intercommunal negotiations under the auspices of the United Nations, but no agreement has been reached. Also, there have been some (unofficial) positive contacts and bicommunal efforts, organized by civil organizations to promote trust, peaceful coexistence, and reconciliation, but the impact of the civil societies remains quite low (Hadjipavlou, 1993, 2007a). Since the 1974 conflict the Green Line that divides the island separates the two communities and deepens further the status quo, feelings of mistrust, stereotyping, and psychological distancing between Greek and Turkish Cypriots. This decades-long physical and cultural separation has rendered the division in Cyprus almost complete—socially, emotionally, and politically—resulting in what Bryant (2004) described as "ethnic estrangement." Since 1974, ethnic estrangement has also been reinforced by intensive processes of nation-building on both sides, and these activities have heightened the groups' respective "Greekness" and "Turkishness," while constructing the other community as the "ethnic-other" and "arch-enemy" of the collective Self. The contentious issues that form the backbone of the official adversarial narratives in the two communities—such as, for example, the settlers' problem, the militarization of the island, and the violation of human rights—prevent the building of a peace culture based on mutual understanding and respect.

In the spring of 2003, the permission granted by the Turkish-Cypriot side for unfettered access across the Green Line (although with the requirement of showing a passport or identity card) rekindled hopes for a final settlement before the accession of Cyprus into the European Union in May 2004. A few days before the accession, a comprehensive UN proposal for reunification on the basis of a bizonal, bicommunal federation—known as the *Annan Plan*[2]—was put to simultaneous referenda on both sides, but it led to failure, with a 65% "yes" vote by the Turkish Cypriots but a 76% "no" vote by the Greek Cypriots. This failure seems to have strengthened the feeling that no solution is expected any time soon (see Varnava & Faustman, 2009). There are Cypriots from both communities who continue to cross the Green Line for various reasons (Dikomitis, 2005), but there are also those (more than half, according to some estimates) who consistently refuse to do so.

The Role of Education in the Cyprus Conflict

Looking at the history of Cyprus, one can easily find competing discourses of trauma and suffering within both communities. The Greek Cypriots and the Turkish Cypriots construct narratives that are different with respect to how the other is portrayed, but the common themes focus on the victimhood, violence, and historical trauma that one side has inflicted on the other (Kizilyürek, 1999a; Mavratsas, 1998). Greek Cypriots choose to talk about the suffering from the "1974 Turkish invasion," and Turkish Cypriots focus on their suffering in 1963 and the enclave period

The "chosen traumas" (Volkan, 1979; Volkan & Itzkowitz, 1994) of each community are particularly reflected in their educational systems (which have always been segregated). The "negative face" of education (Bush & Saltarelli, 2000) has influenced the conflict in Cyprus and seems to have contributed to the perpetuation of division. There is now ample evidence from various studies that school textbooks and curricula, as well as ceremonies and symbols used in schools of both communities, create dehumanized images of the other in each community and inspire negative stereotypes and hatred (Bryant, 2004; Kizilyürek, 1999b, 2001; Spyrou, 2006; Zembylas, 2008a). For example, it is shown that school textbooks implore students to remember each side's glories and to honor the heroes who fought the other (Papadakis, 2008). There is also ethnographic evidence indicating how individuals as well as organized groups from both communities in Cyprus systematically attempt to nationalize suffering and highlight the need to remember what "the enemy" perpetrated in the past (Loizos, 1998; Sant Cassia, 2005).

In the Greek-Cypriot community, the educational objective of *Den Xehno* [I don't forget] became prominent in the school curriculum in the years after the

Turkish invasion of 1974. This objective aimed at teaching children and youth to preserve memories so that they would never forget the occupied territories and that they would care enough to carry on the struggle to liberate those territories. The most prominent themes of the *Den Xehno* campaign focused on remembrance of the Turkish invasion, the thousands of refugees, the missing, those who live in enclaves in the occupied north, the violation of human rights, and the destruction of ancient Greek archaeological sites in Cyprus. At the elementary school level special textbooks were produced to aid teachers in creating lesson plans on the themes of *Den Xehno* and integrating them into courses such as Greek language, history, geography, music, and the visual arts (Christou, 2006). In general, the other community's perspective was systematically excluded and demonized (Zembylas, 2008a).

In the 1980s and 1990s, *Den Xehno* was manifest in school life through references to the losses of 1974, photographic material from the occupied territories, and commemorations during "occupied territories week" (Christou, 2007). According to Christou, the main task of *Den Xehno* became the production of unlived memories for the younger generations born after 1974. In 2001, the *Den Xehno* rhetoric expanded to "I know, I don't forget, and I struggle," to render explicit both the cognitive ("knowing," "remembering") and the prescriptive aspects of the goal ("struggling"; see Christou, 2006). Today, *Den Xehno* remains an active goal of Greek-Cypriot education, although its patriotic militancy has been softened considerably during the last few years (Christou, 2006).[3]

It is also important to recognize that within the Greek-Cypriot community there has been a long conflict between two political identity-discourses: *Hellenocentrism* (which emphasizes the Greekness of Greek Cypriots and is mainly supported by the political right) and *Cypriocentrism* (which emphasizes the Cypriot identity and is mainly supported by the political left) (Spyrou, 2006). Still, Hellenocentrism has been the norm in Greek-Cypriot education, which classically has promoted the strengthening of the national Greek identity within the Greek-Cypriot educational system, leaving little room for alternative discourses (Papadakis, 2008). Greece also provided educational materials (e.g. textbooks) and other assistance to schools, a tactic that continues to be employed (Persianis, 2006).

In this historical context, then, perhaps it was not surprising that the educational objective promoting "peaceful coexistence" (introduced by a leftist government in 2008 for the first time) stirred intense public and educational debates within the Greek-Cypriot community. In a circular sent out by the Minister of Education and Culture, this educational objective highlighted "the development of a culture of peaceful coexistence, mutual respect, and cooperation between Greek Cypriots and Turkish Cypriots, aiming at getting rid of the occupation and re-unifying our country and our people" (Ministry of Education and Culture, 2008, p. 1). This particular recommendation generated considerable debate and controversy, not only among teachers and teacher organizations, but also among members of Parliament, the government, and the wider Greek-Cypriot society. Among other things, the debate and controversy raised the issue of whether teachers and the educational system as a whole have a right to promote reconciliatory ideas through education while a large part of Cyprus is still occupied by Turkey.

In addition to the political problem in Cyprus, immigration has grown over the last few years, bringing to Cyprus immigrants and labor workers from East Asia, Eastern Europe, the former Soviet Union, and the Middle East; there has also been some internal movement of Turkish Cypriots from the north to the south part of Cyprus, especially after the partial lift of restrictions in movement in 2003. Of the current population, almost 20% are non-Cypriots (Statistical Service of the Republic of Cyprus, 2011). Naturally, the changing profile of the population in the Republic of Cyprus has affected schools and the educational system. In the school year 1995–1996, the percentage of "non-indigenous"[4] students was 4.41%, whereas in 2011–2012 this percentage had risen to almost 12% (Ministry of Education and Culture, 2011). There are now some schools in the Republic of Cyprus where non-indigenous children constitute the large majority (80%-90%) of the school population. As a result, there is a growing number of so-called multicultural schools, those attended by children from various cultures, including children whose parents are migrant workers. Occasionally, there are a few Turkish-speaking children,[5] that is, Roma/Gypsies and Turkish Cypriots who stayed in the south after the war of 1974 or who have moved there recently.

Although policy documents and official curricula of the Republic of Cyprus include strong statements about humanistic ideas and respect for human rights, justice, and peace, in practice non-Greek-Cypriot children are seen as deficient and needing to be assimilated (Panayiotopoulos & Nicolaidou, 2007; Zembylas, 2010a). Although individual teachers and schools are implementing inclusive practices, such practices are not the official policy. The model of intercultural education now being implemented in Cyprus is a mainstreaming program in which language learners attend classrooms with indigenous Greek-speaking children. There are a number of schools that have become part of a Zone of Educational Priority (ZEP) (following the example of the French Zones Educatif Priorité, and less of the Educational Action Zones in England). The ZEP networks have some schools with high numbers of non-indigenous students, but this is not the rule; a number of other schools in Cyprus enroll high numbers of non-indigenous students but are not in a ZEP network. Students in ZEP schools receive additional help—such as extra hours for assisting non-indigenous students to learn the language—yet the work of ZEP schools is not only to provide language support but also to promote multiculturalism and to foster closer links between the schools and the community.[6]

It is also important to point out that, although the official policy of the Ministry of Education and Culture is against segregation of non-indigenous children, there is a trend toward segregation in schools with high concentrations of migrants, minorities, and Greek Cypriots from poor backgrounds (Trimikliniotis & Demetriou, 2006). Parallel to the growing number of these students, most of those schools at the same time see a significant reduction in the number of typical Greek-Cypriot students (i.e., white, middle-class). Although there is increasing evidence of racial prejudice against minorities, the Ministry of Education and Culture purports not to have the necessary mechanisms for providing proper figures on racist incidents in schools (Trimikliniotis, *The state of education and racial discrimination for 2007–2008 in Cyprus,* unpublished, 2008). In their study, Panayiotopoulos and Nicolaidou (2007) acknowledge that their semistructured interviews pointed to racist incidents; non-indigenous children were targeted mostly because of the manner in which they dressed, the financial difficulties of their families, and their skin color. My own ethnographic research in recent years (e.g. Zembylas, 2008a, 2012b) shows how emotions of resentment, fear, and hatred at the nation-state level are infectious and travel to constitute and maintain emotional distance between Greek-Cypriot children and those who come from different cultures.

Research also shows that Greek-Cypriot teachers are ill prepared to deal with the challenge of multicultural education (Panayiotopoulos & Nicolaidou, 2007; Trimikliniotis, 2004; Zembylas & Iasonos, 2010). There are no special criteria used to choose teachers for multicultural schools; in fact, teachers are asked by the Ministry of Education and Culture to implement the same curriculum for all public schools regardless of whether a school is multicultural or not. Not surprisingly, the teacher's task becomes even more complicated in schools where Turkish-speaking students are enrolled. Although there are few such schools in the south and the Turkish-speaking student population in those schools is small (usually between 5 percent and 10 percent, except in one school where the Turkish-speaking children represent almost 50% of the student population), the situation is complex in light of the unresolved political problem in Cyprus. The school settings of chapters 3–6, which constitute Part II of this book, are multicultural schools in which Turkish-speaking students are enrolled. In the south, there are also international private schools in which growing numbers of Turkish-Cypriot children are enrolled; the school setting of chapters 7 and 8 in Part III represents one of these international private secondary schools.

After this brief review of the Cyprus Conflict and the role of education, I move on to present the methodological approach followed in my research.

Researching Emotions in Schools: The Methodological Approach in This Book

Empirical attention to emotion in education has grown in recent years; emotion is now recognized as an important feature of school life (Schutz & Zembylas, 2009). However, little attention has been given to emotion *methodologically*—that is, how emotion might be investigated in schools, what methodological problems arise in such investigations, and how to overcome them. Needless to say, the issue of researching emotion poses challenges associated with the difficulties of doing empirical research in schools; it also draws attention to more general methodological, theoretical, and political concerns concerning how emotion is defined and in what ways it should to be investigated (Zembylas, 2007b). Clearly, such issues are highly contested, so some choices need to be made.

The position adopted in this book is broad. Following Burkitt (1997), emotions are understood as multidimensional (thinking, feeling, acting) "complexes" that are both cultural and individual, and that arise in power relationships. This means that emotions are part of the relations and interactions between humans rather than an individual or internal phenomenon; thus power works through social relations "as a structure of actions that aims to affect a field of possible actions" (Burkitt, 2005, p. 683). Therefore, it is argued that emotions need to be understood in terms of the sociospatial dynamics of movements and relations. Specifically, the study of *emotional geographies* (Davidson, Bondi, & Smith, 2005) suggests that there are different repertoires of emotions that arise in particular locations (see Figure 1.1).

The idea of emotional geographies emphasizes again that emotions are understood—experientially and conceptually (Bondi, Davidson, & Smith, 2005)—in terms of how they are sociospatially constituted and articulated rather than as entirely interiorized subjective mental states (see chapter 3). As Figure 1.1 shows, emotional geographies at school are constituted by different "worlds" that are interconnected. The term *worlds* here—which alludes to the phenomenological concept of "lifeworld" (Husserl, 1970)—refers to the world as it is experienced or lived in relational flows. This intersubjective experience is arranged in historical and political, physical and spatial, social and cultural, and subjective and emotional dynamics that cannot be easily separated (hence the dotted line linking the different "worlds" in Figure 1.1). These worlds, therefore, are not taxonomies, classifications, or abstracted categories but rather schematic

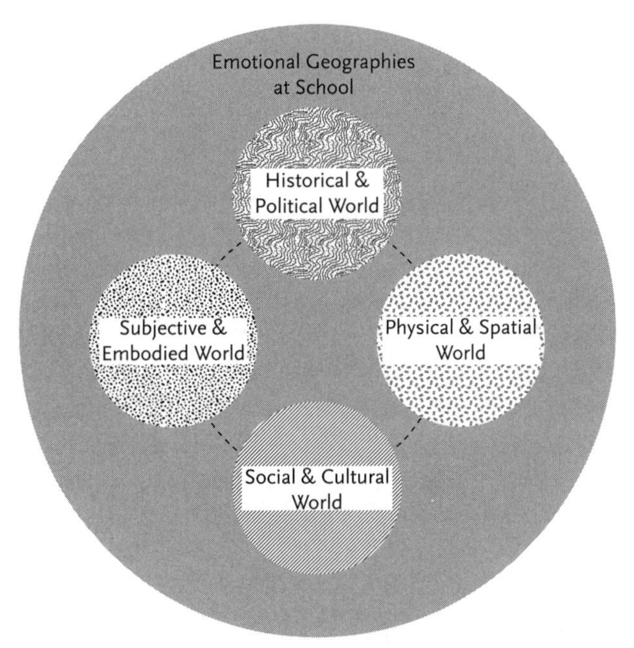

FIGURE 1.1 The different "worlds" constituting emotional geographies at school.

manifestations of the geographical dynamics of emotion and how they are entwined with the fabric of life.

Scholars in the recently emerged field of emotional geographies (Davidson, Bondi, & Smith, 2005) seek to understand emotions in particular spatial contexts, because it is argued that an understanding of the spatiality of emotion can only be gained through careful study of the location of emotion in specific settings—for example, schools, hospitals, workplaces. These settings might include particular locations, such as workplaces in which individuals are exploited and excluded, conflict areas around the world in which an oppressive regime limits the freedom of its people, or contexts in which women are victims of trafficking. My research casts the school as a setting in which symbolic and discursive violence employed by the nationstate to stake out its symbolic borders translates into daily practices of exclusion and hurt for the (ethnic or migrant) other.

For example, previous research has highlighted the prevalence of nationalist and racist attitudes and perceptions of Greek-Cypriot people (including children) toward the Turks, whom they consider responsible for past trauma and ongoing occupation of their homes and land in north Cyprus (e.g. see Spyrou, 2006; Zembylas, 2008a). Discourses at the state and national level do not differ much compared to school discourses, although not all such commentaries are expressed in primitive-racist or nationalist terms. As it is shown generally, wider national discourses of race, ethnicity, and class, among other categories, often become reflected in the ways that majoritized and minoritized children position themselves in school; in fact, these discourses provide inclusion/exclusion criteria on how majoritized children behave toward minoritized children (Troyna & Hatcher, 1992). Through racialization and ethnicization processes in schools, "sameness" and "otherness" are reified and assume a naturalized form (Connolly, 1998).

An important question, then, that arises within the methodological frame of emotional geographies in schools is this: How, exactly, are teachers' and students' emotional practices and discourses racialized and ethnicized? Emotional geographies focus on the ways through which power relations involved in constructions of race and ethnicity produce (and are produced by) particular emotional practices and discourses that *include* some students and *exclude* others. Investigating the sociospatial dynamics of racism and nationalism, as shown in the chapters of Part II, for instance, will indicate how exclusion (on the basis of race and ethnicity) is manifest in the emotions that arise when students and teachers talk and move within school spaces.

In other words, larger social/political forces and discourses influence school practices of exclusion and inclusion, but what seems to be important is *how* this transactional process takes place and what consequences it has. This process apparently connects some bodies to other bodies; it involves seeking proximity to certain bodies (which are perceived to be similar) and distance from others (which are considered dissimilar). Therefore, this process can be traced in the ways in which individuals (e.g. schoolchildren and teachers) learn to construct and implement inclusion/exclusion criteria through their emotional practices and discourses. If we accept this conceptual framework, the next question that has to be posed is this: Which research methodologies are suitable for the investigation of emotional geographies in schools?

Research Methodologies

In terms of research methodologies that can adequately investigate emotional geographies in schools, ethnographic methods in general (Denzin, 1997; Holstein & Gubrium, 2000) draw attention to the dynamic and interactive nature of verbal and nonverbal expressions of emotions through the study of social interaction *over time* (Sturdy, 2003). Ethnographic methods allow for rich data collection—for example, through documents, field notes, interviews, observations—that reveals different dimensions of participants' emotional expressions. The collection of these data is conducted by staying in the field for a considerable amount of time, ranging from a few weeks to several months. In particular, the analysis of such rich data through the lens of "critical ethnography" (Carspecken & Walford, 2001; Madison, 2005; St. Pierre & Pillow, 2000) allows the establishment of links between specific sociospatial terrains and larger political forces, because it is shown how the empirical evidence at the micro-level is entangled with sociopolitical discourses and practices at the macro-level. Critical ethnography is appropriate for the study of emotional geographies in schools, because it is grounded in the commitment to be critical about existing power hierarchies and to advocate change where needed. In other words, through the use of a critical ethnographic lens I want to expose the implicit values and ideologies expressed in school emotional geographies and the taken-for-granted biases that may result from such implicit values and ideologies.

In the context of the research reported in this book, then, I engaged in a series of qualitative case studies grounded in ethnographic methods.[7] In all of the chapters (except chapter 9), the Greek-Cypriot student population (the majority) attended school with Turkish-speaking and other minority students; my main interest was to capture the emotional complexities of this coexistence, so I chose schools (from different districts in Cyprus) in which there was this diverse student population. There were four major sites (case studies): three public primary schools and one private international secondary school; the case study presented in chapter 9 comes from a fifth-grade classroom in a mainstream Greek-Cypriot school. In all of these case studies, critical ethnography was used as a lens through which to explore two major issues: First, I was interested in how emotions were constituted in specific sociospatial terrains yet in relation to larger political forces, and thus any emotions about race and ethnicity were not merely understood as individual actions but as the construction of practices, discourses, spaces, and flows (Zembylas, 2008a). Second, insights from critical ethnographic methodologies helped draw attention to school discourses and practices in relation to perceptions about race/ethnicity with the purpose of exposing the entanglement of emotion with exclusion/inclusion criteria and traumatic conflict.

Furthermore, I chose a case study approach (Merriam, 1998; Stake 1995) as the basis for data collection and analysis. My research team (five research associates) and I spent between two and three months in each school to gain an in-depth understanding of how issues of trauma, emotion, healing, and reconciliation were manifested in participants' everyday lives. Access was gained after informing the Ministry of Education and Culture of Cyprus and each school principal about the project's goals. Data were collected through in-depth interviews, ethnographic observations, and school documents. Semistructured interviews (tape-recorded and fully transcribed) were conducted with the school principal, teachers, and parents, and there were focus groups of children (Greek-Cypriot and Turkish-speaking children separately) at various grade levels; unofficial discussions were also conducted with the rest of the teachers and several other children. Collectively, the data reported in this book were based on 200 hours of interviews and focus groups, 700 hours of observations of teaching/learning activities in schools, and scrutiny of hundreds of pages of policies and school documents (samples of student work and teachers' planning).

Interview questions focused on personal goals, feelings about and experiences with students from different cultures and Turkish-speaking students (and vice versa), and teaching practices that dealt particularly with Turkish-speaking students (in the case of the teachers and the principal). At numerous points throughout the interview process, participants were asked to describe the emotions they experienced and how those emotions were or were not related to their perceptions of race, ethnicity, and the traumatic conflict in Cyprus. The research associates and I recorded ethnographic observations in field notes (through the help of an open or semistructured protocol) and focused on the ways in which Greek-Cypriot students and teachers and Turkish-speaking and minority students expressed their emotions with regard to one another; observations also covered the manifestation of these emotions in organization structures and spaces of the classrooms and the school in general. Specifically, the observations focused on the interactions between Greek-Cypriot students and Turkish-speaking students, as well as on the teacher's instruction and the nature of the teacher's disciplinary responses, particularly toward Turkish-speaking students. The possible bias this process might occasion was counterbalanced by cross analysis of the data conducted by different members of the research team.

An issue that needs to be addressed is the ethics of doing research grounded in ethnographic methods in schools. First, all the participants interviewed were told the purpose of the research and the duration of the interview(s). They were given the option of withdrawing at any time, if they felt that they could not continue for any reason; nobody withdrew from the process. Second, permission was granted on the basis of the ethics procedures followed for research on human subjects in my university. Third, all names used throughout this book are pseudonyms. Finally, the participants were given opportunities to confirm what they had said through member checking. There were also unofficial discussions with some participants that might have revealed sensitive information, and so it was decided that this information would not find its way into this book.

Data analysis was grounded in the theoretical framework (chapter 2). For example, the research assistants and I constantly looked for evidence that showed how emotions were related to teachers' and students' perceptions and practices with regard to race and ethnicity. The theoretical framework was particularly helpful in allowing multiple interpretations of incoming data as an ongoing part of the data-collection process, because attention was paid to the ways in which teachers' and students' emotions were constituted within the sociospatial terrain of each school. To ensure validity, members of the research team worked separately and collaboratively, using an interpretive method of coding (Erickson, 1986) to ascertain confirming and disconfirming evidence of assertions arising from our data sources. We independently read and coded the data following the open-coding techniques outlined by Strauss and Corbin (1994). Building on this analysis (see also Miles & Huberman, 1994), we interpreted the data by developing themes, categories, and tentative hypotheses. Analysis and theory are woven together throughout to establish stronger links between the data and its theorization. Parts II and III of the book analyze the empirical data from this research project, and Part IV takes a step back and theorizes about the emotional tensions, dilemmas, and complexities that arose in the process of that analysis, and it considers ideas and practices that might promote the role of education in healing.

Structure of the Book

As discussed in the previous section, there are four major parts of this book. Part I, which contains this introduction and chapter 2, situates contextually and theoretically the exploration that is undertaken in this book. Chapter 2, in particular, theorizes about the basic constructs—emotion, trauma, healing, reconciliation, critical pedagogy, critical peace education, critical emotional praxis—that comprise the backbone of this book. The theoretical framework draws from psychoanalytic, critical, feminist, and sociopolitical perspectives of emotion and examines how the notion of "critical emotional praxis" may serve as an overarching theoretical and practical pedagogical tool, strategy, or practice in peace education contexts. The notion of critical emotional praxis is linked to recent and foundational work on critical peace education (e.g. Wulf, Bajaj, Brantmeier). A major challenge for teachers and students in conflict societies and post-conflict societies is that emotions of traumatic conflict are often appropriated by social and political institutions, including schools, to justify particular collective narratives and ideologies. The meanings and prospects of critical emotional praxis are theorized in Part I and then explored in the chapters that follow through particular analyses of evidence from a series of case studies in Cyprus (Parts II and III).

Part II, composed of four chapters (chapters 3–6), is titled The Emotional Spaces of Racism and Nationalism in Schools. Those chapters provide detailed empirical accounts of how emotional spaces of racism and nationalism are constituted and maintained in three Greek-Cypriot primary schools. Chapter 3 focuses on how emotional geographies are manifest in the formation and maintenance of particular racialization and ethnicization processes within one primary school in which Greek-Cypriot and Turkish-speaking students are enrolled. Chapter 4 takes a deeper look at another primary school and explores how emotional spaces are racialized and ethnicized through the majoritized group's feelings of resentment. Chapter 5 engages in a cross-sectional analysis of three primary schools in which Greek-Cypriot (the majority) and Turkish-speaking (the minority) children are enrolled, and it highlights the minoritized children's experience of racism and nationalism. Chapter 6 extends the analysis of the previous three chapters and examines Greek-Cypriot teachers' constructions of Turkish-speaking children's identities, focusing in particular on how Turkish-speaking children enrolled in these schools are racialized, ethnicized, and classed within the dominant discourse of Greek-Cypriot teachers. This chapter begins to suggest the importance of forming an *ethic of discomfort* as a space for constructive transformations in classrooms of conflicted societies (I come back to this later in the book). An ethic of discomfort is theorized as an economy of affect that uses discomfort as a point of departure for individual and social transformation.[8]

Part III, which includes chapters 7–9, is titled The Emotional Complexities of Traumatic Conflict: Openings and Closures. Chapters 7 and 8 focus on analyzing the emotional complexities at a shared secondary school in which both Greek-Cypriot and Turkish-Cypriot students are enrolled. The goal of these two chapters is to provide a detailed case study of this shared school and the pedagogic efforts to promote inclusion, healing, and reconciliation. In chapter 7 the discussion focuses on teachers', students', and parents' perspectives toward the struggles to negotiate co-existence at this school. The findings provide insights into how teachers, students, and parents from the two conflicting communities draw selectively from various discourses and practices on collective identity and ethnic conflict in Cyprus (e.g. refugees, missing persons) that are emotionalized to support the preexisting values and beliefs adopted from the family, as well as from the school and ethnic communities. Chapter 8 builds on the focus of chapter 7 and explores the successes and failures of teachers' pedagogies and school policies at this shared secondary school to establish an emotional culture of peace, inclusion, and healing. The analysis shows that there is emotional resistance to shared education and the formation of peace and reconciliation pedagogies. The last chapter of Part III, chapter 9, takes us to a fifth-grade classroom of a "mainstream" Greek-Cypriot school and describes how Greek-Cypriot students perceived and negotiated the meanings of empathy for the "enemy-other" in the context of the *Den Xehno* campaign. The analysis suggests that the process of engaging with empathy is full of fractures and failures, possibilities and impossibilities. Collectively, the three chapters of Part III show that openings and closures often coexist, and therefore it is important to identify and analyze their possibilities as well as their limits in understanding educational institutions as sites of peace, healing, and reconciliation.

Finally, Part IV of the book is comprised of three chapters (chapters 10–12) and is titled Emotional Tensions and Critical Responses to Peace Education Efforts. In those chapters, I attempt to theorize the emotional tensions and possible responses in peace education efforts as those arise from the empirical analyses of the previous two parts and the review of literature in comparative and international education concerning similar cases (e.g. Northern Ireland and Israel). Chapter 10 takes a step back from empirical data provided in the previous chapters and engages in a theoretical discussion of the politicization of emotion, showing how certain educational policies and pedagogical practices emotionalize particular representations in the school culture. In this chapter, the representation of refugees—a key component of educational discourses and discourses of emotion in previous chapters—is taken up for analysis. Chapter 10 examines alternative possibilities of promoting peaceful coexistence while taking into consideration the affective (re)production of certain representations, but without undermining the asymmetrical emotional experiences of individuals and communities. Chapter 11 discusses the value of "citizenship as shared fate" in sites of ethnic conflict and analyzes its implications for citizenship education. It is argued that what teachers and schools should try to do is make practices of shared fate and compassion possible through creating conditions for children and young people to experience what it means to enact such practices in sites of ethnic conflict. Finally, chapter 12 attempts to complicate the reading of nostalgia in the cultural politics of education, arguing that a blind rhetoric of nostalgia—that has a strong sentimentalized basis, as shown in several chapters of Parts II and III—for an idealized past can and should be critiqued in productive ways. Central to the argument made in chapter 12 is that nostalgia has multiple meanings, some of which promote nationalist agendas while others offer opportunities for critical emotional transformation.

The book ends with chapter 13 (Epilogue), which argues that, although it seems as if peace education interventions are laudable initiatives in conflicted societies and that they can contribute toward unity and democratic state building, the persistence of strongly emotionalized accounts of collective memories and identities could slow and be potentially counterproductive to efforts for peace, healing, and reconciliation. The epilogue recapitulates the argument developed throughout the book and proposes that the much needed space for encouraging critical emotional praxis offers an important contribution to critical peace education efforts.

All in all, the major idea in this book is that, if emotions do indeed play a significant role in constituting identities and communities, then emotions should be seen as central to how schools can break the cycle of enmity and division and promote healing and reconciliation in the aftermath of trauma (Hutchison & Bleiker, 2008). The task of curricula and pedagogies that are critical of normative emotional regimes is to constantly question the practices, strategies, and spaces within which emotions of trauma are appropriated—including the ways that peace education itself may be politically manipulated. Inasmuch as certain hegemonic discourses are perpetuated, pedagogues in conflicted societies need to be constantly looking for ways to disrupt the modes through which emotions of trauma are authorized by, implied, and embodied in pedagogies and curricula. In this book I make a systematic attempt to expose these disruptive pedagogies.

Notes

1. *Peace education* is a field of social education that is concerned with war and violence in the world. It and has experienced considerable growth over the past four decades (Burns & Aspeslagh, 1996; McGlynn et al., 2009; Salomon & Nevo, 2002). At its most basic level peace education is taken to be the process of promoting the knowledge, skills, attitudes, and values needed to bring about behavior changes to prevent conflict and violence, both physical and structural; to resolve conflicts peacefully; and to create the conditions conducive to peace (Fountain, 1999).
2. The Annan Plan was named after Kofi Annan, UN Secretary-General from 1997 to 2006. It was the UN's proposal to resolve the *Cyprus Problem* and reunite divided Cyprus into what would be a federation of two states.
3. Interestingly, however, the newly appointed minister of education in 2013 brought back the *Den Xehno* educational objective as "*Den Xehno, Agonizomai, Diekdiko*" [I don't forget, I struggle, I contest].
4. The term "non-indigenous" (μη γηγενείς) is used by the government in reference to children who are not Greek Cypriots; although increasing numbers of immigrant children are born in Cyprus, these children continue to be identified as "non-indigenous" by the majority group (i.e. Greek Cypriots). Other terms used are "foreigners" (ξένοι), "aliens" (αλλοδαποί), and "other-language" (αλλόγλωσσοι).
5. The term "Turkish-speaking" (τουρκόφωνος) is preferred because it is more inclusive than the term "Turkish Cypriots" or "Roma/Gypsies." It is not always easy to distinguish who is "ethnically" Turkish Cypriot and who is Roma/Gypsy (see Trimikliniotis & Demetriou, 2006); therefore, the term "Turkish-speaking" is used to refer to all Turkish-speaking groups. When it is important to make a distinction and highlight who a Turkish Cypriot is, this is explicitly stated in the text.
6. The policy of ZEP schools is currently undergoing comprehensive evaluation and revision by the Ministry of Education and Culture of the Republic of Cyprus.

7. I acknowledge the work of my research associates, Galatia Agathocleous (in chapters 3–6); Stalo Lesta, Nefi Kameri, and Christiana Aravi (in chapters 7–8); and Andri Michaelidou (in chapter 9).
8. The *theory of cognitive dissonance* (Festinger, 1957) and the *conflict theory of majority and minority influence* (Moscovici, 1980; Moscovici & Facheux, 1972) are relevant in discussing the concepts of "discomfort" and "ambivalence"; however, these theories are grounded in different theoretical frameworks from the one adopted in this book. Dissonance theory basically says that an individual experiences discomfort when he or she holds contradictory beliefs, ideas, or values at the same time. Dissonance will lead the individual to self-protective motives that aim at reducing dissonance and avoiding situations that increase dissonance. The conflict theory of majority and minority influence proposes that all attempts (either by majorities or minorities) at influence create a conflict. Confronted with this conflict, the individual tries to make sense of the confusion and uncertainty emanating from this situation. Dissonance theory is grounded in a cognitivist psychological framework, whereas conflict theory is grounded in a social psychological framework; both frameworks differ from the sociopolitical framework of emotions within which discomfort and ambivalence are theorized in the present book (see chapter 2).

2 THEORETICAL POSITIONING

The study of Education and Conflict has received increased attention within the media and the academic field in recent years (Novelli & Lopes Cardozo, 2008). This field of study explores the complex relationship between conflict and education and attempts to understand how conflict influences education and vice versa. On the one hand, conflict affects education in various ways: Through loss of life and destruction of property, violent conflict directly influences the access of children to safe schools and creates economic and social situations that deprive children of educational opportunities (Davies, 2004); on the other hand, education can influence conflict situations, either by contributing to the violence or working against it (Novelli & Lopes Cardozo, 2008; Smith, 2005). Thus, education may contribute indirectly to conflict, for example, by teaching children to hate, fear, and resent others and by promoting social and political conditions that perpetuate various forms of violence and conflict. Education, though, can also be a catalyst for peace, healing, and reconciliation, if it teaches tolerance, respect, compassion, and nonviolence. Bush and Saltarelli capture these "two faces" of education, when they write that:

> The negative face shows itself in the uneven distribution of education to create or preserve privilege, the use of education as a weapon of cultural repression, and the production or doctoring of textbooks to promote intolerance. The positive face goes beyond the provision of education for peace programmes, reflecting the cumulative benefits of the provision of good quality education. These include the conflict-dampening

> impact of educational opportunity, the promotion of linguistic tolerance, the nurturing of ethnic tolerance, and the "disarming" of history. (2000, p. v)

Davies (2004) also distinguishes three major roots of conflict in which education plays a role: first, education contributes to the reproduction of economic and class relations through exclusion of marginalized groups; second, education can perpetuate gender violence and other forms of violence through reproduction of conflicted relations; and finally, education can reinforce essentialist identities based on ethnicity, race, religion, and nationalism through teaching that identities are immutable and are grounded in blood, heritage, or other cultural links. There is now plenty of evidence that educational systems, especially in conflict areas, promote xenophobia, nationalism, and racism toward ethnic or religious groups and minorities. However, as Davies points out, there is also encouraging evidence that education can have beneficial effects, leaning toward more peaceful and just societies by offering programs and curricula that promote peace, healing, and global citizenship and that are resilient, even in the face of the conflict around them (2004).

Needless to say, education cannot solve a conflict on its own; it would not only be unfair to place such a burden on education and educators, it would also be unwise to have such an expectation in light of the "negative face" of education. Especially, with regard to the challenges in undoing the emotions of hatred, resentment, humiliation, and anger that are embedded in a traumatic conflict (see Lindner, 2009a; Smith, 2006), one wonders what forms of pedagogical engagement may be developed to promote healing and reconciliation. To formulate such pedagogical opportunities, I argue in this book that teachers and students need to develop a critical understanding of emotion and trauma in conflict situations. Such an understanding will provide a compelling basis for a critical pedagogical exploration of traumatic conflict and its implications—an understanding that pays attention to emotions and is critical enough to develop pedagogical theories and practices that contribute to healing and reconciliation. Such critical understanding of reactions to conflict must also take into consideration the emotional scars and dilemmas of those experiencing traumatic conflict, either as primary or secondary witnesses. But, first, how do we understand "trauma"?

Understanding Trauma

Generally speaking, *trauma* refers to the effects of unthinkable catastrophic events that, when witnessed, evoke painful feelings and disrupt one's understanding of how the world works. For either a direct witness or a secondary witness, the traumatic experience ruptures normal habits and expectations and defies meaning (Caruth, 1996). Traumatic events rupture life in part because of their powerful emotional nature; they cannot be processed emotionally in the same way as other experiences (Hutchison & Bleiker, 2008). Emotions associated with trauma, such as pain, grief, fear, and awe, are difficult to communicate, and thus it is a challenge, both for victims and witnesses, as well as for societies in general, to work through trauma and create conditions of healing. Although emotions are central to processes of healing and reconciliation, as Hutchison and Bleiker note (2008), relatively little is known about how, exactly, emotions operate in these processes (see also, Gobodo-Madikizela & Van Der Merwe, 2009).

Psychoanalytic theories have usually treated trauma as an unclaimed individual experience that needs somehow to be dealt with, using therapeutic strategies (Caruth, 1996). Kristeva (1993, 2000), in particular, teaches us that the psychic origins of unclaimed experiences are linked to identity and its affective meaning. What this means in specific terms is that, if we have suffered from a traumatic experience (e.g. war violence), the affective meaning of that experience is not only psychic but also relational because it makes sense through our attachments to other members of "our" collective with whom we feel aligned. What this tells us is that emotions align the individual and the collective (Ahmed, 2004, 2005).

Two concepts from the psychoanalytic theorization of emotion are particularly helpful throughout this book. The first one is the concept of *emotional ambivalence*, that is, the presence of both positive and negative emotions. Positive and negative, however, are not attributes of emotions or bodies, they are provisional readings and judgments of situations and people that have implications for how the world is categorized in a person's mind (Ahmed, 2004). Hence in hating the "enemy" who caused "us" unimaginable pain, "we" also love ourselves and come together as a group made up of other "me's" (who may also have suffered at the hands of the same enemy), of others that are loved as if they were me (Ahmed, 2005). The terms and conditions of this emotional ambivalence, however, are not fixed; a differentiation of the psychic dimensions of personal attachments and a re-articulation of trauma can provide the beginning of alternative affective meanings about "we" and "they." This idea can be better understood using another psychoanalytic concept, that of "revolt."

By *revolt*, Kristeva (2000) points to a challenge to authority and tradition that takes place within an individual. Revolt has a psychic dimension that provides an opportunity for new affective meaning. A traumatized individual who has repressed something cannot have meaningful experiences but only traumatic ones, because meaningful experience requires some assimilation into the social order (Oliver, 2005). Because it provides the conditions for reassessment and rearticulation, revolt is the return of the repressed that opens the possibility for meaningful experience. Re-evaluating the emotional remainders of past trauma, for example through critical strategies deployed not simply for survival but to question the dehumanization that takes place (regardless of whether this involves one's self or the other), creates new social spaces. Revolt as a return or questioning of the past for the sake of renewal in the future, enlivens both the psychic and social dimensions of the individual who belongs to a community. Questioning the normalization of emotions of trauma is what creates openings to overcome its fossilization and operates as an invitation to find new ways of relating to one's self and the other. Through this questioning of who the "we" and "others" are, the negativity of trauma may be transformed from a destructive or merely discriminatory force that separates self and others into a positive force of creativity and rearticulation (Kristeva, 2000; Oliver, 2004).

In addition to the psychoanalytic lens, work in the post-Holocaust era has begun to engage the social and political implications of trauma (Alexander et al., 2004; Bennett, 2005). Trauma enters the social and political terrain as an expression of personal experience, explains Bennett (2005), but "it is always vulnerable to appropriation" (p. 6). As Kansteiner (2004) also notes, trauma after the Holocaust has risen "as one of the key interpretive categories of contemporary politics and culture" (p. 193). The political appropriation of emotions of trauma contributes to building a sense of identity and community that rests on stark us-and-them dichotomies (Ahmed, 2004). A recent case in point is the terrorist attacks of September 11, 2001, and the ways that the US government politicized trauma to gain support for its wars in Iraq and Afghanistan. Similar patterns of the political appropriation of trauma are found almost on a daily basis in the Middle East conflict, as well as in other conflicts around the world.

Understanding trauma in both its psychic dimension and its sociopolitical basis within particular historical conditions (e.g. nationalism, racism, religious fanaticism) calls attention to the educational, social, and political discourses and practices that contribute to hostile and monolithic emotions—such as feelings of superiority about one's own group and inferiority for an adversary group (Card, 2002; Eisenstein, 1996; Scheff, 1994). Emotions of trauma, understood as the persistence of past memories that have led to difficulty in dealing with otherness, return to reveal their darkness but can also provide conditions for reassessment. This reassessment is not fixed on the repressive power of trauma but involves questioning the multidimensional implications of trauma in everyday life.

For example, reassessment implies that it is important for teachers and students to engage in critical reflection on the emotional connection between the individual and the large group, and between personal grief and collective trauma; with such reflection it becomes possible to analyze the consequences of creating us-and-them dichotomies that perpetuate hatred and resentment (Bekerman & Zembylas, 2012). Revolt, then, against the oppressive normalization of trauma halts the repetition of destructive strategies that remain stuck in negativity and opens up possibilities for rearticulating constructive ways of considering trauma—such as restoring the humanity of subjects who have been stripped of it and building solidarity on the basis of common suffering (Georgis & Kennedy, 2009). An important component of peace education, therefore, is to explore both the restrictive and the productive forms of engagement with emotions of traumatic conflict in schools and to critically expose how trauma and conflict are emotionally appropriated by ideological-political forces and limit opportunities for healing and reconciliation.

Defining *Healing* and *Reconciliation*

It is not an easy task to define *healing* and *reconciliation*, in part because the terms are often used vaguely and are deployed to discriminate between "bottom-up" and "top-down" approaches to peacebuilding (Parent, 2011). *Healing* is usually synonymous with recovery (psychological or social) from an overwhelming traumatic experience, explains Parent, and *reconciliation* is considered a political process "that symbolizes peace, post-traumatic reconstruction and the end of antagonisms" (2011, p. 379). Parent critiques the ambiguous use of these terms and argues that the complex connections between individual healing and political reconciliation are not made adequately visible in the academic literature and public discussions on peace. For example, the healing of individuals or communities may be subordinated to the political project of reconciliation; however, by neglecting the healing of trauma, one may jeopardize the process of reconciliation too (Green, 2009; Staub, 2000).

Rather than describing the differences between healing and reconciliation in an effort to draw a sharp distinction, I am in agreement with Parent (2011), who argues that it may be more productive to identify the inextricable links between the two. It is "in the uncertain and indeterminate space between (individual) healing and (political) reconciliation that one should find and build peace" (Parent, 2011, p. 380). Importantly, one can also talk about "social healing," an emerging concept that is broadly defined "as the reconstruction of communal relations after mass violence" (Green, 2009). One can employ the concept of social healing as "broader, more spacious and perhaps more appropriate in scope for what is realistic in the immediacy of postwar recovery" compared to reconciliation, which "may be years or decades in the making, more demanding than many victims can manage early in the recovery process, and counter-productive if pushed on societies too quickly by outsiders" (Green, 2009, p. 77). In light of definitions about "reconciliation" as a (complex, multifaceted, and long-term) process of restoring harmony and transforming hostile relations and emotions between rival sides after a conflict (Kriesberg, 1998; Lederach, 1997), one can understand that the line between the "individual" and the "social" (or the "political") is blurred in understandings of healing and reconciliation (Bar-Tal, 2000a). This blurring does not imply, however, that individual suffering is not separate from collective representation (Alexander et al., 2004; Eyerman, Alexander, & Breese, 2011); as it has been argued by Alexander and his colleagues, emotional experience is often channelled via social, cultural, and political processes relatively independent of the trauma's origins. The bottom line in this analysis is that the distinction between "healing" and "reconciliation" should not be taken for granted; it is important to take into account how victims feel and recover from a traumatic experience, while considering the social and political spaces available for this process (Parent, 2011). But let's look at each concept in more detail.

Healing can be a long, complex, and non-linear process (Green, 2009; Lopez, 2011; Parent, 2011). One of the most widespread models in the literature that describes the process of healing is Herman's (1997) fundamental stages of recovery from trauma. These stages include (1) the creation of a safe environment, (2) remembrance and mourning, and (3) reconnection with "ordinary" life. The first stage of healing requires that security concerns take precedence over other needs; security concerns include basic healthcare needs, food, a safe refuge, and a social network that can provide emotional and practical support. The second stage of healing consists of talking about the traumatic events so that they can be integrated into day-to-day life. Herman argues that to encourage healing, victims of trauma need opportunities to tell their stories, confront and uncover difficult questions, and recreate some meaningful explanations for the traumatic event. Importantly, as it is argued, forms of remembrance and mourning that are not limited to polarized explanations of us-the-good and them-the-evil lay the basis for interpretations of one's victimization as less destructive and disempowering (Parent, 2011). Not surprisingly, healing practices can become deeply political, because remembrance and mourning, especially in schools, are often nationalized after a traumatic conflict (Bekerman & Zembylas, 2012; Staub, 2003). However, alternative practices and discourses of mourning (divergent from nationalized accounts) can be developed, if space is provided for critical dialogue. The process of healing can be strengthened when individuals and communities acknowledge their emotional wounds, integrate them through community efforts, and imagine new possibilities for social reconstruction.

Finally, the third stage of healing refers to the reconnection of survivors with ordinary life, including contact with the perpetrator(s); thus it involves a number of emotionally difficult and discomforting experiences for the survivor(s). As in the previous stage, educational institutions in particular have an important role to play by helping younger generations re-humanize broken relations, work against violence, rebuild trust, and restore hope. In sum, the healing process is not linear and does not occur in a social and political vacuum (Parent, 2011). Scholars conducting trauma studies emphasize that there is no such thing as complete "closure" of a traumatic event (e.g. Caruth, 1996), because the term *closure* evokes an ahistorical fantasy that it is possible to emotionally undo a traumatic event. Nevertheless it is possible for survivors to go through the various steps of healing outlined above (in a non-linear manner), come to terms with a traumatic event, and tolerate the remaining emotional ambivalence. Most important, people who are able to move beyond trauma may find meaning in assisting others facing similar situations and in striving to build a better world (Lopez, 2011).

As noted earlier, the process of healing is intertwined with the process of reconciliation. In fact, reconciliation is often confused with healing, because a broad understanding of reconciliation includes social healing (Green, 2009; Long & Brecke, 2003). In addition, there are several dimensions of reconciliation that overlap with the healing process, such as the need for security or peace, the search for truth, the building of new relationships, expressions of forgiveness, and the need for some form of justice (Kriesberg, 1998; Lederach, 1997; Parent, 2011). In general, reconciliation is not an endpoint that marks stability and peace, but rather an ongoing sociopolitical process that is associated with a set of actions by antagonistic parties like the following: "They acknowledge the reality of the terrible acts that were perpetrated; accept with compassion those who committed injurious conduct, as well as acknowledging each other's sufferings; believe that their injustices are being redressed and anticipate mutual security and well-being" (Kriesberg, 1998, pp. 351–352). In this sense, reconciliation is understood as an emotional process that involves changing the motivations, beliefs, attitudes, and emotions inferred about the rival side (Bar-Tal & Bennink, 2004). Recognizing each other's suffering, developing mutual trust and positive attitudes, expressing empathy, considering the other's needs and interests, assuming responsibility for past mistakes, providing restitution, and granting forgiveness are some of the most important aspects of the process of reconciliation (Auerbach, 2009). In sum, Cole (2007) summarizes five major aspects of reconciliation: (1) reconciliation is a dynamic, complex, and long-term process; (2) it is a spectrum rather than a definition; (3) it is an ongoing struggle to engage and manage difference rather than harmony; (4) it is not synonymous with amnesia and forgetting; and (5) it should be seen in realistic and practical terms rather than in idealist and sentimental ways.

An understanding of reconciliation becomes even more complex, if one also considers the level—local, national, international—at which reconciliation ought to take place or whether reconciliation should take a bottom-up or a top-down approach (Parent, 2011). These debates over level, or top-down versus bottom-up approach, argues Parent, seem to obscure some important connections between healing and reconciliation, and especially the intimate connection between individual well-being and sociopolitical structures. At the same time, it is essential to recognize, continues Parent, that individual healing does not necessarily synchronize with national reconciliation; similarly, national reconciliation may even delay or hinder individual healing.

In the long term, an important point to keep in mind when considering the dynamic between healing and reconciliation is the idea that the development of trauma in each conflicted setting is different, and therefore an understanding of reconciliation cannot be depoliticized, just as an understanding of healing cannot be merely individualistic. In this sense, it is important to emphasize that the dominant narrative of posttraumatic stress disorder (PTSD) about how people respond to trauma entails fallacious assumptions, because it remains stuck to an individualistic notion of trauma (Bracken, 2002).[1] Therefore, the healing process is more likely to limit itself in a psychopathological model rather than acknowledging the strong social, cultural, and political implications of trauma. This medicalization or psychologizing of trauma places the burden of healing on the victim's shoulders and renders invisible the role of communities—e.g. through education, skills training, and other activities—in encouraging social healing and political reconciliation. It is also argued that when trauma is understood as a medical illness "we fail to address basic issues of power and social conflict, which have brought about the traumatic experiences in the first place" (Lopez, 2011, p. 307). As far as education is concerned, then, we need pedagogies that pay attention to issues of power relations and social conflict. We have to consider, therefore, how *critical pedagogy*, as a pedagogy that takes into consideration such issues, is in a position to address traumatic conflict and enrich peace education efforts or whether it needs further enrichment.

Emotion and Critical Pedagogy: Working Through "Troubled Knowledge"

Critical educators are increasingly faced with what Worsham (2006) has described as "posttraumatic" cultural moments that infiltrate our current pedagogical work as teachers, students, and scholars. These moments, marked by "unprecedented historical trauma" (Worsham, 2006, p. 170)—such as genocides, apartheid, September 11, and wars and conflicts around the world—shape a culture's emotional landscape in ways that make us "more likely to abide by reductive binaries and black-and-white solutions and therefore to avoid the ambiguity and discomfort that accompanies genuine inquiry into emotional investments" (Stenberg, 2011, p. 350). It is in the context of such moments that we are offered both the challenge and the opportunity to think more deeply about the complex emotional ramifications of critical pedagogy in relation to issues of conflict, peace, healing, and reconciliation—that is, moments in which the rhetoric of critical pedagogy as we know it might prove inadequate.

Jansen (2009), who writes in the context of post-apartheid South Africa, argues that critical theory and pedagogy in posttraumatic contexts is severely limited "for making sense of *troubled knowledge* and for transforming those who carry the burden of such knowledge on both sides of a divided community" (p. 256, emphasis added). "Troubled knowledge" is the knowledge of a traumatized past, which involves profound feelings of loss, shame, resentment, or defeat that one carries from his or her participation in a traumatized community. As Jansen maintains, critical theory receives and constructs the world as divided (e.g. black/white, oppressors/oppressed) and then takes sides to free the oppressed. The focus of this concern is less on what to do with the racist or nationalist in the classroom and more to do with how to empower the marginalized. Yet, the challenge in traumatized communities is often how to deal with the student who resists or rejects critical perspectives and who openly expresses racist or nationalist views because his or her privileges are being threatened or have been lost; or the student who is so traumatized from racism or nationalism that he or she feels that nothing can be done to rectify the situation. Considered from the vantage point of the students who carry this differential troubled knowledge, how might critical educators weigh "disruption"? What does the notion "teaching to disrupt" mean in the context of working through troubled knowledge in posttraumatic emotional landscapes?

Here I want to begin critiquing, in a constructive manner of course, some of the existing literature in critical pedagogy and the way it tends to overlook or downplay the strong emotional investments of troubled knowledge in posttraumatic situations. This examination of the existing literature in critical pedagogy led to a reiteration of the argument that the discourse of critical pedagogy constructs and sustains its own disciplinary affects—e.g. "noble" sentiments such as "commitment," "devotion," and "faith" (Yoon, 2005)—which may well be repressive (Ellsworth, 1989). My main contention is that some of the theoretical orthodoxies in critical pedagogy can be challenged and may be productively enriched by new ideas on how affect and emotion might be harnessed by teachers to deal with troubled knowledge. This book builds on this argument to highlight the importance of foregrounding rather than backgrounding the emotional complexity of "difficult knowledge" and its pedagogical implications in posttraumatic contexts.[2] Working from the assumption that critical pedagogy in these contexts must engage this terrain of difficult knowledge in ways that have not been sufficiently addressed by the critical pedagogy rhetoric so far, I look to work that gestures toward a discourse of critical pedagogy that considers troubled knowledge as a source of fruitful and responsive learning for the benefit of healing and reconciliation.

In general, *critical pedagogy* refers to any number of oppositional pedagogies promoting educational experiences that are transformative, empowering, and transgressive (Giroux, 2004; Kincheloe, 2005; McLaren, 2003). Drawn from many theoretical streams (Darder, Baltodano, & Torres, 2003) but influenced greatly by the Freirean paradigm (e.g. Freire, 2000, 2001, 2005), critical pedagogy seeks to expose and undo hegemonic values and taken-for-granted conceptions of truth that privilege the oppressor and perpetuate domination and social injustice (Darder et al., 2003). Two central aims of critical pedagogy, then, are, first, to engage teachers and students in a critical, dialectical examination of how power relations (particularly connected to the construction of knowledge) operate in schools and society and create or sustain hegemonic structures; and, second, to equip teachers and students with the language of critique and the rhetoric of empowerment so that they might become agents who recognize, challenge, and transform injustice and inequitable social structures.

Although there have been accounts in the critical pedagogy literature that critique the overemphasis on cognition or rationality and reason (e.g. Giroux, 1991; McLaren, 1994), emotion and affect have not been particularly underscored or substantially pursued in much of this literature (Jansen, 2009; Liston, 2008; Seibel Trainor, 2002). More important, though, it has been argued that the discourse of critical pedagogy functions as a "pedagogy of affect" that mobilizes dominant tropes, especially in anti-racist pedagogies (Worsham, 2001). These dominant tropes are associated with certain affects such as commitment, devotion, and faith that may become normalized and even repressive (Ellsworth, 1989). In other words, if these affects are not present among teachers or students in the context of critical pedagogy, then an anti-racist pedagogy may be considered a failure.

These critical accounts, however, have also prompted some critical scholars to suggest that we should be more careful when we examine the affective dimensions of critical pedagogy discourse. For example, Yoon (2005) has written that if affective dimensions were to be left unquestioned, they "would undermine our ability to understand the ways institutional discourses, even radical ones, keep our work and our imaginations and other real possibilities bound" (p. 743). Also, Amsler

(2011) has wondered about the affective dimensions of critical pedagogy when students' desire for individual transcendence and social change appears to be absent, rejected, or devalued. "What might *conscientization* mean," asks Amsler, "when exposing power relations affirms fatalism rather than inspiring hope?" (2011, p. 53). Or what happens when a student rejects conscientization altogether and insists on expressing racist views in the classroom? What are the implications when critical pedagogy's rhetoric of affect fails because it serves exclusionary ends?

There is already empirical evidence showing students' resistance and rejection of critical pedagogical efforts for a variety of reasons (Berlak, 2004; Boler, 2004b; Boler & Zembylas, 2003; Ellsworth, 1989; Zembylas, 2008a). This evidence exposes how some assumptions that are made in critical pedagogy may overlook the complexity of students' emotional investments in particular social positions and discourses. The lack or rejection of desire for empowerment and resistance also indicates how pervasive some dominant pedagogies of affect and emotion are in schools and the society—that is, how some school, workplace, and societal discourses and practices function in ways that sustain the forms and effects through which hegemony is lived and experienced; these dominant pedagogies of affect and emotion undoubtedly play a structural role in the constitution of subjectivities and in the justification of subjection (Worsham, 2001). For example, as Worsham states, critical pedagogy's rhetoric often seems to perceive student agency as little more than resistance, overlooking the role of affect or emotion sufficiently or in a compelling and holistic manner (2001). What is suggested here is that critical pedagogy's rhetoric of affect needs to be demystified and the emotional complexities of difficult knowledge have to be analyzed more deeply.

The scholars who have already acknowledged the emotional power and tenacity of various pedagogies of emotion—including critical pedagogy as a pedagogy of affect—wonder whether critical pedagogy rhetoric is implicated in serving exclusionary and, ultimately, conservative ends (Yoon, 2005). For example, Worsham (2001) asks (rhetorically) whether critical pedagogy eventually contributes unwittingly to sustaining hegemonic structures around class, race, and gender by ignoring the affective implications of transformation and by simply attempting to change students' rational understandings through replacing faith with reason and belief with knowledge. Lindquist (2004) also questions whether critical pedagogy works to produce a new affective life and culture that takes into careful consideration the deep emotional structures of faith from which critical pedagogy itself works. These concerns reiterate that there are important tasks that need to be further delineated in critical pedagogy, particularly in contexts within which there are strong traumatic experiences.

Consequently, part of "demystifying" critical pedagogy's rhetoric of affect is delving deeper into understanding the implications when students carry a traumatized past—a past that is a source of strong emotions such as shame, guilt, resentment, nostalgia, or loss. For example, traumatic experiences such as genocides, the apartheid, September 11, and wars and conflicts, require a more nuanced understanding of the consequences of the emotional burden carried by students' affective investments in particular ideologies, especially when the desire for empowerment and humanization seems to be rejected or eroded. A more nuanced understanding of critical pedagogy's rhetoric of affect and its implications implies two important things.

The first is recognition that the work of dominant pedagogies of emotion in society and in schools has a powerful negative impact on the affective struggle for empowerment and resistance (Worsham, 2001). That is, critical pedagogues need to be more critically aware of the emotional consequences when they categorize individuals into "oppressors" and "oppressed"; failing to understand how students' emotional attachments are strongly entangled with traumatic historical circumstances and material conditions will undermine teachers' pedagogical interventions. For example, a teacher who takes sides very quickly in a posttraumatic context in which two conflicting communities have been both "oppressors" and "oppressed"—and presumably students coming from both communities are present in the classroom—will not advance a critique of binary logic and universalizing tenets of fear and loathing toward each other (see Zembylas, 2008).

Second, as Worsham (2001) further states, there are many emotional manifestations of disempowerment and lack of resistance, such as boredom, apathy, resentment, hatred, anger, nostalgia, sorrow, loss, shame, guilt, and humiliation, and generally the ways those emotions are organized and practiced across differences of race, class, and gender.

A form of critical pedagogy that does not apprehend its own limitations of the complex discourses and practices of emotion that are embedded in posttraumatic situations is less likely to acknowledge emotion as a crucial aspect of political struggle for change. Thus the desire for empowerment and resistance cannot be taken for granted as a "natural resource" for critical pedagogy (Amsler, 2011); rather, the emotional tensions around issues of empowerment and resistance must be placed at the heart of critical pedagogy.

"Feeling" the Tensions of Troubled Knowledge in Conflicted Societies

What, then, are the emotional tensions of troubled knowledge in conflicted societies and what do those tensions imply for critical pedagogy? I want to suggest two ideas here: first, we need to acknowledge the consequences of the emotional complexity of difficult knowledge in conflict and post-conflict situations; and second, it becomes necessary to argue that it is precisely this acknowledgment that enriches the radical potentiality of critical pedagogy so that it can inspire transformative emotional practices in the struggle to fight structural inequalities. The notion of troubled knowledge as a *technology of affect* (Hook, 2005) is particularly helpful in further understanding the power and tenacity of troubled knowledge in posttraumatic situations—that is, how troubled knowledge implies certain mechanisms that work through the body, conduct, and being to establish particular ideological and affective investments.

Before we continue, it is important to clarify what is meant by the term *technology*, a key term in Foucault's later work that refers to any assemblage of knowledges, practices, techniques, and discourses used by human beings on others or on themselves to achieve particular ends (Foucault, 1977; Hook, 2007; Rose, 1998). "Technology of affect," in Hook's (2007) terminology, refers to the mechanisms through which emotions come to be instrumentalized, containing certain social norms and dynamics of inclusion/exclusion with respect to one's self and the other. Given that emotion is never simply individual or internal (Ahmed, 2004), troubled knowledge can be understood as a form of affective technology, a mode of self-practice situated in a circuit of social and political meaning.

For example, consider the context of post-apartheid South Africa. The troubled knowledge of the traumatized white or black student—who is traumatized for different reasons and in different ways, of course (Jansen, 2009)—is manifested affectively on the basis of norms that appeal to feelings of whiteness or blackness. White and black students carry the burden of this troubled knowledge with considerable consequences for pedagogical purposes. White students may feel resentment for being vilified for their parents' history; black students may feel resentment when they realize that very little has changed since the apartheid era. The complexity and diversity of these feelings have to be acknowledged by everyone involved in this process, especially in terms of the forms of exclusion and inclusion they create. As Hook writes:

> It is important to acknowledge here that we may ready our affective postures in how we position ourselves in given social encounters. We may as such assume certain affect-positions (fear, anger, irritation, love) which then become the proof of affect for a given ideological proposition, for a categorical relationship of entitlement, exclusion, belonging, etc. So: that I feel threatened by an influx of immigrants is proof enough of their moral dubiousness, proof enough also of why they—and others like them—should be prevented any rights of access. (2005, p. 93)

Hook's analysis allows for the theorization of troubled knowledge as an affective technology that maintains certain social norms and "structures of feeling" (Williams, 1977). For example, feelings of resentment toward the other (e.g. immigrants, asylum seekers, refugees) within a country that accepts a growing number of immigrants work as an ideological and affective position of exclusion for those who are considered "different" and inclusion for those deemed to be "similar" to the self (e.g. see chapters 4 and 8). An understanding of troubled knowledge and its various complexities and nuances enables a critical consideration of how troubled knowledge is emotionally produced and maintained as forms of inclusion and exclusion. For a critical pedagogue to disrupt resentment, abjection, and other emotions about the other, he or she must understand troubled knowledge as affectively, socially, and politically produced.

This understanding implies that a conception of critical pedagogy that is merely grounded in negative dialectics and counter-affirmation—that is, an emphasis on universalizing tenets about emancipatory forces and oppressive processes, ideologies, and identities—has little value in posttraumatic societies (Jansen, 2009). Needless to say, this is not to deny the systemic and institutionalized character of oppression, identity, and social injustice; rather, it is to highlight that classrooms are not homogeneous environments with a common understanding of oppression, but deeply divided places where contested narratives are steeped in the politics of emotions to create complex emotional and intellectual challenges for teachers. Teachers can themselves be carriers of troubled knowledge, as Jansen (2009) rightly points out, and this has serious implications for the form that critical pedagogy takes in posttraumatic societies.

As a consequence, a basic premise of critical pedagogy in post-traumatic contexts should not simply be to question the dominant educational arrangements (curricula, textbooks, pedagogies); it should also be "the people there, the bodies in the classroom, who carry knowledge within themselves that must be engaged, interrupted, and transformed" (Jansen, 2009, p. 258). These bodies and their troubled knowledge constitute the starting point for critical pedagogy in this context. Thus, taking sides early on based on justice and democracy ideals, maintains Jansen, may not be such a wise move when there is a clash of embodied knowledges and memories. For instance, to turn back to the earlier example, a teacher who takes sides early on in a posttraumatic context in which two conflicting communities have been both "perpetrators" and "victims" may end up intensifying unsafe classroom spaces. It has long been acknowledged in critical pedagogy rhetoric that the classroom is not a safe space and that some teachers and groups of students may be (unintentionally) burdened, for example, through their minority status in the classroom as representatives of their group—e.g., literature that highlights the ways in which students of color in the United States are burdened with the responsibility of teaching white students about diversity (see Boler, 2004a). It is my contention here that critical pedagogy in posttraumatic situations needs to move a step further and be attentive to and cautious of the increased complexity that troubled knowledge adds to (already) unsafe spaces in the classroom.

I want to extend Jansen's (2009) analysis, therefore, by emphasizing in particular the role of critical pedagogy in highlighting those practices through which certain emotions and knowledges become of *most worth*, and how traumatized students and teachers might construct (more) "safe" classroom spaces within which the wounded of either side can engage in critical and productive dialogue. As noted, it is important not to rush to take one side, thus dislodging the participants from a critical involvement with the emotions and the knowledges of one's self and of the other side. Again, this does not imply that "anything goes" and that the recklessness of accusation is simply tolerated (Jansen, 2009). By choosing to adopt a critical pedagogical lens in a posttraumatic context, the teacher is committed to interrogating how received knowledges and reconstructed emotions underlie "structures of feeling" in the teaching of various narratives, without adopting a self-righteous or therapeutic perspective.

In other words, the emotional labor that is demanded for critical pedagogy in posttraumatic contexts is not intended as a self-justified approach or a therapeutic intervention that seeks to validate some selected emotions or to dismiss and pacify some others in the name of healing past wounds (see also Amsler, 2011). The "healing of past wounds" approach, as Mohanty (2003) and Oliver (2001) aptly point out, is problematic because it hides or dismisses the relationship between trauma and power relations. Also, other critics, such as Ecclestone and Hayes (2009), emphasize that therapeutic approaches, introduced under the banners of preoccupation with students' well-being, deliberately decrease the possibility that students will experience complexity, multiplicity, or discomfort in their studies; preoccupation with emotional fragility offers a deeply diminished view of the human subject and undermines the ways in which these feelings contribute unwittingly to the perpetuation of power inequalities and hierarchies.

The critical interrogation of troubled knowledge in posttraumatic contexts marks a valuable intervention in the broad domain of critical pedagogy precisely by focusing on identifying and challenging the affective technologies and emotion-informed ideologies that underlie possible responses toward troubled knowledge—by students and teachers alike—and seeking to make a concrete difference in the lives of those who still suffer from carrying the burden of this knowledge. The process of dissolving categorizations of "us" and "them" in posttraumatic settings is a matter of observing very carefully the consequences of the underlying ideological and emotional attachments of the pedagogies that are being implemented. These attachments need to be engaged and interrupted in sensitive and critical ways. It is precisely in this context that *critical emotional praxis*, as an overarching concept that is theoretically grounded in critical pedagogy in posttraumatic societies, intersects with critical peace education.

Intersections Between Critical Emotional Praxis and Critical Peace Education

A critical consideration of the emotions of conflict and peace in schools enables new directions for a radical reinterpretation of peace education efforts. Principally, this reinterpretation is positioned within the micro-political terrain of the schools and the classrooms, rather than the macro-political structures of a conflict. In this manner, this book is essentially concerned with reconsidering the implications of the macro-political structures of a conflict in micro-political pedagogical encounters and aims to develop capacities for renewed critical approaches in peace education. In particular, this book lays out a "road map" for how critical pedagogies of peace education may use the power of emotion to bring about small transformations and openings in ethical encounters with others. And here is where the notion of "critical emotional praxis" provides the overarching theoretical framework to do so.

Critical emotional praxis is a theoretical and practical tool that recognizes how emotions play a powerful role in either sustaining or disrupting hegemonic discourses about past traumatic events (Zembylas, 2008a). Critical emotional praxis is theoretically grounded in a psychoanalytic and sociopolitical analysis of emotion and trauma and provides a platform from which teachers and students can critically interrogate their own emotion-laden beliefs. This analysis exposes privileged positions of psychic and sociopolitical power and moves beyond the comfort zones in which teachers and students are usually socialized in a traumatized society.

Furthermore, critical emotional praxis recognizes the emotional ambivalence that often accompanies this process and thus creates pedagogical opportunities for critical inquiry into how emotions of uncertainty or discomfort, despite making the world seem ambiguous and chaotic, can restore humanity and encourage healing and reconciliation. Ambivalent emotions—for example, resentment and bitterness with feelings of common vulnerability and empathy—emerge from teaching and learning that recognizes the relationality of trauma; that is, if we can narrate "our" stories of trauma to ourselves and to those who have wounded us and listen to the narratives of those we have wounded, we might set up better conditions for imagining new political

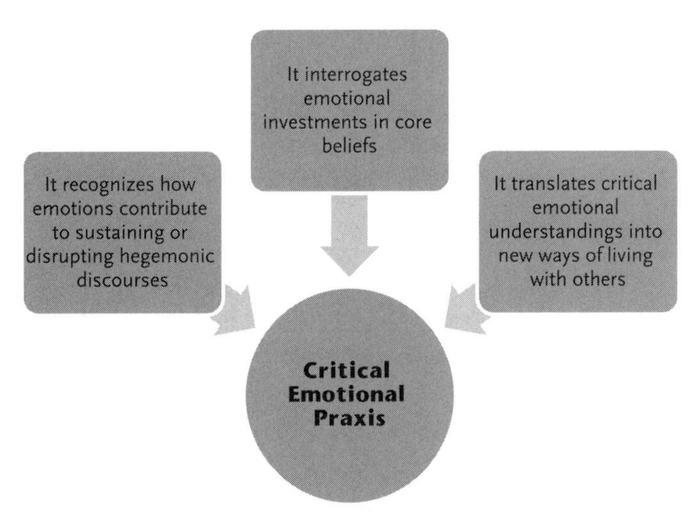

FIGURE 2.1 Summary of the basic components of "critical emotional praxis."

relations (Georgis & Kennedy, 2009; Zembylas, 2008a). The ambivalence of emotion, then, highlights the reality that positive and negative emotions are provisional readings and judgments of others that change when there are opportunities to re-articulate the past in new ways. Critical emotional praxis, therefore, offers opportunities to produce transformative action, because teachers and students are enabled to translate their critical emotional understandings into new ways of living with others. The components of critical emotional praxis are summarized in Figure 2.1.

Emotions of trauma, such as fear, when normalized, impede discourse and action for healing and reconciliation in schools in numerous ways—in the denial of the other's humanity; in the refusal to challenge cherished beliefs; in the perpetuation of the moralistic regime of considering one's self an eternal victim and the other a permanent perpetrator. In order to oppose the normalization of emotions of trauma and to enact peace and reconciliation practices in schools, educators need pedagogical tools that illuminate the interplay between emotions and trauma and critically interrogate their consequences. A critique of the politicization of emotions of trauma in schools offers a deeper understanding of the multifaceted dynamics of trauma; if students and teachers are susceptible to trauma through the normalization of emotions such as fear, then it is incumbent upon educators and policy makers to consider the force of emotions and their implications. Learning from a critical approach to the emotions of trauma is an important departure point for generating new insights into what it might mean to evaluate the prospects and challenges of healing and reconciliation in schools.

As noted earlier, emotions of trauma are inextricably woven into historically based ideologies that teach students and teachers how to perceive themselves and act toward others. This argument indicates how pedagogical practices within a community contribute to the conservation of prevailing psychological and sociopolitical norms in relation to another (the "enemy") community. For example, the teaching of "us-and-them" and "good-versus-evil" narratives from an early age imposes certain affective associations that stick various signs and symbols together—that is, in the case of Cyprus, for Greek Cypriots, the Turkish element is invariably the "fearsome other" and the "evil enemy" and vice-versa. The hegemonic discourses and practices that derive from such thinking systematically build a sense of ethnic identity and community that rests on absolute us-and-them and good-versus-evil dichotomies, and encourage members of one community to define themselves as the only victims of conflict. In this manner, there is no middle ground left for revolt or emotional ambivalence—e.g. to acknowledge that the other community has also suffered and that its members have been victims of the Cyprus conflict too.

It may be argued, therefore, that school discourses and practices that promote the normalization of trauma are *mis-educative* and exert *pedagogic violence* (Worsham, 2001), because trauma is used politically by one group to reject the humanity of the other and perpetuate hostile relations with them (Zembylas, 2008). Research in Israel (e.g. Bar-Tal 2000b, 2003) and Northern Ireland (e.g. McGlynn et al., 2004) confirms the negative pedagogical implications of the political appropriation of emotions to perpetuate divisions and hostilities. If students and teachers in traumatized societies want to create a new psychic and sociopolitical order where they do not simply remain traumatized "objects" of history, they need to re-consider their affective relationship with the other and how it is constructed. An important aspect of reconsideration in this process lies in coming to terms with the emotional remains of past traumatic legacies in schools and in the wider society.

Therefore, instead of taking ideas and feelings for granted, teachers and students begin to interrogate their emotional investments in core beliefs (e.g. the belief in the exclusivity of one's victimhood and the evil nature of the other) and examine the consequences in relation to existing dichotomies and hostilities. These efforts expose monological perspectives and move beyond the comfort zones in which the teacher and her students are often socialized. While engaging in this critical interrogation does not guarantee liberatory action in itself, the process challenges students' understanding of emotions and the ideologies in which they may be grounded (e.g. nationalism). This critical interrogation creates openings for different affective relations—such as empathy, humility, and compassion—that may advance healing and reconciliation in the context of critical peace education.

Critical peace education pays attention to issues of structural inequalities and aims to cultivate a sense of transformative agency to advance peacebuilding (Bajaj, 2008; Bajaj & Brantmeier, 2011; Brantmeier, 2011; Trifonas & Wright, 2013; Wulf, 1974; Zembylas & Bekerman, 2013). Bajaj (2008) discusses Diaz-Soto's (2005) approach to critical peace education as situated in consciousness-raising inspired by Freire (2005). Bajaj and Brantmeier (2011) also argue that one of the most important features of critical peace education is its alignment with a counter-hegemonic paradigm for social change through education. The goal of critical peace education is to empower young people to engage in practices and activism that increase societal equity and justice, which in turn, foster greater peace. As Bajaj and Brantmeier write: "What we term "critical peace education" . . . is that which approaches the particularistic, seeking to enhance transformative agency and participatory citizenship, and open to resonating in distinct ways with the diverse chords of peace that exist across fields and cultures" (2011, p. 222). Both Bajaj's (2008) analysis and Brantmeier's (2011) identification of critical peace education as the cultivation of transformative agency highlight how injustice and conflict are linked. Hence, the transformation of unjust societal structures addresses conflict, just as the reduction of destructive forms of conflict fostered through critical peace education contributes to dismantling unjust structures and eliminating inequities.

More recently, Zembylas and Bekerman (2013) have entered the discussion on critical peace education by arguing that peace education may often become part of the problem it tries to solve, if theoretical work is not used to interrogate the taken-for-granted assumptions about peace and peace education. For this purpose, they put forward a proposition consisting of four elements aiming to reclaim criticality in peace education: reinstating the materiality of things and practices; reontologizing research and practice in peace education; becoming critical experts of design; and engaging in critical cultural analysis. Although their proposition acknowledges the importance of critical ontology and materiality in peace education, there is no explicit attention to the materiality of emotions and its underlying structures that constitute bodily/social/cultural/historical/political arrangements and understandings about peace, conflict, and trauma.

An approach grounded in critical emotional praxis offers critical peace education the conceptual grounding to interrogate the "structures of feeling" that prevent the advancement of peace, because it critically analyzes power relations and entanglements between emotion and traumatic conflict. Critical emotional praxis addresses the ways in which traumatic conflict is manifest personally

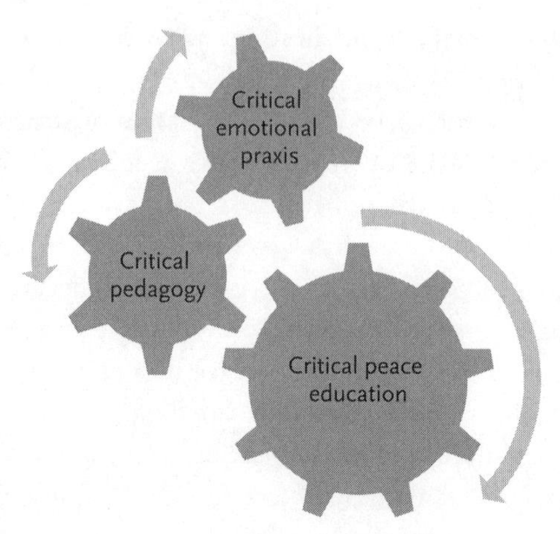

FIGURE 2.2 Intersectional relationship among critical emotional praxis, critical pedagogy, and critical peace education.

and socially and, through the critical analysis of emotion, it encourages action toward the emancipatory goals of critical peace education. At the same time, as noted earlier, critical emotional praxis takes into consideration the emotional tensions and dilemmas in posttraumatic contexts. In this manner, the notion of critical emotional praxis intersects with both critical pedagogy and critical peace education (see Figure 2.2).

Conclusions

So, what do we gain from grounding this book in the notion of critical emotional praxis? First, an approach of critical peace education and critical pedagogy that is enriched by the notion of critical emotional praxis offers opportunities to create spaces for healing and reconciliation in schools—that is, spaces that permit encounters "between the open expression of the painful past, on the one hand, and the search for the articulation of a long-term interdependent future, on the other hand" (Lederach, 1997, p. 29). These spaces allow for the flow of alternative ideas and encourage students and teachers to realize that what they share with those they have classified as "the enemy" may be greater than what divides them. Undoubtedly, these spaces are messy, troublesome, and emotionally discomforting, but they have three valuable features that can promote healing and reconciliation in schools: first, developing a willingness to meet the other in humility and openness; second, acknowledging not only one's own pain but also the pain of the other, as well as admitting responsibility for having wounded the other; and, third, putting into practice strategies that promote empathetic and humanizing ways of reconciling past grievances without establishing new moralistic regimes (Porter, 2007). The emotional complexities of these features will become "alive" through the empirical evidence presented in the upcoming chapters.

Second, an approach of critical peace education and critical pedagogy that is enriched by the notion of critical emotional praxis deepens awareness and criticality about the ways in which trauma stories can be used to teach fear, hate, and mistrust and to perpetuate a trauma-based worldview (Ramanathapillai, 2006). This approach highlights multiperspectivity and the critical emotional analysis of all trauma stories. All stories, according to Kreuzer (2002), even the ones from the perpetrators of violence, need to be considered seriously, because they help us understand the emotional complexities of a conflict. It is in this context, for example, that emotional ambivalence and revolt offer opportunities to revisit one's feelings and re-create emotional connections with others on a different basis. Critical emotional praxis highlights the ability to incorporate other people's perceptions, see and feel with the other's experience, and formulate solidarity bonds on the basis of common humanity and common suffering (Bekerman & Zembylas, 2012; Halpern & Weinstein, 2004).

Therefore, an approach that places psychoanalytically informed perspectives and sociopolitical conceptions of emotions and trauma at the forefront is an important resource for critical peace education. Such perspectives are valuable in developing pedagogical spaces that shift from an uncritical adoption of trauma to an informed insight that "imagine[s] the world altogether differently" (Georgis & Kennedy, 2009, p. 20). Aware of the essentializing features of many pedagogical approaches toward peace education (Zembylas, 2007a), this book emphasizes that rethinking teaching and learning about traumatic conflict, healing, and reconciliation requires a subtle understanding of the ambivalence of emotion and the need to rearticulate the meaning(s) of emotions of trauma as well as their manifestations in practice (Ahmed, 2004). In other words, the effects of emotional injury are powerful, yet they are also temporary and ambivalent, and do not solidify into moralistic law unless the political appropriation of emotions of trauma remains unchallenged. By paying attention to this temporality and ambivalence of emotions of trauma in the context of schools, teachers and students are essentially invited to confront the psychic, social, and political dilemmas of their traumatic histories as "they" encounter "others" who are often defined as "mortal enemies."

Schools are already political terrains in which emotions are ideologically appropriated; however, the role of schools can be further humanized, if they are turned into places of humane connections with adversaries. It is such connections that constitute spaces that oppose polarized trauma narratives and open possibilities for renewing the sense of community and identity. Destabilizing the rhetoric of binary opposites and the hegemonic ways of thinking and feeling about past traumas engages students and teachers in a politics that radically reevaluates the emotional culture in which they live. From this perspective, reframing trauma stories can help restore both one's own and the other's humanity and counteract the confrontational content of competing narratives that lead to dehumanization. The aim is not only to understand what emotions of trauma *do* in everyday school life but also to invent new interpretive approaches and practices of relating with others—critical pedagogies that do not fossilize emotional injury but *move forward*. The richness and complexity of the emotional aspects of critical peace education and critical pedagogy call for more refined and more varied theories, methodologies, and practices.

Notes

1. As an alternative to PTSD, the concept of *posttraumatic growth* (PTG) has been suggested. Posttraumatic growth refers to the process of growth experienced as a result of the struggle with adversity in life (Tedeschi & Calhoun, 1995, 2004). According to previous research on PTG, it is not the event itself that fosters growth but rather the struggle in the aftermath of trauma that leads to such growth. Although previous research has focused almost exclusively on the psychological change experienced as a result of struggling with adversity, my analysis here suggests the possibility that there might be social, cultural, political, and other qualitative transformations that result from a community's struggle with trauma.
2. "Difficult knowledge" refers to the moments when knowledge appears inconceivable to the self, bringing oneself up against the limits of what one is willing and capable of understanding (Pitt & Britzman, 2003; Simon, 2011b). As Simon (2011b) clarifies:

   > [W]hat is difficult about historical knowledge associated with violence and conflict is not just that the materials exhibited elicit anger, horror and disgust, and judgments that past actions were shameful and unjust. More to the point, what defines the difficult in the encounters offered by exhibitions addressing violence and conflict is what happens in that moment when one receives the terrible gift that an exhibition enacts, when one comes face to face with the task of inheriting the troubling consequences of "the otherness of knowledge." Understood on these terms, difficulty happens when one's conceptual frameworks, emotional attachments, and conscious and unconscious desires delimit one's ability to settle the meaning of past events. (pp. 433–434)

What is "difficult," then, is not only a matter of what histories one carries from the past or how these histories are represented, but also the possibility of "encountering the self through the otherness of knowledge" (Pitt & Britzman, 2003, p. 755). That is, the "difficulty" has to do with the affective force provoked by the experience of facing one's experiences in relation to understanding past events.

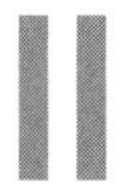

THE EMOTIONAL SPACES OF RACISM AND NATIONALISM IN SCHOOLS

History is that certainty produced at the point where the imperfections of memory meet the inadequacies of documentation.

—JULIAN BARNES, *The Sense of an Ending*

We become just by performing just actions, temperate by performing temperate actions, brave by performing brave actions.

—ARISTOTLE

3 INVESTIGATING THE EMOTIONAL GEOGRAPHIES OF EXCLUSION

Anger, hatred, fear, sadness, and pain often accompany discussions of racial and ethnic matters (Ahmed, 2004; Zembylas, 2008a). Emotions are deemed important in challenging or reinforcing prevailing practices and discourses about race and ethnicity both in schools (Callahan, 2004) and in society (Ahmed, 2004). As Ahmed has argued, emotions circulate between people; they "stick" as well as move, and they involve relations of "towardness" or "awayness" in ways in which race and ethnicity are understood (2004). In particular, the notion of *emotional geographies* (Anderson & Smith, 2001; Davidson & Milligan, 2004; Davidson, Bondi, & Smith, 2005) that has been invoked in recent years signifies a growing concern with the spatiality and relationality of emotions. An emotional geography explained by Davidson, Bondi, and Smith (2005) attempts to understand emotions in terms of the sociospatial dynamics of movements and relations rather than as entirely interiorized subjective mental states. For example, an interpretation of the sociospatial dynamics of racism and other oppressions shows how exclusion is understood as a manifestation of emotions that arise in real or imagined movement between "selves" and "others" (Sibley, 1995).

While emotions have always been acknowledged as important components of discussions about racial and ethnic matters (Srivastava, 2005, 2006), there have been few sustained investigations of how and with what implications emotions are constituted through school practices and discourses in relation to perceptions of race and ethnicity (Zembylas, 2005, 2007a). More important, emotions have remained in the margins of discussions about the sociospatial dynamics of racialization and ethnicization processes in schools, or at best, are regarded as epiphenomena rather than as constitutive components in students' and teachers' lives (Chubbuck & Zembylas, 2008).

This chapter highlights the need to look more carefully at how school practices and discourses are entangled with emotions in relation to perceptions of race and ethnicity in conflicted societies. More specifically, the focus is on how emotional geographies are manifest in the formation and maintenance of particular racialization and ethnicization processes within a multicultural primary school in the Republic of Cyprus. The uniqueness of this school is that the teachers are all Greek Cypriots and the students are both Greek-Cypriot (the majority) and Turkish-speaking children (the minority). The interaction takes place against the background of the long-standing political and ethnic conflict between Greek Cypriots and Turkish Cypriots (see chapter 1). Given that my main interest is to explore how emotional geographies work as spaces of exclusion, I want to clarify at the outset that my focus in this chapter is mostly on the negative emotions rather than the positive emotions (more emphasis on the positive emotions is given in chapter 9). My central argument is that the emotional geographies of exclusion can be understood as manifestations of the racialization and ethnicization processes in schools—a finding that has important implications for how to understand the insidious power and tenacity in certain manifestations of these processes, particularly in divided societies such as Cyprus. Before delving into the case study of the school and the findings as such, I want to highlight a few ideas on the sociospatial dynamics of emotion that are relevant to the present chapter.

The Sociospatial Dynamics of Emotion

In thinking through the sociospatial dynamics of emotion, I find much of value in drawing on recent theorizing in the fields of critical theory, emotional geographies, and the cultural politics of emotions. As noted in chapter 1, my approach to analyzing emotions is informed by critical and poststructuralist concerns with language, power relations, bodies, and social structures (Ahmed, 2004; Lutz & Abu-Lughod, 1990). Critical poststructuralist theories reconceptualize emotions as a public, not exclusively private, object of inquiry that is interactively embedded in power relations; thus these perspectives historicize the ways in which emotions are constituted, their organization into discourse and technologies of power, and their importance as a site of social and spatial control through surveillance and self-policing (Boler, 1999; Zembylas, 2008a). I focus, then, on the relations of language, body, social structures, and power through which emotions are produced and become part of discourses and practices. For example, a relevant question to raise with regard to the concern of this chapter is this: How are emotional practices and discourses racialized and ethnicized in schools? This question focuses on the ways through which power relations and social structures manifested in perceptions about race and ethnicity produce and are produced by particular emotional practices and discourses that include/exclude others. Critical and poststructuralist perspectives highlight the transaction between larger social forces (macro-political) and the internal psychic terrain of the individual (Boler, 1999; Zembylas, 2005, 2007a). Socialization practices and discourses, including corporeal, spatial, and discursive signs and hierarchies of power and position, are critical to shaping the presence or absence—as well as the intensity—of any given emotion. The presence and intensity of emotions, in turn, shape the sociospatial context in which they occur. Within this transactional process emotions are understood as embedded in culture, ideology, gender, space, and power relations.

The notion of emotional geographies draws attention both to the relationality and to the spatiality of emotions, highlighting issues such as the complex range of emotions that emerge as a consequence of movement, that is, the circulation of emotions through individual and collective bodies, shaping social relations and challenging taken-for-granted boundaries of the self (Ahmed, 2004). In addition, emotional geographies emphasize the strong links between emotion and space/place, that is, the emotionally dynamic spatiality of belonging and subjectivity (Good, 2004). A systematic investigation of the movement of emotions and bodies in certain spaces/places would, therefore, be greatly beneficial—e.g. in relation to the nation-state, the border, the boundary, proximity (to sit near, to touch), departure and distance, segregation, separation, occupation, spatial identifications, and disqualifications. This suggestion implies the need to develop concepts and theories that explicitly investigate emotions "in contemporary settings of globalized economic crisis, state violence, exploited migrant communities, and hegemonic gender politics of post-colonial states" (Good, 2004, p. 529). The explicit investigation of emotions in precisely these settings, argues Good, shows that "only through explicating the logic of key emotional constructs do major social dramas become intelligible" (ibid.).

Finally, my approach draws from Ahmed's (2004) "sociality of emotions" model. Ahmed argues that emotions play a crucial role in the ways that individuals come together and move *toward* or *away* in relation to others. Again, this argument challenges the assumption that emotions are "individual" or "private" phenomena and supports the position that emotions are located *in* movement, circulating between bodies. Hence movement is always embedded within certain sociospatial contexts and connects bodies to other bodies; attachment to certain bodies (which are perceived to be similar) and distance from others (which are considered dissimilar) takes place through this movement, through being moved by the proximity or distance of others. To put this differently: emotions do not come from inside us as *reaction* but are produced in and circulated between others and ourselves as *actions* and *practices*. This circulation happens precisely because individuals do not live in a social and political vacuum but *move,* and thus emotions become attached to individuals united in their feelings for something. If emotions shape and are shaped by perceptions of race and ethnicity, for example, then it is interesting to investigate how particular emotions "stick" to certain bodies or flow and traverse space (see e.g. Moreno Figueroa, 2008).

Emotion, Race/Ethnicity, and the Emotional Geographies of Exclusion

Srivastava asks the rhetorical question, "What do emotion and race have to do with one another?" (2006, p. 60). Some scholars have acknowledged the emotional investments and implications of racial oppression (Essed, 1991; Stoler, 1995). This acknowledgment exposes the "deep emotional undercurrents and foundations of racial conflict" (Srivastava, 2006, p. 61). Racial as well as ethnic matters evoke a range of powerful emotions that push researchers to take a more careful look into the relationship between race/ethnicity and emotion (Goodwin, Jasper, & Poletta, 2001).

Taking as a starting point contemporary theorizations of race and racism (Balibar & Wallerstein, 1991; Blumer & Solomos, 1999) and ethnicity and nationalism (Gellner, 1983; Smith, 2004), I argue that classifications of "race" and "ethnicity" must be understood as social and political constructions that are embedded in sociospatial, political, and historical structures and have real and uneven material consequences. That is, the constructed and discursive nature of race and ethnicity is recognized as a political project for the formation of particular individuals and social groups. Race and ethnicity have a materiality that is partly to do with the aspects of racial and ethnic discourses that are constructed as being material (e.g. bodily markers are used to stereotype people) and partly about the emotional practices through which bodies are drawn together or apart on racialized and ethnicized terms (see Riggs & Augoustinos, 2005).

My approach, therefore, demonstrates the importance of examining how race and ethnicity are materialized through emotional practices and discourses and create emotional geographies that legitimate certain inclusions/exclusions. In other words, following Butler (1997), there is no "race" or "ethnicity" prior to its materialization, and if emotion is part of this materialization and occurs through the emotional investment of race and ethnicity with power, then it would seem important to grasp how emotional experiences of race/ethnicity are played out in particular school contexts. This way of thinking can be reframed in the following question: How is it that certain bodies and emotional practices "stick" together, move, and perpetuate certain perceptions about race/ethnicity, and how such bodies and practices occur within racialized and ethnicized processes in schools?

Research shows, for example, how individual fears are cultivated through the intervention of social, political, and educational forces and are less the outcome of direct experience (Zembylas, 2009b). The politics of hatred and fear sustain those emotional practices and discourses that enable anti-immigration attitudes, racism, and nationalism to flourish, curtail civic liberties, and promote the process of attacking everyone who is *different* (Zembylas, 2008a). The formation of social and spatial boundaries aims to protect the integrity of (presumed) racial and ethnic-cultural heritages; this sense of belonging "naturalizes" the concerns of origin and heritage (Penninx, 1988 in Milikowski, 2000) and attaches particular emotions (e.g. pride) to one's own racial or ethnic origin and heritage. The emotional geographies that are created by practices of exclusion and discrimination therefore can be understood as manifestations of the racialization and ethnicization processes (Sibley, 1995).

Given that there has been little research on the emotions embedded in the structures of racialization and ethnicization processes in schools, it is important to study how such processes are entangled with the emotional geographies of exclusion in specific settings. These kinds of investigations urge us to consider how students' and teachers' perceptions about racial and ethnic matters create powerful emotional boundaries between bodies that are read as similar and those that are considered to be different, especially in recent times in which racial and ethnic ideologies become more heterogeneous and extend educational inequalities (Phoenix, 2002; Stevens, 2007).

The School Setting

The data for this chapter are drawn from a two-month case study in a Greek-Cypriot multicultural primary school, according to the procedures described in chapter 1. The Hill School (HS) is a pseudonym for this school; it is located in a small city and has 16 teachers (all Greek Cypriots) and 140 students, 70% of whom are Greek Cypriots, 12% Turkish-speaking, and 18% from various other countries. The socioeconomic background of students is considered low, and the Greek-Cypriot population is mainly comprised of refugees who fled from the north to save their lives in the aftermath of the Turkish invasion in 1974. Free meals are provided to Turkish-speaking students, but no lessons or extra language classes are conducted in those children's mother tongue. Most of these students do not speak or understand any Greek. Also, there is regular migration between the south and the north part of Cyprus among Turkish-speaking students, thus influencing their education and school participation.

The case study at the Hill School focused on the following questions:

1. What emotions do Greek-Cypriot students and teachers express about Turkish-speaking children and what kinds of emotional geographies are constituted in this school?
2. How are those emotional geographies entangled with Greek-Cypriot teachers' and students' perceptions of race and ethnicity?
3. What are the implications of these emotional geographies for Turkish-speaking children's everyday lives?

The Hill School was chosen because of its relatively high number of Turkish-speaking children. As explained in chapter 1, data were collected through in-depth interviews, ethnographic observations, and examination of school documents. Semistructured interviews were conducted with the principal, six teachers, six focus groups of Greek-Cypriot children at various grade levels (approximately four children in each group), and two focus groups of Turkish-speaking children (two children in each group)[1]; unofficial discussions were also conducted with the rest of the teachers and several other children. Three teachers (who volunteered) were observed by a research assistant in their classrooms for almost three weeks, from 7:45 a.m. to 1:05 p.m. per day (i.e. for the duration of the school day). All of the teachers observed had at least eight years of teaching experience. The data sources also included documents of student work and teachers' planning related to various aspects of their teaching.

Analysis

Greek-Cypriot Students' and Teachers' Emotions about Turkish-speaking Children: Toxic and Politically Charged Emotional Geographies

Among Greek-Cypriot students and teachers at the Hill School, perceptions about Turkish-speaking students' race and ethnicity varied. One typical understanding of Turkish-speaking students is captured in the conversation that follows. In this conversation, a Greek-Cypriot female teacher was discussing the cultural characteristics of Turkish-speaking students, explaining why they were not accepted by the majority of Greek-Cypriot students[2]:

TEACHER: First of all, Turkish-speaking students are distinguished by their external appearance. They have a darker skin complexion, they are extremely dirty and untidy, especially the Roma, and they don't speak any Greek. They usually stink and this is a cultural thing. Anyway, they don't have the habit of cleaning themselves and so our children [Greek Cypriots] don't like to play or sit in class with them. [. . .] And there is, of course, the hostility against the Turks.

RESEARCHER: What do you mean by that?

TEACHER: I refer to these children's Turkish identity and the fact that Turks are our historical enemies.

In general, this exchange reflected the toxic and politically charged emotional geographies in this school. National division and hatred in Cyprus was rescaled right down to the school emotional geographies. Emotions of hatred traveled and "pushed away" Turkish-speaking children, who were essentially blamed for the "misfortune" to have a Turkish origin and a relatively "darker" skin complexion. The movement of such emotions from the larger political landscape to this school created racialized and ethnicized emotional geographies and constructed "borders" between Greek-Cypriot and Turkish-speaking students. Interestingly, a large number of the Greek-Cypriot students with whom we spoke confirmed the presence and flow of negative emotions about Turkish-speaking children. The following two dialogues are excerpts from conversations with children of grades 2 and 6 that indicate the emotional specificities of the toxic and politically charged emotional geographies at this school.

Dialogue 1 (grade 2 children)

RESEARCHER: Do you have children from different countries in your school?

MARIOS: We have blacks [*mavrous*]

RESEARCHER: Who are these children? I don't understand.

ALEXIOS: The blacks, miss, the Turks.

RESEARCHER: You mean the Turks are black?

ALEXIOS: Yes, they are not like us.

RESEARCHER: What do you mean they are not like you?

MARIOS: They are not our friends. I don't like them, because they are black.

ALEXIOS: They beat us all the time, we don't like to play with them. They often stink, they are not clean.

Dialogue 2 (grade 6 children)

RESEARCHER: Why don't you play with Turkish-speaking students?

YOLANDA: Because we come from different countries. We play with kids who come from our own country.

RESEARCHER: But why is that? Aren't those kids Cypriots too? (the researcher refers to Turkish-speaking students who are Turkish Cypriots, the majority of Turkish-speaking students at this school)
MARY: No, Miss! They are Turks!
RESEARCHER: OK, why is that a problem in playing with them?
LOLA: Because they fight all the time. They curse us all the time in their language and I don't feel good because the Turks occupy my mother's village. The Turks came and kicked her out and she came here.
MARY: It's the problem of Cyprus with Turkey.
YOLANDA: They took our Cyprus without reason and still occupy it.
LOLA: They come and go all the time from the occupied areas [the north] and they think all Cyprus belongs to them.

Notice the development of children's discourse from the second grade—in which issues of color and cleanliness were predominant—to the sixth grade—in which the ethnic origin of Turkish-speaking children became the center of discussion. In the latter dialogue, the politically charged emotional geographies were more evident and constituted a range of negative emotions toward these children. In these two and other dialogues that the research team documented, there was evidence that national belonging, perceptions about the occupation of Cyprus, and spatial identifications were enmeshed with emotions of proximity and distance about those who were deemed as "similar" (belonging to the Greek group) and those identified as "enemies" (belonging to the Turkish group). The negative emotions toward Turkish-speaking children and the movements of these emotions—as are evident in Greek-Cypriot teachers' and students' discourses—constitute emotional geographies that marginalize Turkish-speaking students.

The segregation and emotional distance between Greek-Cypriot and Turkish-speaking students was also evident in many aspects of everyday school life. Students socialized mainly with those belonging to their own ethnic group—from their sitting arrangements in the classroom to the games they played in the schoolyard. A number of students (both Greek-Cypriot and Turkish-speaking) and teachers essentially confirmed that Greek-Cypriot students' perceptions about the race and ethnicity of Turkish-speaking students were manifestations of emotional geographies that created and maintained segregation and distance. For example, a male teacher explained:

> The cultural differences and the ethnic origin of Turkish-speaking students are major sources of conflict between Greek-Cypriot and Turkish-speaking students. I mean you don't necessarily see them fighting all the time but it's the little things, the details, that make a

> difference. For example, Greek-Cypriot students refuse to sit next to Turkish-speaking students in the classroom or refuse to hold hands in the physical education lessons. Turkish-speaking students do not speak the Greek language and so it's even harder for them to be included in lessons and games. Several of my colleagues have a hard time even accepting these children because of the political problem in Cyprus. This is sad, but it's the truth.

A female teacher demonstrated what the previous teacher meant in his last sentence:

> The Turkish-Cypriot students' national identity and dark skin complexion are major issues for our [Greek-Cypriot] students. Turkish Cypriots are segregated because they don't try to learn Greek or clean themselves. And I don't mean all of them. Greek Cypriots often use expressions such as "I can't stand the Turks" or "These blacks are dirty and stink," but unfortunately they are right. [. . .] We are in a difficult position as teachers because Greek-Cypriot parents and grandparents complain that we have their children sitting next to Turkish Cypriots. One day there was this Greek-Cypriot fifth-grader who told me, "Miss, please do not mention the name "Turkey" ever again, I can't listen to it." When I asked why, he said: "Because Turks occupy our country and I want them to leave. I want the Turks to leave from our school too." He was adamant about it. How could I respond to that?

Such negative emotions about Turkish-speaking children did not just "stick" to individual bodies but came about in the real and imagined movement between "selves" and "others" (Ahmed, 2004, 2005) and played out in the exclusionary aspects (Sibley, 1995) of everyday school life. Thus we documented (through observations) numerous incidents in which the exclusion of Turkish-speaking students was manifest in the negative emotions of the majoritized group, suggesting that there was a consistent segregation and separation of students on the basis of racial and ethnic markers and that several Greek-Cypriot teachers and students acted on that basis. Unable—or perhaps unwilling—to identify the institutional structures that contributed to the segregation of Turkish-speaking students, Greek-Cypriot students and teachers did not recognize their privilege (e.g. majority language, general status, hegemonic Greek culture, etc.) and cast this segregation as entirely the Turkish-speaking children's "problem." One predominant emotion that showed the powerful workings of politically charged emotional geographies was *disgust*.

The Sociospatial Dynamics of Disgust

One of the most frequent emotions described by Greek-Cypriot students toward their Turkish-speaking classmates was disgust. A few teachers expressed sympathy for the hard times that Turkish-speaking students seemed to experience and recognized that the toxic and politically charged emotional geographies stood in the way of building mutual understanding and respect. In general, however, the majority of teachers attributed the Greek-Cypriot students' negative emotions to the Turkish occupation and division of Cyprus. As one female teacher stated:

> I am aware of the intense negative emotions of many Greek-Cypriot students toward their Turkish-Cypriot classmates. Some of us at this school try very hard to change those feelings, but there is not much support and I'll leave it at that. Some Greek-Cypriot students bring those attitudes from home, from their refugee parents, you know what I mean, but those attitudes are cultivated here at school as well. Greek-Cypriot students are not willing to collaborate with Turkish-speaking students and they show those negative emotions overtly on every possible occasion.

In the following conversation, another teacher provided an example of how those negative emotions were manifest in everyday life at school:

RESEARCHER: How do Greek-Cypriot students express their emotions about their Turkish-speaking classmates? Can you provide an example?
TEACHER: They often say "I don't want to be with them."
RESEARCHER: In front of those children?
TEACHER: Yes.
RESEARCHER: That cynical?
TEACHER: Yes. They may not always say it in this manner, but their body movement and facial expressions show disgust or complete apathy toward them.

The following incidents show how emotions of disgust established distance between Greek-Cypriot and Turkish-speaking students. Such "apartness" involved the repetition of stereotypes about Turkish-speaking students. The links between these stereotypes and negative emotions "scripted" the emotional geographies of exclusion. The alignment of bodily and social space was evident in how disgust limited the movement of Turkish-speaking students in social space. Expressions of disgust by Greek-Cypriot students worked to secure social norms and power relations (see Boler, 1999; Lutz & Abu-Lughod, 1990).

Incident 1

The lesson is over and students are waiting for the bell to ring. A Turkish-speaking girl, Emine—who usually sits alone in the last row—makes a move to join a group of Greek-Cypriot girls who are getting ready to read together a Greek children's journal. The Greek-Cypriot girls are laughing and joking and seem to enjoy what they are reading. The teacher is writing something in a notebook and seems absorbed in what she is doing. Emine moves slowly-slowly toward the group of Greek-Cypriot girls. As soon as one of the girls notices the presence of Emine her look becomes angry and she yells at her: "You, leave us right now!" Emine turns back, her face looks very sad, and returns to her seat. I slowly approach the Greek-Cypriot girls' table. They whisper among themselves. "Can you imagine? That stinky Turkish-girl coming to our table?" said one girl, and another responded: "We told her a thousand times, we don't want her to sit with us! She's stupid! She doesn't understand!" A third girl added: "She's incapable of learning Greek."

(field notes, grade 6)

Incident 2

The children have their physical education lesson out in the schoolyard. There are a few minutes left so the teacher tells them to play whatever game they want. The Greek-Cypriot boys form two teams and start playing soccer. Two Turkish-speaking boys stand along the sidelines and wait to be included but nobody pays attention to them. They wave to the other students to be included on the teams, but the Greek-Cypriot boys ignore them. The teacher, who sees what is happening, tells the two boys to choose any other game they want to play by themselves. When I later asked the Greek-Cypriot boys to explain why they did not include the two Turkish-speaking boys, one of them responded: "They are Turks! They get into fights all the time, so we don't want them to play with us."

(field notes, grade 5)

The above incidents, which represented other similar ones, indicate how disgust affected the relations between Greek-Cypriot and Turkish-speaking students. Disgust involved not just corporeal intensities but discourses that made Greek-Cypriot students "pull away" from their Turkish-speaking classmates. The sticking of disgust to Turkish-speaking children worked to affect Greek-Cypriot students by linking emotions to perceptions about the ongoing division and occupation of Cyprus. Once again, it is shown how the division, occupation, and segregation were rescaled right down to the desk, the classroom, and the playground. The following dialogue with a group of fifth-grade Greek-Cypriot students could not show this more bluntly:

RESEARCHER: How do you feel about having Turkish-speaking students as your classmates?
DOROS: Not so good.
PETROS: My parents are refugees.
RESEARCHER: Why don't you feel good? What do you mean by that?
DOROS: Because . . . (long pause) because we have Turks in our school and we should only have Cypriots. But we have Turks.
RESEARCHER: Are they doing something wrong?
PETROS: They kick us and beat us.
CHRISTOS: I feel hatred about them.
RESEARCHER: (turning to Christos) That's a strong word!
PETROS: I want to beat them back. They came to take over our school and steal everything from us, like they do in the occupied areas.

We also collected a wealth of evidence showing that Greek-Cypriot students often used stereotypical names for Turkish-speaking children such as "filthy Turks" [*bromotourtzoi*]. Sometimes, Greek-Cypriot students held their noses when a Turkish-speaking student (particularly any of the Roma students) came close to them, saying aloud, "Yiax" (an expression of disgust; see chapter 4). One Greek-Cypriot student said once, referring to a Turkish-speaking (Roma) student, that "She stinks like a rotted sausage," and several other students laughed. All these examples indicate the extent to which emotional geographies were racialized and ethnicized and the multiple ways in which the larger political terrain and the micro-social and spatial context of the classroom and the playground are entangled (Davidson, Bondi, & Smith, 2005). The boundary formations that were created had considerable implications for the exclusion of Turkish-speaking children.

Implications of the Emotional Geographies of Exclusion for Turkish-Speaking Children

Many Turkish-speaking children talked about their feelings of sadness and fear about being excluded in their relationships with Greek Cypriots. For example, one fourth-grade boy shared his fear about asking for a pencil when he needed one, because his Greek-Cypriot classmates would call him a "thief." Another Turkish-speaking boy recalled being called a "filthy Turk," and a girl stated that she had been told that her parents are "Turkish invaders." The intensity with which these children expressed these experiences seemed to vary depending on each child; yet, the boundary formations between Greek Cypriots and Turkish-speaking children extended the toxic emotional geographies for Turkish-speaking children.

When we asked a sixth-grade Turkish-speaking girl to describe how she felt at her school, she said, "Not so good. Greek-Cypriots tease us all the time. They don't play with us. They call us 'blacks' and 'filthy Turks.'" The following dialogue with two fifth-grade Turkish-speaking girls is indicative of the intensity of the emotional impact that this toxic environment has on these children:

RESEARCHER: Can you tell me how you feel being at this school? Are you OK? Is there something you don't like?
SAFIYE: I don't like Greek-Cypriots.
RESEARCHER: Why is that?
SAFIYE: They don't like us.
RESEARCHER: Why don't they like you?
SAFIYE: They kick us, they call us bad names. They don't want us.
DENIZ: Once I was kicked so hard by a Greek-Cypriot student, it hurt a lot.
RESEARCHER: Did you complain to anyone, to the principal?
DENIZ: No.
RESEARCHER: Why not?
DENIZ: Because they will say [we are] traitors.
RESEARCHER: How does this make you feel?
DENIZ: Not happy. Very sad.
RESEARCHER: You? (turning to Safiye)
SAFIYE: Scared.
RESEARCHER: Why scared?
SAFIYE: (long pause) They can beat us.

The above dialogue is instructive in that it shows the emotional pain experienced by Turkish-speaking children when they are in contact with their Greek-Cypriot classmates. Feelings of pain, expressed here through sadness and fear, have often been described as private experiences. And yet the pain and the resulting exclusion of Turkish-speaking children were continually entangled with the wider political discourses in the Greek-Cypriot community (e.g. with regard to the Turkish invasion and occupation). The emotional geographies of exclusion highlighted the hardship and marginalization caused by the sociospatial dynamics of racialization and ethnicization processes (Sibley, 1995) at this school. These geographies of exclusion were clearly embedded in technologies of power that perpetuated the flows of toxic emotions between "us" and "them" (Ahmed, 2004). This is also evident in the following excerpt from an interview with a teacher; in this excerpt, it is shown how geographies of exclusion could be understood as manifestations of conscious and unconscious feelings that arose in the real and imagined movement between "selves" and "others."

> It's true that Turkish-speaking students don't feel very comfortable in our school. For example, they don't feel close to me like other kids do. The simplest thing: the two girls I have in my class (she refers to the two fifth-grade girls who spoke earlier) never came to kiss me. To be honest, I freeze when I think about it! And I'm sure they freeze too. They are ashamed to tell us where they went on the weekend, and this happens especially when they visit their relatives in the occupied areas. Because they know that if they say they went to the other side and they see the reactions of their Greek-Cypriot classmates, then this will further isolate them. [. . .] But they feel safe when they are hanging out with other Turkish-speaking children. They feel more secure, more comfortable, more spontaneous, more smiley. This is obvious; they are happier when they are with their own people.

Turkish-speaking students confirmed that they felt happier (and in a sense "more included") when they were among other Turkish-speaking students, especially when they were pulled out of the classroom to receive supportive instruction (according to the educational policies of the Ministry of Education and Culture). As the teacher who offered this supportive instruction explained:

> Turkish-speaking children are totally different when they are by themselves. In the regular classroom, they seem isolated and scared and do not participate in discussions because they don't feel comfortable with their knowledge of Greek. When they are by themselves in these supportive instructions, they are happy, expressive, and alive. Their facial expressions are very different. They have my full attention and they feel more comfortable.

One of the Turkish-speaking students we interviewed reiterated this impression and said, "When it's only us, we feel happiness. In the classroom, nobody wants to sit with us." Another teacher tried to provide an explanation for why Turkish-speaking students felt uncomfortable expressing themselves: "They feel shame because the Turkish language is not particularly liked among Greek-Cypriot students. This perhaps influences their relationships with Greek-Cypriot students." It is interesting to note that not even the Turkish language could be disassociated from the toxic and politically charged emotional geographies at this school. At the same time, the example of the students moving from the class to the support session opens up very interesting issues and shows that the emotional geographies of exclusion are not homogeneous. So, at one level, the Turkish-speaking children have to deal with the emotional pain and vulnerability of being racialized and ethnicized, but at another level these boundaries of exclusion are not accepted as "natural" or "inevitable" by these children. Both levels show the complexities of the emotional geographies that underpin issues of racialization and ethnicization in this school (see also chapter 5).

Racialization and Ethnicization Processes in Schools

The analysis in this chapter shows that attending to how emotional geographies come alive offers a promising avenue through which to understand the insidious power and tenacity in certain manifestations of racialization and ethnicization processes in schools. The important intersection of emotion and race/ethnicity is seen in the constitutive role emotions play in the formation and maintenance of particular racialization and ethnicization processes, both historically and sociospatially; in these processes and spaces, emotions work to make various categorizations that include some students and exclude others (Ahmed, 2004). The ethnic division of Cyprus is rescaled down to classroom and school life through the creation of toxic and politically charged emotional geographies. This is not to suggest that all emotions (e.g. those related to nationalism and racism) are simply responses to external occurrences or forces (see also, Barrett, 2006); rather, the emotional geographies of exclusion show how racism and nationalism maintain a pervasive presence in certain social interactions and spaces in which they occur.

A viable theorization of racialization and ethnicization processes in schools requires understanding of emotions for two major reasons, as the present chapter suggests. First, emotions in relation to race and ethnicity in schools need to be understood in terms of their sociospatial transaction rather than as entirely individual psychological mechanisms (and often, pathologies) (see Davidson, Bondi, & Smith, 2005). This need suggests that the constitution of emotional geographies is an inextricable dimension of political processes (see Goodwin, Jasper, & Poletta, 2001) in which ideologies and practices—such as racism and nationalism—adapt and accommodate supremacy beliefs. Second, racialization and ethnicization processes in schools need to be seen as enacted emotional geographies that can be emotionally toxic and politically charged rather than simply socially expressed. In other words, it is important to understand how both emotional geographies and racialization/ethnicization processes are constituted and operate interactively on a range of intersecting levels (Harding &

Pribam, 2004), as shown in the example of the Turkish-speaking students moving from the classroom to the support session.

The issue of why Greek-Cypriot teachers and students either speak or justify racist actions suggests that racism adapts to new ideologies and contexts (e.g. ethnic conflict in Cyprus), accommodating the discourse within a framework of racial and ethnic superiority for security or survival or other justifications. The school in which this research is conducted may be "multicultural" in name, but essentially it remains a Greek-Cypriot school for the majority of teachers, students, and parents; the ongoing Turkish occupation of the north part of Cyprus is used to justify a defensive stance against anything that threatens the "Greek" character of the school (see also Zembylas, 2010a). The teachers take up this idea and justify what seems in many cases as either acceptance of the status quo or failure to acknowledge the racism being practiced every day.

Hence to take seriously the affective politics of racism and/or nationalism in schools is to explore how racialization and ethnicization processes are part of efforts to articulate specific inclusive/exclusive emotional relationships between the "selves" and "others." While the present chapter focuses primarily on the negative emotions involved in such processes, the following chapters consider how particular kinds of school environments construct or prevent the capacity to transform teachers' and children's (emotional) lives. By understanding how racialization and ethnicization are strongly entangled with emotion, it is possible to begin imagining an alternative vision of affective communities (Gandhi, 2006) with others—a vision that is grounded in solidarity, healing, and social justice.

Notes

1. For Turkish-speaking children who could not communicate in Greek, other children, who spoke Greek, served as translators.
2. Transcription notation for this and the following chapters:
   [. . .] Material omitted by the author
   [text] Material added by the author for the sake of clarity
   (. . .) Explanatory comments provided by the author

4 THE POLITICS OF RESENTMENT IN SCHOOL EMOTIONAL SPACES

"Schools . . . have moods, and they . . . display scenes of high drama that those who make policy and who seek to improve practice should know."

(EISNER, *1991, p. 30*)

Since the 1980s, a substantial number of studies have considered the processes of racism and racial discrimination in different educational settings (Stevens, 2007), as well as the role of schools in the formation of the "imagined community of the nation" that excludes and negates minority ethnic and other groups (McGlynn & Bekerman, 2007a). Schools employ a number of "technologies," in the Foucauldian (Foucault, 1988) sense, to create inclusions/exclusions: the distribution of classroom resources; the nature of knowledge and values taught and sanctioned in schools; the organization of time and space in ways that are identical throughout the nation; and everyday practices and policies that often go unnoticed (hidden curriculum) but that contribute to the collective sense of belonging to a particular group (such as saluting the flag, singing the national anthem, or observing national holidays).

However, one of the mechanisms used to create categorizations of the us-and-them form that is often taken for granted is the racialization/ethnicization of school emotional spaces—specifically, the constant fabrication of racial/ethnic identity through the production of spaces of resentment toward the other (McCarthy & Dimitriadis, 2000). As noted in the previous chapter, racialization and ethnicization are not the same as racism and nationalism; the notions of racialization and ethnicization put emphasis on the *processes* (see Miles, 1989) with which school (emotional) spaces are racialized and ethnicized (Barajas & Ronnkvist, 2007). In his thorough review of race and ethnicity research in English secondary schools, Stevens (2007) concludes that instead of using ethnographic research to determine whether teachers or specific processes are racist or discriminating, research in this area should focus more on exploring the processes with which these phenomena are developed and activated in context.

The present chapter builds on the rich tradition of research on racism and nationalism in education by exploring in another multicultural primary school in Cyprus how emotional spaces are racialized and ethnicized through the majoritized group's feelings of *resentment*. Just as in the previous chapter, the uniqueness of the present school lies in the fact that students from the two historically conflicting groups on the island are enrolled—that is, Greek-Cypriot students (the majoritized group) and Turkish-speaking students (the minoritized group). The chapter incorporates and builds on the work of spatial theories (Rose, 1993; Soja, 1989, 1996), critical race theory (Ladson-Billings, 2005; Ladson-Billings & Tate, 1995; Lynn & Parker, 2006; Tate, 1997), theories of emotions in education (Boler, 1999; Zembylas, 2005), and most notably the work of Ahmed (2004) on the cultural politics of emotion. These theories collectively help us explore how emotions work to align individual and collective bodies in the school context of power relations that endow the "other" with particular (often negative) meaning and value. The advantage of this approach is that it moves the emphasis from the outcome of racism and nationalism to an emphasis on the processes and ideologies of emotional connections surrounding inclusion/exclusion. Resentment, in particular, is a key resource for the constitution of racial and ethnic identity in schools through the production of (emotional) spaces of racial and ethnic origins (McCarthy & Dimitriadis, 2000). Essentially, resentment is the process of defining one's identity through the negation of the other. The focus of this chapter, then, is on schools as emotional spaces that are racialized and ethnicized through practices of resentment.

Schools as Racialized and Ethnicized Spaces and the Politics of Resentment

In the previous chapter, it is argued that classifications of "race" and "ethnicity" must be understood as social and political constructions that are embedded in historical and economic structures and have real and uneven material implications. Thus, every phenomenon of racism, argues Miles (1989), involves first of all a process of racialization in which certain people are judged by others as belonging to a separate race category. Similarly, a process of ethnicization refers to the formation of social boundaries aiming to protect the integrity of (presumed) ethnic-cultural heritages. When these categorizations and boundaries are accompanied by practices of exclusion and discrimination, then racialization and ethnicization become racism and nationalism, respectively (Ben-Eliezer, 2008).

An important idea that contemporary theories note is how racism evolved in the second half of the twentieth century to fit with the ideologies of liberal and egalitarian societies. The new type of racism is no longer based on the idea of genetic or biological differences. "New racism" is expressed in ways that are more socially acceptable and is manifested as a judgment of racialized others in relation to the dominant culture's social and moral norms, such as the work ethic, self-reliance, and individual achievement (Dovidio & Gaertner, 1998; Pettigrew & Meertens, 1995). Along with conceptions of ethnicity as the representative of an ancient and deterministic past, in the new racism and nationalism the differences between ethnic or other groups are emphasized and used as a kind of warning to prevent "foreigner" (e.g. immigrants, asylum seekers) invasion into the society and preserve the supposed unity and homogeneity of that society. In contrast to past theories, Ben-Eliezer (2008) explains, new forms of racism and nationalism celebrate difference and, in fact, want to maintain it.

Manifestations of racism and nationalism can be institutional; however, they are also seen in everyday life through *practices*. This idea suggests that although it is important to pay attention to institutional racism and nationalism as outcomes, we also need to take into account the everyday technologies that allow for the persistence of racial and ethnic ideologies. "What for the racist is a slip of the tongue, an occasional practice, a non-binding joke, a case of inattention or even ignorance is for the victims of racism part of an ongoing life experience bearing comprehensive, long-term ramifications" (Ben-Eliezer, 2008, p. 940). An interesting contribution to this discussion is Billig's (1995) idea of "banal nationalism," that is, everyday practices that reproduce national identity in ways so ordinary that they escape attention—small unnoticed words such as "we" and material symbols such as coins and flags. Therefore, Barajas and Ronnkvist (2007) highlight the ways in which school space is racialized through everyday practices and policies and maintains power relations to the benefit of the dominant group.

In general, space is conceptualized as an arena of social, historical, and political relations that imply certain assertions about social and emotional interaction, race, class, ethnicity, gender, identity formation, and power (Rose, 1993; Soja, 1989, 1996). A key idea of spatial theorists is that space is fundamental to social life; social spaces are produced and transformed by social practices (Harvey, 1989). These spaces are manifest through both informal practices and formal policies that render ethnicity and race ambivalent in that, on the one hand, "difference" is deemed irrelevant in order for the school to appear neutral and equal for all and, on the other hand, "difference" is highlighted so that ethnic and racial categorizations are celebrated (see Ben-Eliezer, 2008; Roginsky, 2006). These practices of "ethnocentric consolidation and cultural exceptionalism" (McCarthy & Dimitriadis, 2002, p. 174) characterize much educational effort to promote (naïve) multiculturalism in schools, and thus continuing racialization and ethnicization of school emotional spaces can perpetuate exclusion of marginalized groups.

What seems to be an important contribution of spatial theories, in particular, is the idea that spaces constitute particular "affective economies" (Ahmed, 2004) that are racialized and ethnicized. What characterizes emotional spaces, writes Ahmed, is that they function as economies; that is, they separate "us" from "them" as well as connect us to those who are deemed like us through circulation and distribution of affective energy (Ahmed, 2004; see also Zembylas, 2013c). Thus emotions are viewed as social products that are constituted in cultural and political spaces within which individuals interact with implications for larger political and cultural struggles (Barbalet, 1998). This idea implies that racialization and ethnicization are important mechanisms that are embedded in and define emotional spaces.

It may be argued, then, that emotional spaces in the context of schools could also be racialized and ethnicized by creating and perpetuating power relations that divide "us" from "them," negating the "other" on the basis of racial and ethnic ideologies. The production of emotional spaces of racial and ethnic origins in education is inextricably linked to the *politics of resentment* (McCarthy & Dimitriadis, 2000) as a powerful organizing trope that defines one's identity through the negation of the other. A voluminous literature in sociology, psychology, and philosophy deals with the emotional experience of resentment and its implications (see Barbalet, 1998, for a review of some of this work); however, the mechanisms by which feelings of resentment contribute to the racialization and ethnicization of school emotional spaces need further exploration. The basic notion of resentment is that it constitutes a mechanism by which the "good-us" are separated from the "evil-them." Others are conceived as hostile, as receiving undeserved advantage (Barbalet, 1998), possibly "gained at the expense of what is desirable or acceptable from the perspective of established rights" (Solomon, 1990, p. 137). For example, some native citizens are resentful of the "unfair benefits" offered to immigrants and asylum seekers and voice their concerns in racist insults that "foreigners" have come to take over "our country" and "our jobs" (Zembylas, 2008a, 2012b). Resentment is distributed in discursive practices that come to signify the danger that comes from *them*. Therefore, resentment *does* something in practice, because it has social, psychic, and material implications for those who are its subjects/objects. In particular, alignments between individual and national bodies have important implications for education, because the politics of resentment provides an influential affective orientation for an educational system in a society (Zembylas, 2007a). Schools are caught between reproducing the hegemonic discourses of resentment and approaching them critically (McCarthy & Dimitriadis, 2002).

The School Setting

The data for this chapter are drawn from a two-month case study at a multicultural primary school according to the procedures described in chapter 1. The *Town School* is a pseudonym for this school, which is located in a small town and has 12 teachers (all Greek Cypriots) and 330 students, of whom 70 students are not indigenous students and come from other cultural backgrounds. The Turkish-speaking students number 25, a number that includes Turkish Cypriots and Roma/Gypsies. There is regular migration between the south and the north part of Cyprus among Turkish-speaking students; undoubtedly, this affects their education and school participation. In general, the measures adopted by the Ministry of Education and Culture and the local school administration depend on the number of Turkish-speaking children attending each school (e.g. extra language classes and free meals). In the Town School, free meals are provided; no lessons or extra language classes are conducted in the children's mother tongue. Most of these students do not speak or understand any Greek.

The case study at the Town School focused on the following questions:

1. What emotions does the majoritized group, i.e. Greek-Cypriot students and teachers, express about the minoritized group, i.e. Turkish-speaking children?
2. How are those emotions linked to teachers' and students' perceptions and practices about multiculturalism in their school?
3. What are the implications for school policies and teachers' practices on the lives of Turkish-speaking students?

The Town School was chosen because of the relatively high number of Turkish-speaking students enrolled. Data were collected through in-depth interviews, observations, and school documents (see chapter 1). Semi-structured interviews were conducted with the principal, six teachers, six focus groups of Greek-Cypriot children (four children in each group), and two focus groups of Turkish-speaking children (two children in each group); unofficial discussions were conducted with the rest of the teachers and several other students. Three teachers (who volunteered) were observed by a research assistant in their classrooms for almost three weeks, from 7:45 a.m. to 1:05 p.m. per day (i.e. for the duration of the school day). These teachers (two women and a man) were teaching second, fourth, and sixth grades, respectively, and had at least two Turkish-speaking students in their classrooms (of a total of approximately 20 students in each classroom). These teachers had at least eight years of teaching experience. The data sources also included documents of student work and teachers' planning related to the various aspects of their teaching. In the following pages, I examine a range of incidents and begin to show how those are connected to the racialization/ethnicization of the school emotional spaces, and particularly to feelings of resentment toward Turkish-speaking children. It is important to say that the ethnographic research underlying the data analysis in this chapter did not focus initially on issues of resentment; such issues emerged from the case study.

Analysis

Greek-Cypriot Teachers' and Students' Emotions about Turkish-speaking Children

In many cases, the Greek-Cypriot principal, teachers, and students at the Town School classified Turkish-speaking children according to racial and ethnic categories. For example, the school principal reported:

> Not all Turkish-speaking students are the same. Turkish-Cypriot students are like us [*Greek Cypriots*]. . . . They are clean, tidy, and they sometimes speak Greek. They don't have any problems participating in our religious and ethnic events and commemorations despite the fact that they are Muslim. [. . .] On the other hand, Roma students have a dark skin complexion and they are not very sensitive to cleanliness. . . . As a result, our children [*Greek Cypriots*] do not particularly like to play with them. How can you blame them? The Roma culture is different, they are of a different race, how can I say this? The Roma children are not completely accepted here. . . . (Principal Interview)

Similar comments were made by teachers, who discussed the Roma's outward appearance as a racial and cultural characteristic that was not viewed positively among Greek-Cypriot students and teachers. A female teacher commented:

> The Roma children don't look after themselves, they don't wear their school uniform. [. . .] Generally speaking, they are not clean. Their nails are dirty, their hair is not combed, they have dark skin complexion, they don't bring books with them, and they often steal from our children. (Teacher 1, interview)

Another teacher reported:

> The Roma are different from our children, they are dark skinned. You only need to look at their color to realize that they are different. They are never clean and when they are sick in the winter they have a running nose. (Teacher 2, interview)

In contrast to Roma students, the Turkish-Cypriot students seemed to be "more accepted," according to several teachers, "because some of them behave like us [Greek Cypriots]." It is interesting that when one of the teachers expressed surprise that there were Turkish-Cypriot children at the Town School, another teacher, who overheard the discussion, referred to a sixth-grade girl, saying: "There is this pretty girl in sixth-grade, she's light skinned . . . nobody would know she is a Turkish Cypriot. The others look like genuine Turks, dark-skinned from Anatolia. But she looks like us." In general, however, both the teachers and the principal admitted that Turkish-Cypriot children were not yet fully accepted. "They are becoming more and more accepted, but their ethnic origin always sticks out," said the principal. "They have a Turkish origin, you know . . . with the occupation of our country; this influences our feelings about them. They come here and they have all these benefits from the government. We don't like that."

The teachers' comments as well as the principal's descriptions indicate the extent of negative feeling toward Turkish-speaking children, who were categorized on the basis of their skin color and ethnic origin. Those who could speak Greek or had a slightly lighter skin color were more acceptable, because they seemed to be assimilated. The school space was demographically Greek Cypriot and white, and thus Turkish-speaking students were constituted as the "other." Most of the teachers and the principal negated these students and resented their presence in the south, benefiting from government policies that offer financial support to their families (which were predominantly poor and often unemployed).

Similar negative feelings were expressed by the majority of the Greek-Cypriot students who were interviewed. The following dialogue describes how Turkish-speaking children were perceived by two sixth-graders.

RESEARCHER: How do you feel about Turkish-Cypriot students?
ANDREAS: Many students think that Turkish Cypriots are like . . .
ANDRI: . . . Like animals?
ANDREAS: yes . . .
ANDRI: We are light-skinned and they are dark-skinned, and so we don't like them very much.
ANDREAS: Because of their color . . .
[. . .]

ANDRI: And because they are Turks . . .
RESEARCHER: And why is that an issue?
ANDREAS: They occupy our country . . .
ANDRI: My father says I should not play with them . . . they are bad people
ANDREAS: . . . and dirty.
(Greek-Cypriot student group interview, grade 6)

This dialogue, which was not uncommon with the majority of Greek-Cypriot students, shows what it means to be "different" in a space that was predominantly Greek Cypriot. Both Greek-Cypriot teachers and students used outward markers of race and ethnicity—particularly in relation to the political problem of Cyprus—to express their resentment of the presence of Turkish-speaking children, and especially the Roma. The following dialogue with fourth-graders shows another example of the way in which the school's emotional space was organized on the basis of race and ethnicity.

RESEARCHER: What about Yasemin? She is Turkish Cypriot. What do you feel about her?
DINA: She speaks Greek. She is like us, light-skinned so we play with her.
FOFI: We feel OK about her.
RESEARCHER: Is she different from other Turkish Cypriots?
ORFEAS: I think if you know their race, where they come from, if they come from Turkey, let's say, you won't play with them.
DINA: We know where Yasemin comes from.
LOLA: She has the same skin color as we do.
FOFI: We don't play with other Turkish Cypriots because we don't know them very well and we don't trust them. . . . They steal our things.
(Greek-Cypriot student group interview, grade 4)

The previous two student dialogues, which represented many similar ones, show two things: First, outward markers were used to racialize and ethnicize Turkish-speaking students in the school context. Second, even in the instances in which Turkish-speaking students were accepted because they seemed to be assimilated with the majority, racialization and ethnicization were still present simply by naming who was light-skinned and Greek-Cypriot and who was not. The school emotional spaces were seemingly influenced by racial and ethnic markers and reflected not individual discrimination but a whole cultural terrain that resented the presence of Turkish-speaking students. This resentment became gradually evident through a number of incidents, some of which are described below.

"Yiax," an Expression of Disgust

Evidence from observations showed that there were recurring incidents contributing to the marginalization of Turkish-speaking students, especially the Roma; these incidents were situated in the racialization and ethnicization processes taking place throughout the school. However, such incidents often went unnoticed by the majority of teachers. For example, the principal and several teachers emphasized that, "We teach all students to respect each other regardless of where they come from," and "We help Turkish-speaking students by having them work in mixed ability groups." Yet, the observational evidence indicated the following forms of behavior by the majority group toward the minority Turkish-speaking students:

1. Turkish-speaking students consistently sat by themselves in homogeneous groups; they were isolated during the breaks and school excursions.
2. The majoritized students, regardless of age, were strongly against sitting next to Roma students, despite efforts by a few teachers to have them do so. Even in the rare instances when Greek-Cypriot students accepted being seated next to Roma students, they quickly changed seats or complained to the teacher. The teachers eventually gave up because they did not want Greek-Cypriot parents to go against them.
3. The majoritized students used humiliating and insulting language toward Turkish-speaking students, particularly the Roma; they resented even being near those students and used the expression "Yiax," an indication of disgust and intense dislike.
4. The majoritized students and teachers alike accused the Roma students of being dirty and undisciplined.

These forms of behavior show how the majoritized students and teachers had a less favorable and occasionally resentful view toward Turkish-speaking children. In a few cases, older Greek-Cypriot children named such behavior as "racist," yet when they were asked why they continued engaging in such behavior, they replied "because these children are dark-skinned." The following incidents explore how the whole school emotional space was racialized and ethnicized, and thus the aforementioned behaviors occurred not because of individual prejudice on the part of some teachers and students but because the dominant space was emotionally unwelcoming and hostile to the minoritized students.

Incident 1

The lesson was over and a group of Greek-Cypriot girls, who had sat next to two Turkish-speaking girls during the previous class period (their teacher asked them to do so), went to complain to the teacher and asked her to allow them to change seats. The teacher listened carefully and told them it was time for break and that they would discuss this later. In the next class period, these girls changed seats without receiving permission from the teacher. The teacher did not say anything to them. The two Turkish-speaking girls sat by themselves in the last row of the classroom; nobody interacted with them. They were simply drawing on their notebooks throughout the whole class period. The teacher did not exchange any words with them. At the end of this class period, we asked the Greek-Cypriot girls why they had changed seats. The teacher, who was also present in our conversation, explained that nobody wanted to sit next to these girls. She then asked the Greek-Cypriot girls, in our presence, if anyone wanted to sit next to the Turkish-speaking girls. There was no answer. Then the teacher picked one of the Greek-Cypriot girls and told her to sit next to Melike (one of the Turkish-speaking girls). The Greek-Cypriot girl did not respond and looked down. Then Melike intervened and said, "It's OK here, Mrs. B." Melike's facial expression indicated that she had understood very well what her classmates' feelings were toward her. The teacher then asked another Greek-Cypriot girl if she wanted to sit next to Melike. This girl said "OK, I don't have a problem." Two boys were heard to say "Yiax," while the Greek-Cypriot girl stood up and began walking to sit next to Melike, repeating "I don't have a problem, I don't have a problem." When the Greek-Cypriot girl sat next to Melike and accidentally touched her, one of the boys said to the Greek-Cypriot girl: "The black touched you! Yiax!" The teacher did not say anything.

(field notes, grade 6)

Incident 2

RESEARCHER: Why do you use the expression "Yiax" about some Turkish-Cypriot students?

ZENA: . . . (silence)

KATIE: When something is disgusting.

RESEARCHER: What is disgusting?

KATIE: Sitting next to Gypsies.

TAKIS: Our classmates don't like them. Nobody wants to sit next to them.

RESEARCHER: But why don't you want to sit next to these students?

ZENA: They are dark-skinned.
DAMIANOS: I am afraid of them . . .
RESEARCHER: What are you afraid of?
DAMIANOS: I don't know, they may do something to me . . .
KATIE: I feel strange too . . .
RESEARCHER: What do you mean by that?
KATIE: I don't know. . . . They may steal [from] us, they may hit us . . .
TAKIS: They have diseases. . . . Everyone knows that.
(Greek-Cypriot student group interview, grade 5)

Incident 3

RESEARCHER: How do you feel about some of the reactions of Greek-Cypriot students toward you?
ALEV: I don't care . . . they can say what they want . . . I don't care.
ESMA: Well . . . when they say "Yiax" and "Go away" I feel . . . (silence) . . . I feel sad.
RESEARCHER: Don't you want to tell your teacher they behave like that?
ESMA: No, because then the teacher will be angry.
RESEARCHER: Angry at whom?
ESMA: At them.
RESEARCHER: So what?
ESMA: We don't want to say anything to the teacher. The teacher will be angry. And then, during the break, they will come against us and say, "You told the teacher so and so" and they'll be angry at us.
(Turkish-Cypriot student group interview, grade 6)

When some of these incidents were described to the principal, she maintained that Turkish-speaking students had never experienced any problems in the past. She even called a teacher to come to her office and confirm that in front of us. This teacher explained that there had never been any discrimination or racist behavior against Turkish-speaking students. On the contrary, "our students embrace Turkish-speaking students and include them in their company," the teacher asserted. On the other hand, the principal admitted (once again) that some students in certain classes might not be ready to accept "different" students. Therefore, she suggested that if we wished to see how Turkish-speaking students were "included" (for the purposes of our research), she could temporarily place some of them in a classroom in which she was confident that this would happen.

The above incidents suggest that there was a consistent separation of students on the basis of racial and ethnic markers and that Greek-Cypriot teachers and students acted on that basis. The implications of these actions could be seen in the constitution of a resentful emotional climate against Turkish-speaking students. This resentment was manifest as a complete disavowal of the presence of these students in the name of skin color, ethnic origin, and outward appearance. In other words, the discourse of race and ethnicity was foregrounded in Greek-Cypriot students' and teachers' behaviors and actions toward Turkish-speaking students. In the last section, I took a closer look at the school policies and teachers' practices toward Turkish-speaking students in order to show how they further infused school emotional spaces with resentment.

School Policies and Teachers' Practices

An examination of school policies and teachers' practices at the Town School showed that they were not applied in the same manner for Turkish-speaking students as they were for Greek Cypriots. In fact, the school principal and most teachers believed that there were fair and neutral policies and practices toward all students. However, observations and interviews showed that (1) most teachers had lower expectations when they evaluated the learning performance of Turkish-speaking students, (2) they were less willing to help these students, and (3) they interpreted school policies and rules in ways that favored the majoritized group. One teacher who was working at the Town School as a logotherapist explained the situation as follows:

> Non-native children want attention, and in this school they don't get it. Here the situation is "cool" for everyone. The culture is very Greek Cypriot. . . . The teachers don't talk to Turkish-speaking children with respect. . . . As a result they hurt them constantly. I mean their resentment toward these children is obvious. The teachers stigmatize Turkish-speaking children and the stereotypes are perpetuated among all children. [. . .] I don't hesitate to tell you that there is a lot of racism here. I mean the way that native students are separated from the non-native. . . . "If you are touched by Melike you will get sick," and things like that. This is blunt racism! (Teacher 3, interview)

The principal tried to explain the presence of negative feelings toward Turkish-speaking students, reporting that parents had reacted publicly to the presence of these students, particularly the Roma, and had threatened to remove their children from the Town School. She pointed out:

> When I came to this school four years ago, parents reacted a lot to the presence of Turkish-Cypriot and Roma students. I explained to them

> that it was a government policy and that we gained several benefits from their enrollment, such as extra support for students who had learning difficulties and smaller numbers of students in classes. The parents' concerns were focused on the fact that the standards would go down. . . . They were greatly concerned and I can say that they were right. But now that everything works well and they see that that their children are doing great and there are no negative implications from the presence of foreign students, there are no reactions. (Principal interview)

In other words, the principal justified the negative feelings against minoritized students and highlighted the benefits for the majoritized group as a result of government policies. When our research team discovered (with the help of Teacher 3) that the school administration did not *really* allocate the proper number of hours for the support of Turkish-speaking students to learn Greek and receive help for their lessons, we asked the principal to explain her policy.

> Look, I think it's fairer to our [Greek-Cypriot] children as well to take some hours from the support allocated to Turkish-speaking students. Besides, we were told to allocate these hours the way we think is right. I considered it fairer to do it in this way because I think it's unfair to give all the periods to non-native students and give nothing to Greek-Cypriot children. (Principal interview)

It became evident, therefore, that school policies and practices were "appropriately" bent to increase the benefits of the majoritized group, thus keeping Greek-Cypriot parents pleased. The principal interpreted the government policy in a way that clearly favored the majoritized group while putting aside the needs of the minoritized group.

Turkish-speaking students, who had a real need for the support provided by the government policy, experienced obvious difficulties with participation in class activities. For example, we were present at the time of several incidents in which the teacher was simply teaching the "rest" of the class while ignoring the Turkish-speaking students, who were just sitting doing nothing or drawing pictures in their notebooks. When asked to explain why Turkish-speaking students seemed to be ignored, one teacher reported:

RESEARCHER: Do you do anything different about Turkish-speaking students in class?
TEACHER 4: Not really, I try to put some pressure on them.
RESEARCHER: How do you do that?

TEACHER 4: Look . . . I stopped insisting on having them sit next to our children or putting a lot of pressure on them. It's impossible to include these children as long as they don't learn to speak Greek. They got the message, OK it's our fault too, but they got the message that, "I am here just to be and whether I do something or not, whether I can do something or not, nobody will pay attention to me." This is a common secret among us, so I don't have too many expectations from them and they are, "OK if you don't care, we don't care either," and the time goes by. There is no way I will tell a Turkish-Cypriot student to do something because he/she won't do it. So, they accepted that they are ignored and we [teachers] move on. This is the reality.

This teacher admitted that she had lower expectations of Turkish-speaking students and essentially gave up on providing any support to them. Another teacher, as shown below, claimed neutrality on this matter, yet she asserted that she would not like to see her own daughter sitting next to Turkish-speaking students:

> I try to take a neutral stance on this matter. For example, I don't want the [Greek-Cypriot] parents to be angry so I don't push my native students to sit next to Turkish-speaking students. . . . I am afraid a lot so I don't insist. One reason why I don't insist is that deep down I would react the same, if my daughter's teacher did the same to her . . . I wouldn't want my baby to sit next to them. . . . It sounds racist but if my daughter was forced to sit next to a Turkish-Cypriot girl . . . I would be angry. I would be in a difficult position so I don't want the [Greek-Cypriot] parents to be in this difficult position. (Teacher 5, interview)

Several other teachers expressed the view that "Turkish-speaking students are completely included in this school and they have many benefits that some of our [Greek-Cypriot] poorer students do not even have, such as free breakfast and lunch." Along the same lines, another teacher admitted that "It is great success for us if Turkish-speaking students, especially the Roma, stay at school . . . and [continue to] be physically present. Anything beyond that is unrealistic to expect." Not surprisingly, most teachers were in disbelief when one day a substitute teacher told them how Turkish-speaking students participated in class and seemed eager to learn. When the principal was asked to comment on claims that Turkish-speaking students were in fact "capable of learning, just like everyone else," she explained:

> We do everything possible to support these students. My teachers are very sensitive. . . . I have to go back to the issue of free lunch because

> I feel strongly about this. I have to say that the Greek element is being taken advantage of in this school. There are Greek-Cypriot students who should also receive free lunch. It's provocative to our children that Turkish-speaking students receive free lunch and yet they bring unhealthy food with them, which they buy from outside . . . and it's things that are forbidden by school health regulations. I think this is a discrimination against our children and I resent that a lot. I tried many times to explain this to the Ministry but nobody listens. (Principal interview)

The principal insisted to racialize and ethnicize her student body and engaged in a logic of categorization that clearly favored the majoritized group while further marginalizing the minoritized students. The culture of resentment was fed by school policies and practices that attempted to correct the perceived discrimination of members of the majoritized group yet turned a blind eye on the discrimination against Turkish-speaking students. Another teacher expressed similar views and pointed out that, "Roma students do not need financial support. This is discrimination against our students who come from poor families."

A "resistance" voice was raised by Teacher 3, who emphasized that the policy on allocating support for Turkish-speaking students appeared to be fair and neutral but in fact it was practiced through discrimination against minoritized students.

> The truth is that we [teachers] often discuss about Turkish-speaking students, not because we care about them but because they create problems. This is the truth, in all honesty. I don't ever remember a colleague expressing concerns about these children, coming up with ideas and things to do to help them and include them in the school community. Usually, the discussion is about what "this Turkish-Cypriot student did to me today," and things like that. At a teachers' meeting, I dared once to say that these children were justified to behave the way they did because they knew they were not welcomed here and that we resented their presence. I was fiercely attacked by several colleagues who said I had a "Turkish-friendly" attitude.

Although there was some "resistance" by a few teachers like Teacher 3, the culture of resentment was so dominant that opposition voices had a very hard time to find a public space of expression. Teacher 3 was critical of the school efforts that supposedly offered formal support through government measures, but which failed to address practices of structural racism among teachers themselves.

Interrogating the Politics of Resentment in Schools

Through the description of various incidents at the Town School, this chapter has shown the ways in which racialization/ethnicization of school emotional spaces contributes to the constitution of an affective economy of resentment toward Turkish-speaking students. School emotional spaces are overloaded with feelings of resentment and racial/ethnic markers that aim to define the dominant group's identity through the negation of the "other." Racialization and ethnicization are embedded in the majoritized children's discourses, teachers' practices, and school policies. Thus the issue is not simply about individual discrimination or prejudice against a group of minoritized students, but there is an emotional culture of resentment that feeds school discourses, policies, and practices. This emotional culture of resentment, I argue, needs to be interrogated both in theory and in practice, as an important component of the process that prepares the ground for healing and reconciliation. Although an interrogation of the politics of resentment is clearly not enough—given that the power structures may essentially remain unchanged—such a critique may serve as a point of departure for educators to consider more seriously the emotional complexities involved in the racialization and ethnicization of school spaces and the consequences of these complexities. In particular, engaging in the interrogation of the politics of resentment in schools offers the following opportunities.

First, it is shown that there is a variety of everyday "technologies" in schools that instill resentment and inhibit the creation of emotional spaces that encourage an ethics of friendship, solidarity, and care for the "other" (Zembylas, 2007a). These technologies are racialized and ethnicized modes of emotional engagement and are perpetuated through the cultivation of particular embodiments—such as collective practices and school policies that contribute to the formation of particular inclusions/exclusions (Gillborn, 1992, 2005, 2008). Therefore, it is important to analyze the modes through which resentment is authorized by, implied in, and embodied in these practices and policies. While it is valuable to interrogate the politics of resentment in schools, one should not forget that plain critique does not bring about transformation (Bekerman & Zembylas, 2012); social structures of racism do not change through critique, yet it is important to begin from analyzing how school practices and policies are implicated in structures of resentment.

Second, an interrogation of the politics of resentment in schools shows how structures of resentment are historical and political matters rather than individual and psychological matters. The notion of affective economies links the individual with the social and political formation through practices and energies of affect (Ahmed, 2004). Thus, the affective economies or structures of resentment become important forces that motivate power relations among individuals and social groups. Understanding the complexities and ambivalences involved in structures of resentment and their links to racialization/ethnicization processes in schools illustrates that the implications are not only emotional, psychic, and social for those who are marginalized but material as well. Minoritized groups experience discriminatory practices and policies—that are supposedly fair and neutral—as a result of racial/ethnic ideologies (Barajas & Ronnkvist, 2007; Stevens, 2007).

Lastly, educators, particularly in conflicted societies that also have a flow of migrants, must accept that racism and nationalism exist in schools (Lynn & Parker, 2006) and thus identify practices, strategies, and spaces where affective solidarity, an ethic of care, and social justice may be possible. The "invention" (Deleuze & Guattari, 1994) of alternative practices, strategies, and spaces is important for educators who struggle to de-racialize school emotional spaces. If our commitment is to individual and social change, as Worsham (2001) seems to argue—that is, change that would finally dissolve the normative technologies tied up with the structures of resentment in school policies and practices—then this work must also occur at the affective level.

5 CHILDREN'S CONSTRUCTIONS AND EXPERIENCES OF RACISM AND NATIONALISM

In the last few decades, educational researchers around the world have examined issues of racism (Gillborn, 2008; Mirza, 1992) and nationalism (Bénéï, 2005; McGlynn et al., 2009) in schools. Most studies so far have presented evidence that *either* racism *or* nationalism (as separate processes) exists in schools, yet their intersection—also with genderism, classism, and so forth—has received little attention, particularly in the context of research on children's construction and experience of racism and nationalism. Advances in "intersectionality theory," though, provide the theoretical tools with which to examine more carefully the intersection between "race" and "ethnicity" in schools.

This chapter sheds light on children's construction and experience of racism *and* nationalism in three of the sites where I conducted my research—in all of these sites (primary schools) Greek-Cypriot (the majority) and Turkish-speaking (the minority) children are enrolled. My overall concern was to explore how racism is fused with nationalism and other -isms, such as genderism and classism (e.g. Anthias & Yuval-Davis, 1992; McCall, 2005) within schools. This chapter focuses, therefore, on the constructions and experiences of racism and nationalism among Greek-Cypriot and Turkish-speaking children enrolled in these primary schools.

The Study of Children, Racism/Nationalism, and Intersectionality Theory

Children, Racism, and Nationalism

Research on educational processes from the 1980s onward demonstrates that young children's lives are racialized and ethnicized and that children learn about differential positioning from an early age (e.g. Troyna & Hatcher, 1992; Van Ausdale & Feagin, 2001). This research documents the experience of racism and nationalism among children in their school lives and provides evidence both for racist practices by majoritized groups and the negotiation of such practices by minoritized groups (e.g. Archer & Francis, 2005; Connolly, 1998; Devine, Kenny, & Macneela, 2008).

Children's experiences need to be viewed, therefore, within the ideological framework of racism at its intersection with nationalism, especially in conflicted areas like Cyprus, where both racialization and ethnicization processes are enmeshed to produce particular ethnic and racial identities (see McGlynn et al., 2009). In the context of Cyprus, "racial identities" are considered in relation to children's references to color; however, as seen in the previous two chapters, children's sense of identity and their expressed attitudes toward strangers/foreigners (i.e. non-white) cannot be viewed outside their references to "ethnic identities." Previous research in Cyprus has highlighted the prevalence of nationalist attitudes and perceptions of Greek-Cypriot students toward the Turks, the primary "other" for Greek Cypriots; Greek-Cypriot children do not make any distinction between Turks and Turkish Cypriots but view them as one homogeneous category (e.g. see Spyrou, 2006; Zembylas, 2008a). Also, research investigating the attitudes of Greek-Cypriot children toward immigrants, Roma, and Turkish Cypriots records many stereotypes and racist perceptions (Trimikliniotis & Demetriou, 2009). As some of this research suggests (Spyrou, 2009), the coming together of the ideologies of nationalism and racism provides a socially convincing way of hiding racist attitudes in the name of the nation, which in conflicted areas like Cyprus is more likely to be accepted.

However, there has not been much research examining how the intersection of racialized and ethnicized identities in schools is manifest in children's construction and experience of racism and nationalism in the few Greek-Cypriot schools in which Greek-Cypriot and Turkish-speaking children are co-educated. The investigation of this intersection is valuable because it constitutes a "testament to the (re)productive tendencies within children's peer relations as they construct and negotiate their social identities in line with dominant values and norms" (Devine et al., 2008, p. 370). Wider discourses of race, ethnicity, class, gender, and so forth become reflected in the ways that majoritized and minoritized children position themselves in school. The social categories of race, ethnicity, class, gender, and so forth serve as inclusion/exclusion criteria in children's school lives (Troyna & Hatcher, 1992). Through racialization and ethnicization processes in schools, as documented in the previous two chapters, "sameness" and "otherness" are reified and assume a naturalized form (Connolly, 1998). Therefore, it is pertinent to examine how racialized identities are fused with other axes of identity, and ethnicity is one of the categories to which children appear highly sensitive (Anthias & Yuval-Davies, 1992; Archer & Francis, 2005).

Intersectionality Theory

In light of the goal to investigate the intersection of racism and nationalism in children's everyday lives, this chapter draws from intersectionality theory. *Intersectionality* refers to the notion that subjectivity is constituted by mutually reinforcing "categories" such as race, gender, ethnicity, class, and so forth (Crenshaw et al., 1995). Although intersectionality emerged from critical race studies conducted in the later 1980s, it has since influenced the theorization of multidimensional positioning of subjects' lived experiences in the social sciences, including education (Brah & Phoenix, 2004; Phoenix, 2006). The most important contribution of intersectionality theory is that it rejects the notion that race, gender, ethnicity, class, and so forth are separate and essentialist categories; instead of reducing people to one category at a time, the concept of intersectionality describes the interconnections and interdependence of racialization processes with other social processes (Crenshaw et al., 1995).

Intersectional analysis, therefore, is valuable in describing the power relations that are central to multiple positionings of subjects in social processes (e.g. racialization and ethnicization processes) and how these power relations are constantly shifting (marked by conflicts and resistances) to construct particular identities. Understandably, it is impossible to take into account all significant differences in the intersectional approach; thus, the question that becomes important in the processes in which multiple positions intersect is this: Who defines when, where, and why differences become what they do (Ludvig, 2006)? For example, in the context of this research in Cyprus, how is "the Turk" being demonized as an oppositional identity for Greek-Cypriot children? And by implication, how are different social categories (e.g. racial, ethnic, and cultural) co-constructed to formulate racist and nationalist practices against Turkish-speaking children? As Yuval-Davis explains:

> The point of intersectional analysis is not to find "several identities under one" [. . .]. This would reinscribe the fragmented, additive model of oppression and essentialize specific social identities. Instead, the point is to analyze the differential ways in which different social divisions are concretely enmeshed and constructed by each other and how they relate to political and subjective constructions of identities. (2006, p. 205)

Consequently, intersectional analysis emphasizes how particular identities are lived in the modalities of other categories of identity, such that ethnicity is always lived in the modalities of race and class (McCall, 2005). To paraphrase Matsuda (1991) with respect to her method of asking "the other question," one should say, "When I see something that looks racist, I ask, 'Where is nationalism in this?' " This co-construction of each category takes place in myriad ways, all of which are dependent on social, political, and historical factors (Prins, 2006); these particular intersections produce specific effects, securing both privilege and oppression simultaneously (Anthias & Yuval-Davis, 1992).

Therefore, it is important to explore how identities occur in interactions in particular contexts, such as schools, in order to reveal the complexity of the lived experience within each group (McCall, 2005). The methodological approach favored by McCall to do research on intersectionality "begins with the observation that there are relationships of inequality among already constituted social groups, as imperfect and ever changing as they are, and takes those relationships as the center of the analysis" (2005, p. 1784–1785). This way of theorizing and researching intersectionality uses the categories strategically in the service of displaying the linkages between categories and inequality (Nash, 2008). McCall (2005) suggests that case studies represent the most effective methodological way of empirically researching the complexity of the way that the intersections of categories are experienced and produce certain effects such as racism and nationalism. As noted in chapter 1, all chapters in Parts II and III adopt a case-study approach. This approach, emphasizes Valentine (2007), describes the multiple and shifting ways in which the self and other are represented, the ways that individuals identify and disidentify with other groups, and how one category (e.g. race) is used to differentiate another (e.g. ethnicity) and produce racist and nationalist practices.

The School Settings

The previous two chapters have presented case studies of two of the participating schools in the research project discussed in this book; the present chapter covers all three primary schools that participated in the study. As noted, the choice of these schools was based on the presence of Turkish-speaking children in the student population. The majority of Turkish-speaking children did not speak or understand any Greek. Free meals were provided to these students in all three schools, but no lessons or extra language classes were conducted in the children's mother tongue—except in one school, the one with the highest percentage of Turkish-speaking children. These schools were: the Hill School, the Town School, and the Sea School (pseudonyms); the first and third schools were part of a ZEP (Zone of Educational Priority) network. Throughout Cyprus ZEP schools receive additional help—such as extra hours for assisting non-indigenous students to learn the Greek language (see chapter 1).

The Hill School (HS) is a pseudonym for a primary school located in a small city. It has 16 teachers (all Greek Cypriots) and 140 students, 98 of whom are Greek Cypriots; 17, Turkish Cypriots and Roma; and 25 natives of various other countries. The socioeconomic background of students is considered low and the Greek-Cypriot population is mainly comprised of refugees who fled from the north to save their lives in the aftermath of the Turkish invasion in 1974.

The Town School (TS) is a primary school located in a small town; it has 12 teachers (all Greek Cypriots) and 330 students, 70 of whom are non-Greek-Cypriot students and come from other cultural backgrounds. The Turkish-speaking students number 25.

The Sea School (SS) is a primary school located in a fairly large city (by Cypriot standards); it has 12 teachers (10 Greek Cypriots and 2 Turkish Cypriots; the Turkish-Cypriot teachers are responsible for teaching the Turkish language to Turkish-speaking students). The Sea School has 139 students, 51 of whom are Turkish-speaking; 71, Greek-Cypriots; with the rest from various cultural backgrounds. The socioeconomic status of most students is considered low.

This chapter draws on data gathered from group interviews involving a total of 60 children (47 Greek Cypriots and 13 Turkish-speaking students) aged 7–12 years, ethnographic observations for eight consecutive weeks in each school (from 7:45 a.m. to 1:05 p.m., that is for the duration of the school day), and collection of documents (curriculum and policy documents, school demographic information, teaching materials, and children's work). Children were organized for interviews on a friendship group basis and their grade level, with no interview group larger than five children. Turkish-speaking children were teamed up in smaller groups (two to three children) because of their small numbers; whenever needed, some Turkish-speaking children served as translators for others who did not speak Greek very well. Also, the aim was to have an equal number of children from lower grade levels (grades 1–3) and higher grade levels (grades 4–6).

Intersectional analysis in this chapter is used to examine how children's constructions and acts of categorization constitute acts of power that create particular inclusions and exclusions (of social groups and identities) and depend on assumptions about naturalized realities. First, the analysis is undertaken both per children group interview and per school (within-case analysis). Second, a comparative analysis between the schools (cross-case analysis) is completed. In the following pages I examine a range of interview excerpts highlighting the children's constructions and experiences of racism and nationalism. There are three main sections: the first section examines Greek-Cypriot children's perceptions about Turkish-speaking children; the second section examines Turkish-speaking children's experiences of racism and nationalism; and the third section discusses children's strategies to negotiate racism and nationalism in school.

Greek-Cypriot Children's Perceptions about Turkish-Speaking Children

The majority of Greek-Cypriot children had a limited understanding of what racism and nationalism meant. A few older children provided some explanation of racism when the issue emerged in the conversation, but the younger children had no understanding of the terms. The majority of the older children, however, made connections between their behavior and the segregation of Turkish-speaking children, as the following dialogues indicate:

Dialogue 1 (grade 5 children, the Hill School)

RESEARCHER: Have you ever heard of the term *racism*?
YIANNIS: Yes, it means you don't want others.
RESEARCHER: Why is it that you don't want others?
YIANNIS: Because they are black.
RESEARCHER: Do you have black people in your school?
MARKOS: Yes, the Turks are black.
GEORGE: We don't want to sit with them and play with them because they have diseases.
MARKOS: . . . and they occupy our country.
RESEARCHER: Have you done any lessons in which you are taught how to behave to others who are different from you?
ANDY: We've done once a lesson about racism in our religion course . . . that we have to play with all children.
[. . .]
RESEARCHER: So why don't you play with Turkish-speaking children?
MARKOS: It's not us, it's them; they want to play by themselves and they don't give us their ball.

Dialogue 2 (grade 3 children, the Sea School)

RESEARCHER: Have you ever heard of the term *racism*?
LEANNA: Yes, it's something about your color.
RESEARCHER: How about [the term] *nationalism*?
LEANNA: Um . . . is it about your country?

Greek-Cypriot children in this study found it difficult to define racism or nationalism, yet they had some understanding of racism in color terms and nationalism in relation to one's country of origin. There was ambivalence, however, in the older children's understanding of these terms. Initially, these children admitted that they didn't want to play with Turkish-speaking children; however, later in the discussion one student (Markos) attempted to assert his non-racist credentials by referring to the Turkish-speaking students as being responsible for not playing with Greek Cypriots.

In a sense, then, Greek-Cypriot children blamed Turkish-speaking children for the latter group's marginalization. In Dialogue 1, as well as in other dialogues the research team documented, Greek-Cypriot children distanced themselves from recognizing the power dynamics between different groups (see Devine et al., 2008; Troyna & Hatcher, 1992). This sort of distancing is also shown below in an excerpt from an interview with sixth graders at the Hill School; in this dialogue, which was first presented in chapter 3, issues of race and ethnicity were blended with the political situation in Cyprus as well as with the socioeconomic class of Turkish-speaking children.

Dialogue 3 (grade 6 children, the Hill School)

RESEARCHER: Why don't you play with Turkish-speaking students?

YOLANDA: Because we come from different countries. We play with kids who come from our own country.

RESEARCHER: But why is that? Aren't those kids Cypriots too? (the researcher refers to Turkish-speaking students who are Turkish Cypriots, the majority of Turkish-speaking students at this school).

MARY: No, Miss! They are Turks!

RESEARCHER: OK, why is that a problem in playing with them?

LOLA: Because they fight all the time. They curse us all the time in their language and I don't feel good because the Turks occupy my mother's village. The Turks came and kicked her out and she came here.

MARY: It's the problem of Cyprus with Turkey.

YOLANDA: They took our Cyprus without reason and still occupy it.

LOLA: They come and go all the time from the occupied areas [the north] and they think all Cyprus belongs to them.

[. . .]

RESEARCHER: Do you think there is racism in your school?

[. . .]

MARY: We don't like some people but I don't think there is racism in our school.

Dialogue 4 (grade 2 children, the Town School)

ANNA: They [Turkish-speaking children] should learn Greek so that they can speak our language.

CHRYSTALLA: . . . and they should clean themselves. They usually stink.

The main elements of the stereotypes against Turkish-speaking children focused on a double position of these children as "Turks" (the arch-enemy of the Greeks) and dark-colored and unclean (associated with a lower culture, race, and socioeconomic class). While the Greek-Cypriot children's constructions of such stereotypes were very much grounded in their day-to-day experiences, these understandings were not completely irrelevant to the larger national discourse about the Cyprus Problem in the Greek-Cypriot community. This is shown below in a dialogue that was initially introduced in chapter 3.

Dialogue 5 (grade 5 children, the Hill School)

RESEARCHER: How do you feel about having Turkish-speaking students as your classmates?

DOROS: Not so good.

PETROS: My parents are refugees.

RESEARCHER: Why don't you feel good? What do you mean by that?

DOROS: Because . . . (long pause) because we have Turks in our school and we should only have Cypriots. But we have Turks.

RESEARCHER: Are they doing something wrong?

PETROS: They kick us and beat us.

CHRISTOS: I feel hatred about them.

RESEARCHER: (turning to Christos) That's a strong word!

PETROS: I want to beat them back. They came to take over our school and steal everything from us, like they do in the occupied areas.

This excerpt indicates an interesting blending of personal day-to-day experience with the dominant Greek-Cypriot discourse about the political situation in Cyprus. The perception of stealing and the analogy with the occupation of Cyprus was manifest in other similar examples. In general, all of the examples provided a deeper understanding of the ways that Greek-Cypriot children perceived Turkish-speaking children, their limited understanding of what racism and nationalism mean, yet their awareness that their perceptions and actions are linked to the marginalization of Turkish-speaking children. Such constructions "homogenized" and "naturalized" (Anthias & Yuval-Davis, 1992) Turkish-speaking children's identities.

Turkish-speaking Children's Experiences of Racism and Nationalism

While the majority of Greek-Cypriot children we interviewed did not think that there was racism or nationalism in their school, the views of Turkish-speaking children were different. For Turkish-speaking children, racism and nationalism were present in many aspects of their day-to-day experiences. The following dialogue shows that the minoritized children had a more complex and subtle understanding of racist and nationalist practices than their Greek-Cypriot peers.

Dialogue 6 (grade 6 children, the Town School)

RESEARCHER: How do you think Greek-Cypriot children see Turkish-speaking children?
MELEK: They hate us.
RESEARCHER: Why do they hate you?
AYLIN: They are racist. They blame us for everything. They call us names.
RESEARCHER: But what's the reason they do that?
AYLIN: They don't like that we are Turkish Cypriots.
MELEK: They call us *mavroi* [black] and *bromotourtzoi* [filthy Turks].
RESEARCHER: How does this make you feel?
MELEK: I cry.
AYLIN: I try not to pay much attention but I feel bad.

Many Turkish-speaking students talked about their discomfort and unhappiness for what they perceived as "racist behavior" on the part of their Greek-Cypriot classmates. The following dialogue with two fifth-grade Turkish-speaking girls—which was also presented in chapter 3—is indicative of the emotional impact of such behavior on these children:

Dialogue 7 (grade 5 children, the Hill School)

RESEARCHER: Can you tell me how you feel being at this school? Are you OK? Is there something you don't like?
SAFIYE: I don't like Greek-Cypriots.
RESEARCHER: Why is that?
SAFIYE: They don't like us.
RESEARCHER: Why don't they like you?
SAFIYE: They kick us, they call us bad names. They don't want us.
DENIZ: Once I was kicked so hard by a Greek-Cypriot student, it hurt a lot.

RESEARCHER: Did you complain to anyone, to the principal?
DENIZ: No.
RESEARCHER: Why not?
DENIZ: Because they will say [we are] traitors.
RESEARCHER: How does this make you feel?
DENIZ: Not happy. Very sad.
RESEARCHER: You? (turning to Safiye)
SAFIYE: Scared.
RESEARCHER: Why scared?
SAFIYE: (long pause) They can beat us.

Turkish-speaking children were painfully aware not only of the ways that name-calling fed a racist discourse about them but also of the hurting consequences. However, as several Turkish-speaking children pointed out, not all Greek-Cypriot students engaged in name-calling; some did so more than others. As Erhan, a sixth grader from the Town School, explained: "There is this Greek-Cypriot boy whose parents are refugees and he blames all Turkish Cypriots for that. He calls us "Turkish barbarians" all the time. This hurts me a lot. I understand his situation but this is not fair, what he calls us. [. . .] It's sad that teachers don't do anything. Some just laugh."

Several Turkish-speaking children felt that most teachers were not supportive of them and were essentially bystanders. These experiences seemed to be everyday events for some of these children, as the following vignette, composed from field notes at the Hill School, illustrates.

Incident 1

Most of the time, the two sixth-grade Turkish-speaking girls do not pay attention to the teacher's instruction; instead, they make drawings on their notebooks or play with their pencils and bags. They have a hard time understanding anything, as I have been told by the teacher, because they don't have a good grasp of Greek. There was this one time when the teacher assigned students to do group work at tables, and the Turkish-speaking girls were trying to make contact with the teacher to see if they were also assigned to a group. The teacher was busy talking to other students so she didn't notice the two girls' efforts to make eye contact with her. One of the Turkish-speaking girls, Ayse, decided to move toward a table of Greek-Cypriot students, but then turned back. The other girl continued to draw in her drawing book and paid no attention to what was going on. Ayse made another attempt to approach a group, but a Greek-Cypriot boy yelled an insult at her—"you go away, you filthy Turkish girl." Ayse yelled something back in Turkish and then started crying. She went back to her desk, picked up a pencil and threw it at the boy. At that moment the teacher became aware of what had happened and sent both Ayse and the Greek-Cypriot boy to the principal's office. When the research assistant later talked to Ayse about this incident, Ayse was very upset and hurt and stated that it was not the first time an incident like that happened, but nothing seemed ever to change: "Greek-Cypriot students are always like that. They don't like us. Teachers don't do anything. They don't care how we feel."

This example strengthens the interpretation suggesting that some children are systematically marginalized and recognized "as stranger than others, as border objects that have been incorporated and then expelled from the ideal of the community" (Ahmed, 2005, p. 109). The relationality of emotions that underpins the dynamics of exclusion also produces and sustains the bonds of kinship *within* each group of children.

Although the intersection of racist and nationalist discourses was apparent in the name-calling directed toward Turkish-speaking children, Turkish-speaking children did not understand racist name-calling as being explicitly linked to the presence of "nationalism" in Greek-Cypriot schools, except in a few cases. For example, Zehra, a sixth-grader from the Sea School who spoke fluent Greek, provided her explanation about the intersection of racism and nationalism.

In my school, we never talk about nationalism, but at home my parents taught me that nationalism is responsible for many bad things we suffered in Cyprus. Fortunately, my Greek-Cypriot classmates don't pick on me because I speak Greek like them and I look a lot like them. But I am sad that they call Turkish Cypriots bad names and most teachers don't do anything. I find this very nationalistic behavior because Greek Cypriots consider that they have a right to call Turkish Cypriots bad names as a result of the Cyprus Problem.

What is interesting about this extract is that it acknowledged nationalism as a subtle everyday practice enmeshed with racist name-calling (e.g. *mavroi* [black] and *bromotourtzoi* [filthy Turks]). Zehra saw racist and nationalist behavior not as individual practices but as social and political practices embedded in everyday school life, having painful consequences for Turkish-speaking children.

Children's Strategies to Negotiate Racism and Nationalism

Children who recognized racist behavior or were victims of racist behavior engaged in a range of different strategies to respond to such behavior. In line with the findings reported by Archer and Francis (2005), the responsibility for action was placed on individuals rather than on school structures or anti-racist policies. A few Greek-Cypriot children stood up for what they thought was inappropriate treatment of their Turkish-speaking classmates; for their part, some Turkish-speaking children tried not to pay attention and chose to stick together; others (often the boys but not always) reacted and got into fights with Greek Cypriots; still others tried to approach Greek-Cypriot children and make friends with them; finally, a few Turkish-speaking children (who spoke Greek well) attempted to adopt characteristics of the majority group so that they could fit in.

A few Greek-Cypriot children reacted when their Greek-Cypriot classmates said bad things about Turkish-speaking children, as the following dialogue indicates.

Dialogue 8 (grade 6, the Town School)

ANDREAS: Once I was standing next to my classroom desk and Melek was passing by and my classmates were shouting at me, "Be careful, don't go near her because she stinks." I responded saying, "What's your problem, if she comes near me? What's going to happen to you?" And, then, they shut up.

LOLA: Many children say nasty things about Turkish-Cypriot students, that they occupy Cyprus and so on. I tell them, "What are they going to do to you? Eat you?"

Several incidents were also recorded in classrooms where some Greek-Cypriot children stood up for their Turkish-speaking classmates, either by lending them things (when everyone took the position that these children were "thieves") or by taking a stance against the majority, asserting that it was not fair to always blame Turkish-speaking children for whatever happened.

Among Turkish-Cypriot children, some tried not to pay attention and chose to stick together, as Aylin described in Dialogue 6. As she explained, "If we stick together, they cannot harm us so much. So we try to play together, sit together in class. They don't want us anyway. We don't want to get into fights with them." This strategy was not without emotional cost, because these small groups of excluded children (usually two to three children each) were easily identified, picked on, and teased by the majority. But several Turkish-Cypriot students confirmed that they felt happier and more comfortable when they were among other Turkish-Cypriot students.

Other Turkish-speaking students (often the boys but not always) reacted and got into fights with Greek Cypriots. The following two dialogues show this kind of response and the consequences:

Dialogue 9 (grade 5 children, the Hill School)

ASIL: They [Greek-Cypriot children] call us *mavroi* and *bromotourtzoi* all the time.
ETZEVIT: I get into fights with them. I am not afraid. I am strong. So, I win them.
RESEARCHER: But do you think this is the best way to solve the problem?
ETZEVIT: I don't care.
ASIL: They are afraid of Etzevit so they stop cursing us when he beats them.

Dialogue 10 (grade 6, the Town School)

RESEARCHER: Why do you get into fights with some of your classmates?
AYSE: They don't want us.
RESEARCHER: Is this a reason to get into fights?
AYSE: They curse us all the time. I am not going to sit there and do nothing.

In the previous dialogues, it is interesting to notice that some Turkish-speaking boys played the masculinity card, because they had the physical strength. In this case, hegemonic forms of masculinity intersected with racialized and ethnicized discourses and identities and provided a means for Turkish-speaking boys to respond to exclusion (Archer & Francis, 2005). For girls like Ayse, her fighting back seemed more like a desperate effort to voice her feelings of marginalization.

Other Turkish-speaking children (often the girls but not always) tried to approach Greek-Cypriot children and make friends with them. The following dialogue provides an example of the efforts undertaken by two girls.

Dialogue 11 (grade 3, the Sea School)

FATIME: We try to be friends with them [Greek-Cypriot girls] but they don't like us.
RESEARCHER: What things do you do to be friends with them?
NADIRE: We go to play games . . .
FATIME: . . . go near them to sit together in class.
RESEARCHER: How do they [Greek-Cypriot girls] respond to those actions?
NADIRE: They say nasty things. . . .
FATIME . . . they sometimes ignore us.

This strategy was also followed by a few boys who mixed with Greek-Cypriot children who were also marginalized for some reason. For example, Melios (a Greek Cypriot) and Hasan (a Turkish Cypriot) were hanging out together at the Sea School because nobody else wanted to be with them, as they pointed out.

Finally, a few Turkish-speaking children (who spoke Greek well) attempted to adopt characteristics of the majority group so that they could fit in. For example, they tried to speak like Greek Cypriots and for the most part they were successful in not being excluded. At the same time, they were very aware of what they were doing and why they were doing it, as is evident in Zehra's talk:

> If you don't speak Greek and if you are not clean and tidy like Greek-Cypriot girls, they don't accept you. I am lucky because my parents insisted that I learned to speak Greek from a young age, so everyone thinks I am Greek until they hear my name. [. . .] I don't really think about whether someone is Greek Cypriot or Turkish Cypriot. I think it's stupid to get into fights for this. But I understand why some boys react and want to fight. Many Greek-Cypriot children look down on Turkish-Cypriot children.

In comparison with most of the Turkish-speaking boys who got into fights, girls like Zehra, Fatime, and Nadire responded to racism and nationalism by trying to fit in with the majority group. A notable exception was Ayse, who emphasized that she "could not ignore the curses" and reacted in a different way, although she also tried to fit in.

Further Explorations of the Intersection of Racism and Nationalism in Schools

This chapter has focused on children's constructions and experience of racism and nationalism among a sample of Greek-Cypriot and Turkish-speaking children in three public Greek-Cypriot primary schools. It has highlighted how these children's identities are racialized and ethnicized from a young age, and how such social processes relate to the development of understandings about racist and nationalist practices. As research in this area emphasizes, it is important to understand children's understandings of racism and nationalism before making inferences about the impact of these factors on children's self-esteem and identity development (Stevens, 2008). Power relations are central to racist and nationalist practices and their negotiation, as those are enmeshed in day-to-day experiences at school; power operates to systematically define ways of being, and to mark out who is included and excluded.

Greek-Cypriot children's perceptions about Turkish-speaking children are located within a sociopolitical context in which children experience the intersection of categories, particularly race and ethnicity but also gender and social class.

Greek-Cypriot children are particularly sensitive to skin color, race, and ethnicity, and they have a strong emotional investment in themselves as white Greeks and of Turkish-speaking children as, invariably, "Turks." The only exception is evident in relation to children who speak Greek very well and dress/behave according to the majority group's accepted norms; all other Turkish-speaking children are viewed stereotypically and are marginalized. The present findings confirm Devine et al.'s (2008) study that majority children have a limited understanding of racism and nationalism as opposed to the minoritized children's nuanced understandings. More interestingly, the coming together of nationalist and racist practices provides a socially convincing way for some Greek-Cypriot children to hide their racist attitudes in the name of the political problem in Cyprus.

Intersectional theory helps theorize the ways in which privilege and marginalization intersect, informing each subject's experiences (Nash, 2008). Intersectionality, for example, in this chapter shows how race and ethnicity use intersecting technologies of categorization and control, disciplining children in distinctive ways and coalescing in particular formations to make particular identity positions become more salient, stabilized, or institutionalized. However, some children from both majoritized and minoritized groups come to see themselves differently compared to the hegemonic culture constituted in their schools. In analyzing race and ethnicity both as co-constitutive processes and as historically specific technologies of categorization (Nash, 2008), it is possible for educators to gain a deeper understanding of how certain identifications and disidentifications are simultaneously experienced by children in specific sociopolitical circumstances through the course of their everyday lives. In particular spaces there are dominant social orderings that produce moments of exclusion for particular social groups (Valentine, 2007); power operates in and through these spaces of racialization and ethnicization, but there is fluidity of identities and the possibility of resisting hegemonic culture.

Needless to say, the results of this research cannot be generalized, as they refer to the experiences of only a few schools. But this research has implications for educational policy, classroom practice, and teacher professional development and encourages researchers to further explore the intersection of racism and nationalism in different sociopolitical settings. At the level of policy making, it is important that educational authorities and schools take responsibility for identifying and challenging the intersection of racism and nationalism without losing sight of the distinctive side effects of each of those social processes. As Gillborn (2008) has emphasized, school authorities need to set clear procedures for both the monitoring of practice in schools and a commitment to challenge racism (and nationalism) in all its formations and intersections with other -isms.

More in-depth analysis of racisms and nationalisms, asserts Gillborn, involves more fluid and complex understandings of identities.

At the level of classroom practice (and I will come back to this in Part IV), the data in this chapter suggest that attention needs to be given to activities, curricula, and programs that challenge racism (Stevens, 2008) and its intersection with nationalism. Clearly, the majority group's limited constructions of racism and nationalism need to be questioned, moving beyond the simplistic acknowledgment of color-based racism (Devine et al., 2008) to a more nuanced understanding of how racist practices are enmeshed with nationalist ones and create certain inclusions/exclusions. "This should involve," according to Devine et al., "enabling children to name and explore their behavior with one another and to consider the consequences of such behavior for children who are racially abused" (2008, p. 382–383). Children need to recognize that nationalist beliefs and practices also constitute particular forms of racism; thus naming these beliefs and practices as racist and/or nationalist is an important step in overcoming stereotypes and historical traumas (Zembylas, 2008a).

Finally, learning to recognize and critique the intersection of racism and nationalism is an important aspect of teacher development efforts. This understanding requires the design of teacher professional development opportunities that take into consideration the complex nature of the intersection of race and ethnicity, and how children (as well as teachers) are actively involved in the negotiation of these identities. For example, teacher educators can build constructively on children's ambivalence—i.e. that some children from both majoritized and minoritized groups come to see themselves differently compared to the hegemonic culture—and use this as a point of departure to raise more critical awareness of how identities as well as racialization and ethnicization processes intersect. It is through such opportunities that teachers can be encouraged to identify, challenge, and resist hegemonic representations and practices regarding the intersection of racial and national politics.

6 TEACHERS' CONSTRUCTIONS OF OTHERIZED CHILDREN'S IDENTITIES

From the 1970s onward, a substantial number of studies in different educational settings have shown that teachers hold negative stereotypes and have low expectations of racial/ethnic minoritized children. The literature relating to (negative) teacher expectations and constructions of children from minoritized ethnic/racial backgrounds shows that these stereotypical representations are mapped onto educational policy and everyday teaching practices (Archer & Francis, 2005). In his review of research in England during the last three decades, Stevens (2007) asserts that an investigation on the racialized, ethnicized, and classed constructions expressed by teachers should not focus on whether teachers or specific school processes are racist or discriminating as such, but could explore "the *contextual development* and *activation* of these phenomena" (p. 173, emphasis added).

In response to the call for research on the contextual development of school processes that may be racist or discriminating, this chapter builds on the previous three chapters and examines Greek-Cypriot teachers' constructions of Turkish-speaking children's identities in the Greek-Cypriot educational system through the lens of Critical Race Theory (CRT). Having examined children's constructions and experience of racism and nationalism in the previous chapter, I now focus on how majoritized teachers' constructions of minoritized otherness are racialized and what consequences these constructions have. This is important, because examining teachers' views will make us (educators, teachers, policy makers, researchers) more knowledgeable about how to prepare anti-racist teacher education programs and policies that take into consideration all teacher views without diminishing, dismissing, or over-valuing them. A rich academic agenda already exists toward this end, emphasizing the significance of considering teachers' views in the formulation of anti-racist education (Gillborn, 2008).

This chapter, then, deals with the racialized, ethnicized, and classed constructions of Turkish-speaking children within Greek-Cypriot teachers' discourses. In this context, the following questions are discussed: (1) How do Greek-Cypriot teachers perceive the race, ethnicity, and class of their Turkish-speaking students, and how does the CRT concept of the structural racialization of minoritized groups illuminate these teachers' constructions of Turkish-speaking children's identities within the Greek-Cypriot educational system? and (2) If teachers' views are racialized/ethnicized/classed, are there any pockets of "resistance" (Youdell, 2006) to the "normalized" identities ascribed to Turkish-speaking children, and if so, how are these resistances manifest in school life?

In addition, this chapter analyzes the ways in which emotions are mobilized in teachers' lives and create particular economies of affect in response to racialization and ethnicization processes in schools. Finally, the nature of these economies of affect is analyzed and the ways it is possible to form an *ethic of discomfort* (Foucault, 1994)[1] as a space for constructive transformations in schools is discussed—I come back to the theme of discomfort and its pedagogical implications in the Epilogue (chapter 13).

Critical Race Theory

Critical Race Theory has its origins in US legal scholarship, but it is increasingly used by educators around the world (such as the UK, Europe, Australia, and Asia) to analyze the continued salience of structural racism in educational settings (Gillborn, 2008). According to Delgado and Stefancic (2001), there are six unifying tenets that define the movement of CRT: (1) racism is ordinary; (2) the current system of white-over-color ascendancy serves important purposes; (3) race and races are products of social thought and relations; (4) the dominant society racializes different minority groups at different times; (5) intersectionality and antiessentialism are present, whereas everyone has overlapping, conflicting identities, and loyalties; and (6) there is shared minority experience that people of color communicate about race and racism that white people are unlikely to know is present. Central to these tenets is the notion that racism is pervasive and systemic, not merely an individual pathology. Racism is ingrained in everyday practices, events, institutional policy rules, and administrative procedures in subtle and often unnoticed ways, yet the actions associated with everyday racism are seen as derogatory by persons of color. Critical Race Theory, then, calls attention to the existence of structures in the broader society that are created and maintained through institutions, relationships, and practices.

Throughout this chapter, the majoritized (i.e. Greek-Cypriot) teachers' perceptions of the minoritized (i.e. Turkish-speaking) children are theoretically framed within CRT. Critical Race Theory is appropriate for the case of Cyprus because it offers insights and methodological tools with which to identify and analyze existing evidence of the structural and cultural aspects that maintain dominant racial positions (coupled with ethnic ones) in and out of schools (Spyrou, 2009; Trimikliniotis, 2004; Zembylas, 2008a). The ethnopolitical conflict in Cyprus is very much related to "race"—as shown in previous chapters—because existing evidence highlights how the ethnic "other" is also viewed through racial lenses. According to this research, teachers' racialized/ethnicized/classed constructions inform and reflect the larger (unjust) structures in the Greek-Cypriot educational system, indicating how the Greek-Cypriot educational system performs exclusion. Although the implementation of CRT in a North American, European, or other context would look different from its use in the Greek-Cypriot educational system, there is an important commonality: the challenge of racist practices through investigating the lived experience of minoritized peoples as a defense against universalistic discourses (Gillborn, 2008; Taylor, Gillborn, & Ladson-Billings, 2009).

Although a number of conceptual and methodological tools have grown out of CRT (e.g. whiteness as property, interest convergence), I draw specifically on two ideas that are used in this chapter: (1) the concept of how the dominant society racializes minoritized groups in different ways, and (2) the theme of *resistance*—that is, how some narratives constitute counter-storytelling that aims to upset hegemonic truth. First, CRT is particularly helpful in analyzing how majoritized teachers' racialized/ethnicized/classed constructions are manifest in everyday school practices that perpetuate the uncritical use of race and other categorizations (Taylor, Gillborn, & Ladson-Billings, 2009). By arguing that racism is endemic in both institutional structures and everyday "business-as-usual," CRT helps analyze the ways in which majoritized teachers' constructions about minoritized students' identities constitute racialized, ethnicized, and classed perceptions. Second, the theme of resistance (e.g. through counter-storytelling) refers to challenging myths, assumptions, and received wisdoms grounded in color-blind ideologies and discourses of objectivity and neutrality (Gillborn, 2008; Youdell, 2006). Thus CRT questions liberal views that are deeply embedded in education and society, exposing the racist inequities "that are created and sustained behind an inclusive and progressive façade" (Gillborn, 2008, p. 28).

Teachers' Constructions of Minoritized Children's Identities

The literature in many countries around the world shows that majoritized teachers perceive minoritized children "differently." A full exploration of teacher racism all over the world is beyond the scope of this chapter; however, a brief review of some research evidence is valuable, first in understanding how teachers perceive minoritized children's identities in other parts of the world—including conflict-ridden areas—and, second, in appreciating the implications of these perceptions in teachers' practices.

Studies in England indicate the prevalence of racism in schools, mainly in terms of teachers' (un)intended attitudes, behaviors, and practices (Gillborn & Mirza, 2000; Gillborn, 2008). In particular, it has been found that teachers treat black, Muslim, and Asian students in stereotypical or hostile ways and assume that these students have behavior problems (e.g. Archer, 2003; Connolly, 1998); teachers' constructions are found to be grounded in racialized, gendered, and classed assumptions (e.g. Archer & Francis, 2005). Similarly, research in other European countries (e.g. Belgium and the Netherlands) shows how Belgian teachers discriminate against Turkish children (e.g. Stevens, 2008), or how Dutch teachers disregard Moroccan children (e.g. de Haan & Elbers, 2004). Also, research in the United States shows that teachers' negative stereotypes and low expectations of minoritized children partly explains the overrepresentation of culturally and linguistically diverse students in special education programs, which, in turn, affects the eventual educational outcomes of these children (e.g. Harry & Klingner, 2006). All these representations of minoritized children are grounded in homogeneous perceptions of identity and color-blind perspectives, and they place the burden for adaptation to the majoritized norms on minoritized children (Phoenix, 2002; Stevens, 2007). Most of these studies argue that teachers are de facto running racist regimes in their classrooms either without realizing it, or meaning to, or while they deny it to researchers (i.e. speech and practice are different) (see also Zembylas & Chubbuck, 2012).

Research on race and ethnicity in England, other European countries, the US, and so on has parallels in conflicted areas such as Northern Ireland and Israel. In particular, it has been found that teachers tend to "homogenize" minoritized children and disregard them without realizing it, even in integrated school settings (e.g. see Bekerman & Maoz, 2005; Donnelly, 2004). However, there is evidence that the politics of conflict adds to the complexity of the situation, in that issues of in-group/out-group classification and hierarchy become more intense (see McGlynn et al., 2009). Similar evidence on the entanglement of issues of race and ethnicity also exists in the Cyprus conflict, as noted in previous chapters (see also Spyrou, 2009; Zembylas, 2008a). In general, studies from conflicted societies indicate that racialized discourses coupled with ethnicized discourses operate through processes of classification and hierarchy, differentiation and homogenization, exclusion, and entitlement

(Bekerman, Zembylas, & McGlynn, 2009). These findings confirm anthropological and sociological findings in other disciplines that ethnic, racial, and class identities, too, are social and cultural constructions, not biologically determined (Jenkins, 1996; Woodward, 2002). These ideas emphasize that ethnicity and other identity constructions are neither static nor monolithic; rather, they are shifting, plural, fluid, relational, constantly negotiated, and embedded within power relations. Recognizing the idea that children have a range of identities, with different ones acquiring salience in different contexts, can be useful in understanding how particular social positions—for example, race, class, ethnicity—are ascribed to children through discursive formations and ideologies such as racist talk and discriminatory practices (Phoenix, 1998; Ross, 2007).

The School Settings

The school settings and the research design have been described in previous chapters. As a reminder, the three focus schools are: the Hill School, the Town School, and the Sea School. This chapter examines data collected in semi-structured interviews with 18 teachers (12 women and 6 men) in these schools and their principals (two females and one male), all Greek Cypriots. In following pages I examine a range of interview excerpts highlighting the Greek-Cypriot teachers' constructions of Turkish-speaking students' identities and their feelings of discomfort about diversity of the student population in their school. First, I provide evidence for the discomfort felt by the majority of Greek-Cypriot teachers who participated in this research, highlighting their emotional ambivalence about the presence of Turkish-speaking and minority students in their schools. Second, I explore data exposing the racialized, ethnicized, and classed perceptions of the majority of Greek-Cypriot participating teachers, showing how their perceptions are linked to larger structural, systemic issues of race, ethnicity, and education. Finally, I highlight the resistance that is present in the discourse and enacted curriculum of a few teachers; these teachers use their discomfort to enact an "ethic of discomfort" in their teaching. I close with a discussion of some of the possibilities that are opened from enacting an ethic of discomfort in schools.

Teachers' Discomfort about the Growing Diversity in Schools

One typical response to the question "How do you feel about the growing diversity and multiculturalism in your school?" is captured in the following conversation—part of which was introduced in chapter 3—with a female teacher from the Town School.

TEACHER: I feel uncomfortable, of course! Foreign children bring with them totally different customs and habits from ours. Cyprus cannot integrate all these immigrants and our cultural and national identity is threatened by them. So, to be honest, I don't feel comfortable with the presence of foreign children and especially the presence of Turkish Cypriots.

RESEARCHER: Why do you feel uncomfortable especially with the presence of Turkish-Cypriot students?

TEACHER: You know, because of the Cyprus Problem, the Turkish invasion, the ongoing occupation of our country. Yes, they are children but I can't take off my mind that they are also of Turkish origin.

In this short conversation, this teacher identified the two major emotional issues that concerned many teachers who taught in the three multicultural schools examined in the present study: first, *discomfort* with the presence of immigrant children and especially Turkish Cypriots (because of the political situation in Cyprus); and second, *fear* that immigrants (in general) threaten the national and cultural identity of Greek Cypriots. Other teachers specified further their discomfort—citing, for example, discomfort with not knowing how to deal with immigrant and minority children's lack of Greek language and communication skills as well as these children's low performance compared to the majority's academic performance. A female teacher from the Sea School explained:

> Honestly, I have been thrown into this school without any training how to deal with foreign children. Putting aside the fact that these children are often undisciplined and create all sorts of problems, I don't have a clue how to teach them because they don't know a word of Greek! I mean, what do you do in a case like this? Naturally, I only work with Greek-Cypriot children, while foreign students stay behind. This makes me frustrated; it doesn't make me feel good about myself. But we [teachers] are put in an impossible situation. We need professional support but also emotional support to cope with these challenges because dealing with this situation is emotionally very difficult.

This teacher argued that she—and other colleagues at the Sea School—needed emotional and professional support to cope with the teaching of immigrant and minority children. Her inability to teach these children in appropriate ways made her feel discomfort. In spite of the stereotypes that one could identify in this teacher's talk (e.g. "these children are often undisciplined and create all sorts of problems"), there was a sense of powerlessness to cope with diversity and multiculturalism. In general, our data show that while teachers felt they were put in an unpleasant situation, they felt powerless to cope with the resulting emotional and professional demands.

At the same time, a small group of teachers from the three schools talked about their discomfort for having to deal with the negative emotions and attitudes of their colleagues and Greek-Cypriot children toward immigrants and Turkish-speaking students. A male teacher at the Hill School pointed out the following.

> I feel sad and disappointed because many of my colleagues express extremely negative feelings about immigrant children and especially Turkish-speaking children. [. . .] Some of us at this school try very hard to change those feelings, but there is not much support and I'll leave it at that. . . . In addition, many Greek-Cypriot students bring negative attitudes from home, from their refugee parents, yet those attitudes are also cultivated here at school. Greek-Cypriot students are not willing to collaborate with Turkish-speaking students and they show those negative feelings overtly on every possible occasion. [. . .] Sometimes I am in despair, because I feel there is nothing that can be done to change this situation. On the other hand, I have to find the emotional strength to move on and try to change things, because this unfair treatment of immigrant and Turkish-speaking children is unacceptable to me.

Another source of teachers' discomfort came from Greek-Cypriot parents' negative reactions to the presence of immigrant and Turkish-speaking children in Greek-Cypriot schools. As a female teacher at the Hill School noted:

> Greek-Cypriot parents complain that foreign children pull back the level at which their children should be and so, for example, they don't want Turkish-speaking children in our classrooms. We are pressured to show that Greek-Cypriot children are not left behind as a result of the low level at which Turkish-speaking students are permanently. [. . .] We are working hard to reach the same standards as other schools that do not have foreign children, but the truth is that we are falling behind.

Finally, a number of teachers discussed their anxiety regarding the changing working conditions. For example, they feel pressure to keep the educational standards high despite the presence in the classroom of immigrant and minority children; pressure from Greek-Cypriot parents not to ignore Greek-Cypriot children; and sometimes, their own self-ethical pressures to treat all students fairly. The following excerpt from an interview with a teacher at the Town School shows the "toxic" economy of discomfort in this school and its implications for their students.

> Not all of us feel the same pressure or ethical responsibility toward these children. Unfortunately, many of my colleagues have given up on immigrant and Turkish-speaking children. But their feelings of resentment and even cynicism are present and poison the school culture and our relationships with these children. I can't begin to tell you how distressed this situation makes me. Recently, we organized a multicultural week, essentially to put on a show for the parents and supposedly show that we do multicultural education. In reality, during the whole time we were organizing this event, most teachers were complaining that immigration and multiculturalism would signal the end of Greek culture in Cyprus.

Overall, the majority of Greek-Cypriot teachers in the three participating schools expressed their discomfort, anxiety, and ambivalence with the increasing presence of immigrant and minority students (especially Turkish-speaking ones) and the lack of teacher training and support to cope with the growing diversity and multiculturalism in their schools.

The Racialized, Ethnicized, and Classed Perceptions of Greek-Cypriot Teachers about Turkish-Speaking Children's Identities

Also, the majority of Greek-Cypriot teachers (13 of the 18) in the three participating schools classified Turkish-speaking children according to racial, ethnic, and class categories. One typical understanding of Turkish-speaking children is captured in the conversation that follows. During the conversation, a female teacher at the Hill School discussed the cultural characteristics of Turkish-speaking students, explaining why they were not accepted by the majority of Greek-Cypriot students:

TEACHER: First of all, Turkish-speaking students are distinguished by their external appearance. They have a darker skin complexion, they are extremely dirty and untidy, especially the Roma, and they don't speak any Greek. They usually stink and this is a cultural thing. Anyway, they don't have the habit of cleaning themselves, and so our children [Greek Cypriots] don't like to play or sit in class with them. [. . .] And there is, of course, the hostility against the Turks.

RESEARCHER: What do you mean by that?

TEACHER: I refer to these children's Turkish identity and the fact that Turks are our historical enemies.

RESEARCHER: How does this influence you as a teacher?

TEACHER: It gives you an awry feeling. . . . I mean they are children but they are also of Turkish origin. It's impossible to get this out of your mind.

In this short exchange, this teacher identified almost all of the issues raised by most teachers when they referred to Turkish-speaking students. She talked about Turkish-speaking children being poor, dark-colored, unclean, and of different ethnic origin and argued that the sensitivity about these issues was further accentuated as a result of the historical conflict with the Turks. Importantly, these issues were used to justify the rejection of Turkish-speaking children; however, the burden of rejection was placed on the minoritized children. Yet, the majority of the teachers we interviewed admitted that Turkish-Cypriot children were not yet fully accepted. "They are becoming more and more accepted, but their ethnic origin always sticks out," said the principal at the Town School, and added: "They have a Turkish origin, you know . . . with the occupation of our country; this influences our feelings about them. They come here and they have all these benefits from the government. We don't like that." Several teachers in all three primary schools referred to the financial aid that Turkish-speaking families received from the government and expressed resentment for this. "I am sorry but this makes me very angry," said one male teacher at the Sea School. He then continued: "I know how it's going to sound but I'll say this anyway. They [Turkish-speaking families] come here and go to the occupied areas [the north] whenever they like, they are extremely poor and uncivilized, and yet they receive more financial aid than our [Greek-Cypriot] poor families. This is not fair."

Many teachers in all three schools talked openly and freely about the language and culture "deficiency" of Turkish-speaking children. As a female teacher at the Hill School admitted:

> We do everything possible to help these children learn the language and become a bit more civilized because they have no manners from home. But no matter what we do, these children are incapable of learning the Greek language. [. . .] We are pressured to show that Greek-Cypriot children are not left behind as a result of the low level at which Turkish-speaking students are permanently.

The Turkish-speaking students' difficulties with participating in class activities were obvious through our ethnographic observations. For example, we were present for several incidents in which the teacher was simply teaching the rest of the class, ignoring the Turkish-speaking students who did not do anything or simply drew pictures in their notebooks. When asked to comment why Turkish-speaking students seemed to be ignored, one teacher at the Town School admitted that he had lower expectations from these students and stopped "putting a lot of pressure on them" (see chapter 4).

Most teachers denied the existence of discriminatory and racist perceptions or practices—either systemic or solely individual—against Turkish-speaking children. More important, embedded in these assumptions about the absence of any racial discrimination in the three schools was a belief that the majoritized group (i.e. Greek Cypriots) had the right to determine "the rules of the game" and even to be "racist." As one female teacher at the Hill School asserted, "We do everything possible to be fair. But it's their [the Turkish-speaking children's] responsibility to learn the rules of the game and adapt to our way of life. Why should we change for them?" Another (male) teacher at the Town School put it more bluntly: "Look, given the threat we face to become extinct as Greeks, I think we are justified to be a bit racist. It's a matter of survival." In general, these teachers failed to recognize the systemic, structural component of the Greek-Cypriot privilege in the Greek-Cypriot educational system and its unequal implications for Turkish-speaking children. Instead, these teachers were free to express their decidedly racist views under the cover of the "threat" of extinction as a (Greek) community.

At the same time, however, most teachers (regardless of school) claimed that Turkish-speaking students were mostly integrated in Greek-Cypriot schools without major problems. These claims, in conjunction with the "racist" assertions identified earlier, indicated that there were conflictual or ambivalent discourses "within" individual teachers. Consider, for example, the following two interview excerpts by the same teacher at the Sea School:

> The most important thing is to treat all children equally. When you have a conflict, for example, between Greek Cypriots and Turkish Cypriots, you don't approach the incident as a problem between two ethnic groups. You don't make distinctions between them on the basis of their ethnic or cultural origin.
>
> To tell you the truth, Turkish Cypriots are the most disruptive and unfocused children in the whole school. They always find ways to avoid learning and engage in misbehavior. [. . .] Our children are polite, diligent, attentive, and clean. They are completely the opposite from Turkish Cypriots. [. . .] The Turkish-Cypriot families are poor and don't really

care about their children's education; unavoidably, this lack of interest passes on to the children themselves.

Like teachers in the other two schools, this teacher distinguished between two types of students on the basis of their origin. Greek-Cypriot students were "normal"—well behaved, diligent, and polite—whereas Turkish-speaking students were aggressive, unclean, poor, and did not care about their education. However, this normalization seemed to be grounded in a "color-blind" and "equality for all" rhetoric. In other words, there was an admixture of claims about the educational system's being objective, equal, and color-blind with perceptions that Turkish-speaking students misbehaved, and were poor and somehow deficient. The majority of teachers brought out the issues of "low socioeconomic status" and "being dirty" as characteristics of Turkish-speaking students; therefore, to some extent there was evidence that the "racism" of teachers involved class issues, too. Interestingly, these forms of "new racism" at school (see Gillborn, 2008; Youdell, 2006) were discussed in terms of "normal" school behavior and "school hygiene"; thus racism "mutated" into more "politically correct" forms of speech, yet the result (i.e. exclusion) is the same.

Resistances in the Dominant Discourse and the Enacted Curriculum of Some Teachers

Teachers' discomfort—including the role of the principal in the constitution and circulation of this discomfort—in the Town School and the Hill School created very hostile economies of affect for Turkish-speaking students and other minorities. At the Sea School, however, the principal played a key role in the constitution of an economy of affect that used discomfort in constructive ways. Here, I highlight some of the resistances enacted through the teaching practices of five teachers in the three participating schools and the leadership of the principal at the Sea school. Although the racialized, ethnicized, and classed constructions are difficult to change, unraveling resistances to "normalized" teachers' perceptions creates openings (e.g. see Gillborn, 2008; Youdell, 2006) for alternative constructions of Turkish-speaking children's identities. Some of the resistances in the discourse and practice of these teachers are discussed below.

First, it is important to acknowledge how the principal at the Sea School assumed at activist role in the community and engaged in practices that struggled to create a school culture grounded in social justice and anti-racism. For example, this principal referred to the importance of being committed to social justice values and beliefs that aimed at changing school structures and practices that "are unfair to some students." His vision was "to create a school that works in a just way . . . so that student outcomes are not related to students' ethnic or cultural background, color, language, or race. I want my school to be successful for all students." Discussions with this principal highlighted the negative implications of teachers' racialized, ethnicized, and classed constructions, referring specifically to the marginalization of Turkish-speaking children. He also emphasized that it was his "moral duty" to engage in challenging stereotyped perceptions, no matter where they came from.

Furthermore, the principal at the Sea School took a clear stance against discourses and teaching practices that were discriminatory toward Turkish-speaking children. Just as CRT theorists point out, this principal highlighted that racism, nationalism (especially in Cyprus), and classism "were not problems of individuals but of societies" and that stereotyped perceptions were constructed to maintain the privilege of the hegemonic group (i.e. Greek Cypriots). Clearly, the majority of teachers we interviewed defended themselves as not being implicated in racism/nationalism/classism, yet this principal insisted that teachers' stereotyped perceptions were present. Thus he challenged his teachers at every opportunity (e.g. staff meetings, breaks, one-to-one basis) and encouraged them to consider: "Why is it that Turkish-speaking children are always framed as failures and then eventually fulfill these expectations?" Or, "What are the consequences of rendering Turkish-speaking students as 'misbehaving' or 'backward'?" As he further explained:

> My school staff and the parents need to be convinced first that it is morally unacceptable to subscribe to deficit thinking for minority students or students who come from low socioeconomic background. It's not the students' fault but the system's failure that sustains failing results for these students. You know, it's not easy to convince parents and teachers that all children have the potential to do well in school. Naturally, there is a lot of resistance from those who belong to the dominant culture. Non-indigenous students, for example, are blamed for everything. For everything unpleasant that happens in school. Fights, misbehavior, everything is their fault. So, I encourage my staff to attend workshops, conferences, and seminars and bring back specific ideas they can implement to change these perceptions and the ways we deal with these challenges. We need to constantly examine our practices, take responsibility for what we do, and not blame others or the system for everything.

The economy of affect at the Sea School constitutes an example of what was termed earlier an "ethic of discomfort." The principal at this school engaged his teachers in systematic efforts to use their discomfort as a point of departure for individual and social transformation. An important affective space was provided for reflexivity on teachers' emotional experiences and pedagogical practices so that teachers could embrace more empathetic positions and challenge their normative ideas about diversity and multiculturalism. Individual and social transformation was not guaranteed by the presence of this economy of affect; an ethic of discomfort was not an end result, but rather a space and a process of building on individual and collective discomfort as a source of enrichment rather than a stumbling block.

Another example of resistance was found at the Town School. A teacher expressed repeatedly her public disagreement at the ways her colleagues treated Turkish-speaking children. As she explained in an interview—an excerpt of which was first presented in chapter 4:

> Non-native children want attention, and in this school they don't get it. Here the situation is "cool" for everyone. The culture is very Greek Cypriot. . . . The teachers don't talk to Turkish-speaking children with respect. This situation stigmatizes Turkish-speaking children and the stereotypes are perpetuated among all children. [. . .] I don't hesitate to tell you that there is a lot of racism here. [. . .] Children say things like "If you are touched by Melike you will get sick." This is blunt racism! And some teachers and the principal herself witness such incidents and they just laugh.

This teacher also emphasized that discourses about fairness and neutrality were essentially rhetorical ways of covering discrimination. In the following excerpt—which was also presented in chapter 4—she talks about how her efforts to resist racialized, ethnicized, and classed perceptions turned the majority of her colleagues against her.

> The truth is that we [teachers] often discuss Turkish-speaking students, not because we care about them but because they create problems. This is the truth, in all honesty. I don't ever remember a colleague expressing concerns about these children, coming up with ideas and things to do to help them and include them in the school community. Usually, the discussion is about what "this Turkish-Cypriot student did to me today," and things like that. At a teachers' meeting, I dared once to say that these children were justified in behaving the way they did because they knew they were not welcomed here and that we resented their presence. I was

fiercely attacked by several colleagues who said I had a "Turkish-friendly" attitude.

Finally, another teacher at the Hill School resisted the "normalization" of Turkish-speaking children by sharing with colleagues her experiences from providing individualized instruction to these children in pull-out sessions. As she pointed out in an interview:

> When they are by themselves in these supportive instructions, they [Turkish-speaking students] are happy, expressive, and alive. [. . .] I try to communicate this to my colleagues but [. . .] they don't believe that these children have the potential to learn if you show them love and respect. I feel uncomfortable with the attitude of my colleagues, and we often get into arguments about this, but they say I have these views because I am supportive of rapprochement between Greek-Cypriots and Turkish-Cypriots and so I am blinded and don't see the low potential of Turkish-speaking students.

Teacher resistance, although isolated and small, attempted to provide alternative constructions about Turkish-speaking children's identities through highlighting the problematic features of fixing these children to particular static descriptions. The positioning and counter-positioning of Turkish-speaking children's identities had important implications for these children's survival and success in the Greek-Cypriot educational system. The dominant discourse of racialized, ethnicized, and classed perceptions about Turkish-speaking children and the normalization of these children's identities showed how the dominant group racialized this particular minoritized group. The teachers and the principal who resisted this dominant discourse were critical of racialized, ethnicized, and classed perceptions and the mechanisms through which such perceptions occurred in systemic ways. By applying a counter-construction of Turkish-speaking children's identities, an oppositional praxis was enacted and turned the "normal" identities of these children into contested spaces, even in minor ways.

Enacting an Ethic of Discomfort in Schools

There are two key issues that I discuss as this chapter comes to an end. The first issue has to do with how Greek-Cypriot teachers perceive Turkish-speaking children; the second issue highlights the openings that are manifest through teacher resistance, particularly in relation to enacting an "ethic of discomfort" (Foucault,

1994). An *ethic of discomfort* may be understood here as a particular economy of affect that captures not only the circulation of certain emotions between individuals (e.g. anxiety about the increasing presence of immigrants), but also the way in which discomfort serves as a medium for individual and social transformation. Let's discuss one issue at a time.

First, this chapter shows that Greek-Cypriot teachers perceive Turkish-speaking children in racialized, ethnicized. and classed ways, and that the sociopolitical structures in Cyprus influence teachers' negative discourses and practices toward these children. Most of the classic studies on teacher racism suggest that teachers are running racist regimes in their classrooms either without realizing it, or meaning to, or while they deny it to researchers. The remarkable finding of this research project is that several teachers say they are "racist," claiming that they are justified to act in these ways in light of the political situation in Cyprus; in other words, there is not a "mismatch" between spoken account and actual practice. Teachers' perceptions, then, entail a sense of a "right" to be racist, because this "right" is perceived as a defense mechanism against Turkish efforts to dominate all over Cyprus and change its demographic character. Clearly, this claim reveals the intensely negative representations of the Turks and how these representations are influential to the ways teachers behave toward all Turkish-speaking individuals, including children.

Previous research (e.g. see Vaught & Castagno, 2008) has shown the range of social and structural components that influence the common phrase "I don't think I'm a racist," as well as the discursive functions of self-justification and disarming criticism about accusations of racism. However, an important sociological point emanating from the use of CRT in the present research is that while this position (i.e. "I don't think I'm racist") exists, there is additionally the position of some teachers who admit it is their "right" to be racist when their country is perceived to be in danger. This finding complicates theoretical understandings of teachers' ambivalent justifications of their racialized, ethnicized, and classed practices; contextual concerns are manifest in simultaneous claims that there should be equal opportunities for all children (see Rattansi & Phoenix, 2005), yet it is rightful to be racist under some circumstances.

The second key issue is that despite negative discourses and practices toward Turkish-speaking children, there is resistance on the part of a few teachers and a school principal; this resistance is expressed through *liminal performance* (McKenzie, 2003) such as counter-discourses and counter-practices that challenge or temporarily suspend the "normalized" identities of Turkish-speaking children. This liminal performance is a fundamental component of critical emotional praxis, because it provides the emotional space to enact alternative practices and discourses about the "other." Although teacher resistances do not seem to have any major effect on transforming the structural inequalities that persist on an everyday basis (Gillborn, 2008; Taylor, Gillborn, & Ladson-Billings, 2009) and are often veiled as formal equality for all (Vaught & Castagno, 2008), it is important that the "normalized" identities of Turkish-speaking children do not remain unchallenged. These (small) openings are essentially possibilities for cultivating individual and collective political consciousness and critical emotional praxis against fixed and reified identities of the past. The case studies of primary schools discussed in Part II of this book teach us that these openings exist because individual teachers or school leaders enact their agency to invent leadership practices and pedagogies that challenge essentialist identity categories (Bekerman & Zembylas, 2012).

In general, an important issue emerging from the case studies in Part II is that the capabilities of teachers to cope with growing diversity and multiculturalism may be enhanced, if an "ethic of discomfort" is constituted in schools. The case of the principal at the Sea School, for example, demonstrates how an economy of affect grounded in an ethic of discomfort can be used to problematize taken-for-granted daily habits with regard to why particular discomforts persist or these discomforts may be dealt with productively (Boler & Zembylas, 2003). Discomfort, in other words, is used as a point of departure that encourages teachers to reconsider diversity and multiculturalism (Boler, 1999). The principal at the Sea School demonstrates this process when he attempts to critically engage his teachers without dismissing their emotional ambivalence, uncertainty, or even uneasiness toward Turkish-speaking and minority children. Feelings of discomfort do not necessarily block action or paralyze us; they may, in fact, offer opportunities for reconsidering affective connections with others. Using discomfort productively—e.g. through critical dialogue and negotiation—teachers may become able to engage in a process of transforming their emotional experiences of frustration, anxiety, and ambivalence rather than remain trapped in those (see chapters 10–13).

In conclusion, by looking through teachers' constructions in the three schools, we are able not only to see what is problematic but also to discover a window of opportunity for addressing the problematic aspects of the racialized, ethnicized, and classed framework in schooling. For example, teachers' discourse on equality and fairness can be used as a point of departure to identify practices through which solidarity might become possible (Anthias & Yuval-Davis, 1992). Critical Race Theory provides the conceptual framework within which to problematize how perceptions and practices establish, assert, and reinforce power differentials and hierarchies, and how individuals draw on the resources of stereotypes to reproduce racism/nationalism/classism. Racialized/ethnicized/classed discourses are facilitated by relevant modes of engagement and are perpetuated through the cultivation of particular practices—such as collective behavior and school policies that contribute to the formation of inclusions/exclusions (Gillborn, 2008). Unavoidably, then, it is important to analyze the modes through which such perceptions are authorized by, implied in, and manifest in teacher practices and school policies. Therefore, providing systemic opportunities for teachers and school staff—in conjunction with implementing equal treatment of Turkish-speaking children—to problematize exclusive practices, and considering what those practices *do* to Turkish-speaking children, are crucial elements in developing alternative "pedagogies of emotion" marked by compassion, caring, and social justice.

Note

1. Foucault (1994a) defines an ethic of discomfort as,

> never to consent to being completely comfortable with one's own presuppositions. Never to let them fall peacefully asleep, but also never to believe that a new fact will suffice to overturn them; never to imagine that one can change them like arbitrary axioms, remembering that in order to give them the necessary mobility one must have a distant view, but also look at what is nearby and all around oneself. To be very mindful that everything one perceives is evident only against a familiar and little known horizon, that every certainty is sure only through the support of a ground that is always unexplored. The most fragile instant has its roots. In that lesson, there is a whole ethic of sleepless evidence that does not rule out, far from it, a rigorous economy of the True and the False; but that is not the whole story. (p. 448)

The ethic of discomfort that Foucault seeks to introduce into our relation to the present is one that emphasizes the proactive and transformative potential of discomfort. The aim of an ethic of discomfort is to make problematic manifestations of discomfort "without portraying them as acts of bad faith or cowardice, to open a space for movement without slipping into a prophetic posture" (Rabinow & Rose, 2003, p. xxvii).

THE EMOTIONAL COMPLEXITIES OF TRAUMATIC CONFLICT

Openings and Closures

There is no flag large enough to cover the shame of killing innocent people.

—*"Terror Over Tripoli" (1993), from The Zinn Reader (1997)*

History isn't the lies of the victors. . .; I know that now. It's more the memories of the survivors, most of whom are neither victorious nor defeated.

—JULIAN BARNES, *The Sense of an Ending*

7 NEGOTIATING COEXISTENCE AT A SHARED SCHOOL

I wake up everyday and I see the Turkish flag on the [Pentadaktylos] mountain and you tell me to reconcile with the Turks?

—MINAS, *Greek-Cypriot student*

Some teachers and students are racist in this school. And I don't think anything can be done, unless people admit this and are willing to change. People have to see us as human beings.

—GÖNÜL, *Turkish-Cypriot student*

In a country that is troubled by protracted ethnic conflict, *shared* or *integrated* education[1]—that is, schooling that is grounded in the idea of educating together children who come from conflicting communities—would seem like a good idea. In Cyprus, although there have been previous examples of shared education between students from the two conflicting communities of Greek Cypriots and Turkish Cypriots, the idea of shared education is relatively new and has recently gained increased attention (Zembylas, 2013a). The increased attention in Cyprus has come as a result of the partial lift of restrictions on movement through the checkpoints that still divide Cyprus into its north side (where Turkish Cypriots live) and its south side (where Greek Cypriots live). The partial lift of restrictions in 2003 made possible the shared education of Greek-Cypriot and Turkish-Cypriot students in a rudimentary yet politically and socially important manner.

Existing research on shared and integrated education in conflict-ridden societies shows that there are numerous (social, emotional, political) challenges influencing the success or failure of shared and integrated education (Bekerman, 2009; McGlynn, 2009; McGlynn, Zembylas, & Bekerman, 2013; McGlynn et al., 2004). In particular, existing stereotypes and prejudices are considered one of the most serious challenges for teachers, students, and parents involved in shared and integrated educational efforts (McGlynn, 2009). This particular challenge has been primarily evaluated through psychological paradigms, whereas more recent theoretical approaches, such as critical multicultural theory (Kincheloe & Steinberg, 1997; May, 1999), have been used to theorize the complexities of interactions that occur in shared and integrated schools (McGlynn & Bekerman, 2007b). Research on these complexities of interactions through the use of theoretical approaches like critical multicultural theory is extremely valuable, if educators are going to find more appropriate educational policies and pedagogical practices for promoting shared education.

This chapter introduces yet another site of my ethnographic research—a shared secondary private school on the south side of Nicosia, the capital of Cyprus—and focuses on teachers', students', and parents' perspectives on the struggles to negotiate coexistence between Greek-Cypriot and Turkish-Cypriot students. Chapter 8 continues the analysis that begins here and delves deeper into the pedagogical struggles to enhance inclusion and reconciliation in the context of this school. At this particular school, Greek-Cypriot students (the majority) and Turkish-Cypriot students (the minority) have been educated together since September 2003. Every morning, approximately 100 Turkish-Cypriot students (roughly 10% of the school's population) cross the dividing line from the north part of Cyprus and go to the south side to attend this secondary international school and then return to their homes in the afternoon. How do these students feel about attending a school on the "other" side? How do Greek-Cypriot students perceive this experience and behave toward their Turkish-Cypriot classmates? What possibilities are there for constructing new affective connections between students from the two rival communities?

Being a Greek-Cypriot researcher and educator who grew up and was educated in a segregated educational system (see chapter 1), I have always been puzzled by the prospects and possibilities of shared education in a divided country. Needless to say, the findings of this case study cannot be generalized in any way, yet they provide interesting indications for the prospects and challenges of coexistence of students in this particular setting. If nothing else, the mere opportunity of shared education within a society in which schooling has always been segregated is a provocative event in itself, and thus an investigation of some of its workings is valuable. Yet, as I will argue, the results of this case study help us make interesting connections with some of the ideas that are highlighted in this chapter, chiefly, critical multiculturalism. Looking at shared and integrated education through the lenses of these ideas enriches the theoretical foundations with which shared schooling has thus far been viewed in conflicted societies.

Shared and Integrated Education

My analysis begins with a brief review of the theoretical approaches that have been most commonly applied to shared and integrated education; my intention is not to conduct a comprehensive review, but rather to provide an overview of the foundational perspectives of each approach—namely, contact theory and social identity theory. More attention is paid to discussing critical multicultural theory and its connection to the idea of critical emotional praxis.

Contact Theory

The "contact hypothesis" (Allport, 1954) has been used to investigate the impact of intergroup contact on attitudes and identities, especially in the context of conflicted societies. Contact theory suggests that contact between members of conflicting groups can promote positive intergroup attitudes in individuals and improve intergroup encounters. Allport (1954) argued that, under certain conditions, contact between groups in conflict will break down the barriers of prejudice and stereotypes. Four such conditions of contact have been identified as factors of reducing intergroup conflict: the equal status of groups, the requirement for co-operation, the avoidance of social competition, and the institutional support for legitimate contact (Pettigrew & Tropp, 2006). Allport's theory relies on the assumption that the origins of conflict lie in the existence of ethnocentric personalities; in other words, Allport's approach suggests that the problem is at the level of the individual.

Since Allport's initial theoretical formulation, the contact hypothesis has been developed over the years, and in addition to the conditions proposed, attention has been turned to how and why contact works. Thus, for example, specific strategies have been proposed to introduce successful contact such as the need for "decategorization" of group (e.g. ethnic) identity (Brewer & Miller, 1984) and "recategorization" on the basis of broader (common) social categories (Gaertner et al., 1993). More recently, Hewstone (1996) and Pettigrew (1998) have analyzed possible outcomes of different contact strategies, suggesting that there is potential benefit in the order in which contact approaches are introduced. For example, interpersonal contact should first be introduced, followed by intergroup contact, and then by decategorization and recategorization.

Contact theory has often been used to analyze the shared education of students from conflicting groups (Niens, 2009). Thus, shared and integrated education has been proposed as a way to promote positive contact between children from conflicting communities. For example, shared and integrated education has been established in Israel (Bekerman, 2007), Northern Ireland (McGlynn et al., 2004), and South Africa (Vandeyar & Esakov, 2007) to promote intergroup contact and reduce prejudice (McGlynn, 2009). Review of research on shared and integrated education in Northern Ireland (Niens, 2009) and elsewhere (Dovidio, Gaertner, & Kawakami, 2003) indicates that contact in shared schools can be effective in fostering positive intergroup attitudes and identities if Allport's conditions of contact are upheld. Also, a number of other factors seem to influence the effectiveness of contact, including the approach taken to diversity and inclusion, the educational and sociopolitical context, as well as the involvement of parents and the wider community in school affairs (Brown & Hewstone, 2005; Niens, 2009).

Social Identity Theory

Allport's approach to the value of contact has been challenged by subsequent social psychological work in conflict and intergroup relations. There is now substantial literature on social identity theory (Tajfel, 1978; Tajfel & Turner, 1979, 1986) and self-categorization theory (Turner, 1991), emphasizing that social identification plays an important role in both maintaining and exacerbating the conflict (McGlynn et al., 2004). These perspectives challenge the assumption that conflict is rooted in individual prejudice and personality, and they highlight that there are social psychological factors that contribute to conflict. Both social identity theory and self-categorization theory acknowledge the interconnections between the social and individual aspects of conflict and reveal the significant influence of the collective on the individual. In particular, the investigation of the link between large-group psychology and individual psychological aspects is important in showing how social identity is inextricably intertwined with self-categorization (Zinner & Williams, 1999) and the politicization of identity (Hammack, 2011). This kind of investigation has contributed to social psychological explanations of shared and integrated education, highlighting the impact of shared education on identity as the socialized part of self (McGlynn, 2009).

However, the increased complexities of multicultural politics make social psychological paradigms alone inadequate to account more fully for the political aspects of identity and the multifaceted interactions between individuals coming from conflicting groups (Al-Haj, 2005; Hammack, 2011; Bekerman & McGlynn, 2007). In light of the potential impact of multicultural politics on integrated schools, social identity theory by itself seems insufficient to consider how power relations are involved in the recognition of diversity as it is linked to social inequalities and the political structures of the nation-state (Bekerman & Zembylas, 2012). Bekerman (2004, 2007), in particular, argues that integrated educational approaches grounded in social identity theory are lacking if the nation-state is not sufficiently accounted for in cross-cultural encounters. Therefore, educational interventions that draw on social psychological and interpersonal perspectives—e.g. that focus on the contact of members of conflicting groups aimed at creating familiarity, acceptance, and recognition—have a low level of success and a low level of critical interest, if encounters ignore existing social structures and power relations. For this purpose, Bekerman and Maoz (2005) suggest that both our research approaches to integrated education and our pedagogical practices that promote meaningful coexistence may have better chances to succeed if the assumptions about monolithic identities and cultures are somewhat relaxed, not only at the social psychological level but also at the structural political level as well. According to Bekerman and Maoz, strengthening coexistence needs to consider alternative options to the ones dictated in the past—such as, the critical consideration and theorization of the tight relationship between essentialist perspectives of identity and the larger sociopolitical context.

Critical Multiculturalism

Most modern states today face the challenges of multiculturalism in that they need to deal with modes of interaction between majority groups and minority groups in the context of a complex set of social, cultural, and political factors (Kelly, 2002). Al-Haj (2003) identifies two major approaches: mainstream and critical multiculturalism. Mainstream multiculturalism emphasizes difference and the importance of recognizing diversity; however, it fails to consider the role of power relationships in society and the majority's control of minorities (Giroux, 1993). By contrast, critical multiculturalism adopts a comprehensive view of diversity, challenges inequalities, and acknowledges the role of power relations in shaping dominant discourses and practices (Kincheloe & Steinberg, 1997; Mahalingham & McCarthy, 2000; May, 1999; Nieto, 2000). Attention is not focused on superficial differences (e.g. food preferences, traditional dances, cultural customs) but on those differences that are linked to social injustices and unequal social and political structures. More specifically in relation to education, critical multicultural theory recognizes the ideological mission of schooling and the role of teachers as cultural gatekeepers who transmit values of the dominant culture (Kincheloe & Steinberg, 1997).

Furthermore, critical multicultural theory differs fundamentally from both a (naïve) liberal emphasis on similarities between groups that avoids sensitive and controversial issues and a "harmonious empty pluralism" (Mohanty, 1994, p. 146) that amounts to nothing more than celebration of diversity or what has become known as the "3S's: Saris, Samosas, and Steelbands" (Troyna & Williams,

1986). Ethnicity, nationality, religion, and race are acknowledged in critical multicultural theory as powerful markers that are used to legitimate inequality; thus critiquing these categories and their consequences is an important component of research and pedagogical approaches that are grounded in social justice ideas (Bekerman & Zembylas, 2012).

Contact theory and social identity theory offer frameworks for explaining construction of identity and how this affects cross-cultural contact as a means of counteracting stereotype, prejudice, and conflict. However, it is critical multiculturalism that informs educative practices to address the effect that contact does or doesn't have on breaking down barriers between students. Unlike contact and social identity theories, critical multicultural theory makes it possible to move beyond individual and social psychological aspects and acknowledge how children and youth can critically confront their stereotypes and prejudices within a specific context of social inequalities and the political structures of the nation-state.

The struggle over religious, ethnic, and other rights has particularly become a major source of debate and tension in conflict-ridden societies and thus critical multicultural theory is particularly pertinent in gaining a deeper understanding of issues of recognition, conflict, contact, and prejudice. The question often asked in this regard is whether the struggle for recognition of difference and preservation of national ethos of a specific group "goes hand in hand with multicultural ideology" (Al-Haj, 2005, p. 49). On the one hand, cultivating a national ethos is considered important for maintaining recognition of collective rights in societies in which those rights are perceived to be threatened by interethnic conflict. On the other hand, focusing only on recognition and national ethos promotes further segregation and marginalization, because each social group cares about its own culture and puts aside concerns about unequal social and political structures (Al-Haj, 2004; Steiner-Khamsi, 2003). Writing in the context of the Middle East conflict, Al-Haj concludes that the introduction of mainstream multiculturalism seems to be an impossible task when a specific national ethos stands at the center of the school curriculum: "This is especially true in states that are experiencing an "intractable conflict" in which the past is used to justify the present" (2005, p. 47). Along similar lines of thought, Bekerman (2004) emphasizes that mainstream multiculturalism "might not be a good formula for countries that are still unstable. These might be in need of a much more careful and critical approach. [. . .] [I]interethnic tensions are aggravated by educational reforms that highlight each ethnic group both sequentially and in isolation" (p. 603).

In conjunction with critical multiculturalism, the notion of critical emotional praxis offers the opportunity to explore emotion and its link to traumatic conflict in the context of a shared school. In particular, attention to both psychoanalytic and sociopolitical aspects of emotion (chapter 2) allows the acknowledgment and critical analysis of the emotional complexities involved in the co-education of children from antagonistic communities. The intersection of critical multiculturalism and critical emotional praxis acknowledges the affective basis of power relations in shaping dominant discourses and practices and encourages a critical stance toward the troubled knowledge carried by students who feel traumatized, resist coexistence with students from an antagonistic community or openly express their racist and nationalist views.

The School Setting

In Cyprus, there have never been shared or integrated schools, along the lines of initiatives in Northern Ireland and Israel, because of the very real geopolitical boundaries that divide Cyprus (Johnson, 2007). In my recent work, I have posed the question of whether integrated schools are essentially impossible or indispensable in the present context of Cyprus, suggesting that there is not an easy yes or no response to this question, because there are powerful structural obstacles that prevent even shared educational experiences in Cypriot schools (Zembylas, 2013a). As Johnson (2007) explains, establishing integrated schools as a means of systemic peace education in Cyprus is not practical at this time; although the partial lift of restrictions in movement in 2003 made crossing to and from the south/north easier, there are still many other barriers, including political, cultural, and psychological ones. Nevertheless, after 2003, a few international (private) schools have accepted Turkish-Cypriot students, and so children from the two communities can enroll in the same school, if they wish. Among these schools is the international private school in which the case study presented in this chapter took place.

This shared secondary school is situated on the south side of Nicosia. Since the time it was founded, this school accepted students from all communities of Cyprus. (I am deliberately vague about the date of the school's establishment and other details as it would then be easily identified because there are relatively few such schools). After the 1974 conflict, there were no Turkish-Cypriot students enrolled at this school until September 2003, when a small number of Turkish-Cypriot students from the north side enrolled. The enrolment of Turkish-Cypriot students was encouraged and supported by the government of Cyprus, which sought to revive the school's bicommunal character. The parents we interviewed for the purposes of this study said that they sent their children to this school because it had always had a reputation of being "a good school" with "a multicultural character." The school has always been multicultural in terms of the student population. At present, Turkish-Cypriot students constitute approximately 10% of the student body, and Greek-Cypriot students are the majority at 85% of the 900 students enrolled in the school. English is the language of instruction. Besides Turkish-Cypriot students, this school also hosts students from other countries and cultures. These include Armenians, Maronites, Europeans, Russians, Australians, and Filipinos. Most of the teachers are Greek Cypriots, although there are teachers from several other countries (especially the United States and the United Kingdom); there are also a few Turkish-Cypriot teachers, who teach Turkish language and literature to Turkish-Cypriot students. The academic program of the school is based on the model of British independent secondary schools and mostly aims to prepare students for UK universities. Entrance to this school is highly competitive (through special exams) and the school charges fees; this constitutes a limitation of this study because the students who are educated together come from middle and upper socioeconomic classes.

The Case Study

The overarching question that drives the case study discussed in this chapter is this: How do teachers, students, and parents from the two conflicting communities in Cyprus perceive their shared education and negotiate their coexistence? To answer this focus question, two sub-questions were addressed:

1. To what extent do stereotypes and prejudice affect the contact and relationship building between Greek-Cypriot and Turkish-Cypriot students at this shared school?
2. To what extent do formal and informal discourses on collective identity and ethnic conflict in Cyprus influence the prospects of coexistence among students from the two conflicting communities?

To explore these questions, a case study approach was chosen; it used a critical ethnographic perspective and qualitative analysis, as described in chapter 1. The research took place over a period of three months in the fall of 2007 and the winter of 2008 and data were collected in two stages. The first stage involved collecting documents that included official aims and policies of the school and course syllabi. The second stage focused on ethnographic data collection through in-depth interviews with ten teachers (7 Greek-Cypriot teachers and 3 teachers of other nationalities), the school principal (British), forty students (28 Greek Cypriots and 12 Turkish Cypriots), and ten parents (7 Greek Cypriots and 3 Turkish Cypriots). All of the participants were interviewed individually, yet in a few cases some students were interviewed in groups (separate Greek Cypriot and Turkish Cypriot groups). There were also participant observations of six classrooms in four different subjects (English, Religious Education, Economics, and Geography) across five grade levels (7th, 9th, 10th, 11th, and 12th). These observations took place on a daily basis in the chosen classrooms (a total of 120 hours) and also included staffroom interactions (a total of 35 hours) and schoolyard interactions between students (a total of 20 hours). The research was carried out by three researchers.

All interviews (with teachers, students, and parents) were semistructured and focused on the following issues: (1) past and present personal experiences of inclusion-exclusion; (2) past and present experiences of coexistence and/or reconciliation with individuals who come from the other community; (3) perceptions about diversity and coexistence in the particular school context; (4) perceptions about the relationship between diversity and conflict; (5) ways of dealing with conflict inside and outside the classroom; (6) practices and policies that promote (or not) coexistence and reconciliation. All interviews lasted between 60 and 90 minutes, and were taped and transcribed. All participants were interviewed once, except the six teachers whose classrooms were observed; those teachers were interviewed three times. The teachers whose classrooms were observed volunteered to participate, after the research team visited the school and informed the school authorities about the goal of the research project. Interviews with these six teachers focused on events happening in their classrooms during observations (always in relation to the research questions of this case study). The final summaries of each interview and each observation were checked for validity and reliability through member checks; the teachers were given the summaries and asked to comment on them. Observations were carried out for nine consecutive weeks in the school staffroom, the schoolyard, and in six classrooms, and were conducted based on an observation protocol, with particular attention to recording: (1) rich descriptions of students' interactions and (2) teachers' pedagogical practices in relation to promoting (or not) coexistence. Finally, a last round of member checking was conducted through presentations of the findings to a group of teachers, the parents' association, and the school administrators (in three separate sessions). All claims made and assertions provided were validated by the participants.

First Impressions

One's first impression from visiting this school was that there are no problems between Greek-Cypriot and Turkish-Cypriot students; there are no fights in the schoolyard, students seem to hang out peacefully, and everything seems to run smoothly. However, after extensive ethnographic observations and interviews, things were shown to be somewhat different. There was a strong lingering animosity, particularly on the part of many of the Greek-Cypriot students the research team interviewed, toward Turkish Cypriots. For example, some typical phrases that Greek-Cypriot students used to describe Turkish Cypriots were: "The Turkish Cypriots are barbarians," "they are backward-thinking," "they are filthy," and "they don't belong to a Greek school." The use of these stereotypes was also confirmed by some of the teachers. For example, Andreas (GC)[2] admitted that the prevailing situation constituted "a smoldering problem. You won't see children fighting if you stroll through the schoolyard during recess time." However, as he stated, "the problem manifests itself in different ways and surfaces every so often, either as hostility in some students in the classroom, in the way they speak or in the degrading manner the Greek Cypriots refer to the Turkish Cypriots." Interestingly, no similar stereotyped language was used by Turkish-Cypriot students to refer to their Greek-Cypriot peers; in rare cases, a few Turkish Cypriots characterized Greek Cypriots as being "racists" and "nationalists."

These impressions were also confirmed by a number of different incidents that occurred during the research team's presence at this school. For instance, the research team took pictures of a number of abusive slogans against Turkish Cypriots found on walls and desks, and on one occasion some Greek Cypriot students wore Greek flags and shouted slogans against Turkish Cypriots (in the context of protests against the Turkish-Cypriot anniversary of their own state). Segregation between Greek-Cypriot and Turkish-Cypriot students was very obvious. Students socialized mainly with those belonging to their own ethnic group. Many Turkish Cypriots were usually found to hang around the so-called Turkish Room (the room where they took intensive English-language courses during their first year of study). Talent show nights organized by the school ended up as separate events, one for the Turkish Cypriots and one for the Greek Cypriots. None of the students in the two groups agreed to cooperate in hosting a joint event; more important, students from the two communities refrained from attending each other's talent show. Also, some Greek national days were celebrated, yet Turkish-Cypriot holidays were not. A number of incidents that occurred in and out of the classroom are discussed below and analyzed.

Incidents of Stereotyping and Prejudice

During a discussion in the context of a religious education class (only attended by Greek Cypriots)[3], Minas (GC) stated that he would never reconcile with his Turkish-Cypriot classmates because his mother was a refugee:

> I wake up everyday and I see the Turkish flag on the mountain and you tell me to reconcile with the Turks? How can I abandon these feelings at

> home when I see them here in my own school? My mother is a refugee. At home, she talks about the home she once had and lost because of them. Living with the Turks is impossible.

Minas's tone of voice was quite intense and he was visibly upset. He referred to his Turkish-Cypriot classmates indiscriminately as "Turks" despite the subtle interventions from his teacher to make a distinction and refer to them as "Turkish Cypriots." During recess time, one of the researchers interviewed Minas and some of his classmates. Minas mentioned that his family had frequent discussions at home about their lost home and property on the north side. He referred to a party he had organized in which he invited all his classmates except the two who were Turkish Cypriots. As he explained: "They [Turkish Cypriots] took my house once, do you think I will simply stand by and let them take this one too?" Interviewing other students, the research team discovered that some of Minas's classmates had criticized him for his decision not to invite their Turkish-Cypriot classmates to his party, given that they celebrated their team's victory (during school competitions)—a team that included these two Turkish-Cypriot students who, according to several comments made by students and teachers, had made a significant contribution.

Other observations confirmed some of the stereotypical perceptions and prejudices that existed among Greek-Cypriot and Turkish-Cypriot students at this school. The following two incidents occurred in English Literature classes. The students involved were 15–16 years of age. In the first incident, the teacher assigned a group activity to the students, asking them to work in pairs or groups of three, according to the way they were seated in class. George (GC) and Aylin (TC) sat next to each other. Throughout the duration of the 40-minute group activity the researcher observed that the two students did not exchange a single word or a single glance. Each of them took separate notes in his notebook. On three different occasions, George turned to another Greek-Cypriot classmate who was sitting behind him; they talked briefly and then George continued taking notes on his own. When the researcher interviewed the two students (separately) and asked them why they did not cooperate, George mentioned that he did not cooperate "with Turks," and Aylin stated that "the Greek-Cypriot pupils usually don't want to cooperate with us." This unwillingness to cooperate was also confirmed by the teacher, who admitted that she had faced serious reactions when she had attempted to encourage group work between Greek-Cypriot and Turkish-Cypriot students.

In the second incident, the topic of the day referred to pensions and the existing provisions in Cyprus. When the teacher asked what the provisions were in the north side of Cyprus regarding this issue, Tasos (GC) replied: "How can we know miss? Those are the occupied territories." The teacher repeated the question, looking at Ceylan (TC). Ceylan began to mention some of the provisions, however, Tasos and Petros's (GC) voices overshadowed her, saying: "This is so pathetic! They don't even have taxis! They don't have a culture!" A short disruption followed and the teacher went on with the lesson, ignoring the students' comments.

Similar incidents indicating stereotypes and prejudices were narrated by several Turkish-Cypriot students interviewed by the research team.

> The first year I was at this school, there was a girl who told me in public, "I don't want to sit next to you, because you're a Turkish Cypriot." So, okay it was a bit, you know, it made me feel upset, feel bad. (Turkish-Cypriot student, female, 15 years old)
>
> Last year there was this guy. I used to enter the classroom saying to everyone "good morning." He would always have this angry look when I said that. One day he swore back to me and I felt very bad. He said things in Greek so I didn't understand, but my Greek-Cypriot friends told me later not to talk him again because he didn't like Turkish Cypriots. I can't tell you what he said. It was very offensive. (Turkish-Cypriot student, female, 14 years old)

On the other hand, two other Turkish-Cypriot students pointed out that not all Greek-Cypriot students had prejudices against Turkish Cypriots:

> Because there are racist Greek people who don't want to be with Turkish Cypriots, we shouldn't just say that we are not doing well with Greek Cypriots. We are not doing well with most of them, but there are good ones too. Ones who are not racist. (Turkish-Cypriot student, male, 17 years old)
>
> I feel very included by the Greek Cypriots. I am very good at sports and my Greek-Cypriot friends communicate with me because I do sports. I don't have any problems with them. You cannot say that all Greek Cypriots are racist; this would be a false generalization. (Turkish-Cypriot student, female, 17 years old)

Responses to the Prospects of Coexistence and the Role of Family and Education

An important theme that came up in the research team's interviews with teachers, students, and parents at this shared school was the participants' perceptions about the prospects for coexistence and the discourses that essentially fed these perceptions. First, it is important to acknowledge that there were diametrically opposed responses to the prospects of coexistence between many Greek-Cypriot and Turkish-Cypriot students interviewed by the research team. Given that Turkish-Cypriot students consciously chose to cross the checkpoints on an everyday basis and enroll at this school, they were naturally more positively inclined to the idea of coexistence with Greek Cypriots. In contrast, most Greek-Cypriot students interviewed by the research team expressed negative feelings about the prospects of coexistence with their Turkish-Cypriot schoolmates. The following incident shows some of these feelings.

During a discussion in the context of a religious education class, the religion instructor asked the Greek-Cypriot students (16–17 years old) to talk about the prospects for coexistence with Turkish Cypriots. Most students mentioned that they did not want to accept Turkish Cypriots as equal or to reconcile with them, because of the past trauma and suffering and the unresolved political problem. As one student stated, "We do not want to forget. We have a debt to our ancestors not to forget what the Turks did to us, so coexistence is out of the question." Another Greek-Cypriot student asked, "All those atrocities they did to us, should we just dismiss them?"

The teacher made an effort to bring the discussion to the context of the students' own school so he asked them how they felt about their Turkish-Cypriot schoolmates. Many students spoke and insisted that it was impossible to reconcile with them. A few students expressed a different view: "The idea is not to remain stuck in the past," said one student, "but to move forward." Another student stated: "What is important is that we must look at the present and the future. We are here with Turkish Cypriots, we have to find ways to coexist with them. Is it their fault because some fanatics from their side did what they did? Didn't some fanatics from our side commit similar atrocities to innocent Turkish-Cypriot women and children?" The majority of students, however, presented various arguments, such as: "We cannot be friends with Turkish Cypriots, because at school we learned to say *Den Xehno* (I do not forget)," and "We do not want them here; we know they are here for political reasons so we simply ignore them."

Similar negative views about Turkish Cypriots were expressed in a group discussion with three 14–15-year-old Greek-Cypriot students. When these students were asked why they had negative feelings toward their Turkish-Cypriot classmates, they made the following response:

> Is it our fault that in history we are told all the bad things about the Turks? Naturally, this is what we know about them. It is difficult to change these beliefs. (Greek-Cypriot student, male)
>
> This is what we have been learning all these years. What, now we are going to change history? They have wronged us and now we are going to

> become friends with them simply because they attend our school? (Greek-Cypriot student, female)
>
> We know the kind of barbaric group the Turks have been throughout history. Nothing will change that. I do not understand why they were brought to a Greek school. (Greek-Cypriot student, female)

Some of the Turkish-Cypriot students (16–17 years old) who were interviewed also talked about their feelings concerning the prospects of coexistence in their school and the role of the family and education in forming perceptions of coexistence:

> My family believes in coexistence; otherwise I wouldn't be here. But you have to realize that nationalistic education, especially on the Greek-Cypriot side, threatens any possibility for coexistence. (Turkish-Cypriot student, male)
>
> Greek Cypriots grow up believing they are always right and the Turkish Cypriots are wrong. Greek Cypriots never talk about the atrocities committed against the Turkish-Cypriot community in 1963. It's hard to talk about coexistence when the other side just can't get over this strong belief that they are the only ones who suffered. [...] The school tries to promote coexistence through some activities, but the influence from the family and the educational system is very strong. (Turkish-Cypriot student, female)

When the research team asked two teachers to comment on the aforementioned views, they provided some reasons in an effort to explain Greek-Cypriot students' animosity:

> Based on my experience from my daughter's attendance in public schools, and despite the fact that she has grown up meeting my Turkish-Cypriot friends, she has developed this fear and a particularly hostile attitude. I think that the primary school is the one that takes the first step in making our students so prejudiced against Turkish Cypriots. (Maria, interview)
>
> Do not forget the impact of six years of primary school and children's indoctrination with the campaign of *Den Xehno*. This mentality is evident in school celebrations, marches, slogans. All these things are not necessarily wrong, but they are a form of education in believing that "All Turks are barbarians!" I mean, I grew up learning that, "A good Turk is a dead Turk." That is how our society is educated. Similarly, Turkish Cypriots were educated in the same manner to consider every Greek as someone who wants to squeeze them up, to rip them apart, to take up their space. It is this "us" and "them" mentality. On the other hand though, I have

> seen Greek-Cypriot students approaching Turkish Cypriots, yet Turkish-Cypriot students seem to have some kind of—justifiably or not—fear that does not allow them to get close to Greek Cypriots. I think that Turkish Cypriots themselves have a certain prejudice against Greek Cypriots. It just happens that the majority here, the Greek Cypriots, has the upper hand and sets the rules of the game. (Chris, interview)

Two parents (one Greek Cypriot and one Turkish Cypriot) also mentioned the unresolved political problem of Cyprus and feelings of past trauma and hatred as issues that have important implications for the formation of friendships between Greek-Cypriot students and Turkish-Cypriot students at this school:

> It is particularly difficult for our children to feel the same kind of friendship with Turkish Cypriots; especially if the Greek-Cypriot parents are refugees or they lost people in the Turkish invasion of 1974 or if they have family members who are still missing. (Greek-Cypriot parent)
>
> For 30–40 years we have lived separately and both parents and children have not had a lot of contact. Some do have contact now, but there are many others who still don't; many Greek Cypriots and Turkish Cypriots do not want any contact as long as the Cyprus Problem is unresolved. But without contact, we will never learn to live with each other. (Turkish-Cypriot parent)

A Greek-Cypriot parent mentioned that she did not approve of friendships between Greek Cypriots and Turkish Cypriots and therefore she did not encourage her son to develop such relationships:

> I could encourage my son to hang out with his Turkish-Cypriot classmates but for now I choose not to do such a thing. I will not do such a thing, because I do not trust this type of friendship as long as the Cyprus Problem is not resolved in some way, so that our children can feel safe.

Even stronger feelings were expressed by another Greek-Cypriot parent. As he explained, even though this was not done consciously, he had affected his daughter's attitude toward Turkish Cypriots.

> It is true that I feel hatred toward the Turks because of what I and my family suffered during the Turkish invasion. Personally, I do not talk to

my daughter about this issue, but she knows how I feel. I will not tell her, "Do not hang out with your Turkish-Cypriot classmates" or something like that, yet she notices that when I see Turkish Cypriots on the street I curse at them. I am adamant about this. With her other classmates, of other ethnic groups, it is okay to be friends, but not with them.

Friendships with Members of the Other Community

Finally, a number of teachers and students emphasized that despite the challenges, there were friendships being developed between Greek Cypriots and Turkish Cypriots at the school; the issue focused on the degree to which this was taking place rather than whether it was happening at all. Two teachers stated the following:

> Among some of the students there are friendships. But this is not the rule. I cannot say that this has been achieved to the degree that it could have been achieved. (Chris, interview)
>
> There are friendships. For example the first Turkish Cypriots who came and got involved in [club name], I know them for some time now, they became very good friends with some Greek Cypriots. They bonded, went out together, ethnicity was not an issue. Just imagine that the Greek-Cypriot students of the club voted a Turkish-Cypriot student as their president! (Andreas, interview)

Two Greek-Cypriot parents also referred to the existence of cross-community friendships, even if of a limited scope:

> Once, when my daughter was invited to interview with UK universities, a Turkish-Cypriot girl, Gül, was very willing to share some of her experiences and give us information and tips. And later, when my daughter bought a new type of a math calculator, Gül, bless her heart, was once again very willing to help my daughter because she already had this calculator and knew its use.
>
> One Turkish Cypriot from my son's class is one of his best friends. They hang out a lot, they talk about their grades and their tests, they talk about their teachers and their girlfriends (smiles). To be honest, I wasn't very keen on this kind of friendship but my son helped me gradually to see things a bit differently.

The friendship of his daughter with Greek Cypriots and the resulting implications were also raised by a Turkish-Cypriot parent. As he stated: "Sending my daughter to this school has helped her to become more open-minded and make friendships with Greek Cypriots. She used to have some negative opinions about Greek Cypriots but I see that she is changing some of these ideas. As a parent, I welcome this."

The existence of friendly relations between Turkish Cypriots and Greek Cypriots emerged as a topic in several students' interviews. The following are excerpts from interviews with Greek-Cypriot students (14-15 years old):

> We hang out together a little, but when we go out or when you ask who our best friends are, most of us will tell you those who have the same ethnic background as us. Very few of us are close friends with our Turkish-Cypriot classmates. (Greek-Cypriot student, male)
>
> I think some Greek Cypriots have good friendships with Turkish Cypriots, even though many Greek Cypriots underestimate and ignore Turkish Cypriots. For example, the other day I asked a Turkish-Cypriot classmate for a pencil and he gave it to me. When I gave it back to him, he told me that if I needed something again to feel free to ask him. I was surprised; I didn't expect that. (Greek-Cypriot student, female)

Soner, a 17-year-old Turkish Cypriot boy, pointed out that strong friendships between Greek Cypriots and Turkish Cypriots took place mostly in higher grade levels:

> There are people with whom I mix and do projects with; for example, we debate together. Also, I always go out with my Greek-Cypriot friends, I go downtown to Makariou Avenue at night or even, for instance, yesterday after the exams we went out with them. My Greek-Cypriot friends also visited my house in the north. This kind of friendship is more common among older students. Young students of 13 or 14 years of age are still influenced by their previous education and their family, so I think they may not be as mature to develop friendships and overcome existing prejudices.

Beginning to Make Sense of the Emotional Complexities of Coexistence

The contact hypothesis (Allport, 1954; Pettigrew & Tropp, 2006) has been an unspoken guiding principle behind shared and integrated schools (McGlynn, 2009). Educators and stakeholders are convinced that the daily contact is adequate to develop friendships and break down ethnic and other divisions (McGlynn & Bekerman, 2007b). However, research in the context of shared and integrated schools (e.g. see McGlynn et al., 2004; Niens & Cairns, 2008) shows that mere contact may reify difference and group salience. The present case study also confirms that the mere co-existence of Greek-Cypriot and Turkish-Cypriot students at a shared school in divided Cyprus does not necessarily break down existing divisions although it provides some opportunities to do so. This chapter reveals the emotional challenges encountered by teachers and students when they are unwillingly thrown into a situation in which they have to negotiate their coexistence with individuals coming from a conflicting community and with whom they have never had any contact before. Social identity theory (Tajfel, 1978; Tajfel & Turner, 1979, 1986) helps us theorize that the participants' ethnic identity is inextricably intertwined with their own self-categorization, however, it is inadequate to account more fully for the political aspects of identity and the role of power relations in the interactions that occur at this school. Therefore, I will make a first attempt here (and continue in the next chapter) to theorize the findings of this case study using critical multicultural theory in conjunction with the notion of critical emotional praxis. My argument is that this combination has some important advantages compared to the use of contact theory and/or social identity theory.

First, it is important to acknowledge the unwillingness on the part of many Greek-Cypriot teachers, students, and parents to participate in a shared education settlement at this school. In their narratives, Greek Cypriots express strong views and consider this school to be essentially "a Greek school" that accommodates Turkish Cypriots for political reasons. These strong views are influenced by students' peer groups and societal views that express animosity toward Turkish Cypriots, identifying Turkish Cypriots with Turkish invaders (Bryant, 2004; Loizos, 1998). This unwillingness to enroll at a shared school constitutes a major difference with the practice followed during the establishment of integrated schools in other settings (e.g. Northern Ireland and Israel) in which all the participant teachers and students *choose* to be in such schools. Therefore, it seems that power relations—and especially the fact that Greek Cypriots constitute the majority in this school located on the south side in which the overwhelming majority of the population is also Greek Cypriot—are involved in the ways that Turkish Cypriots are (*mis*)recognized and are essentially defined as members of an enemy group rather than as "human beings," as one of the introductory quotations in the case study suggests. These power relations, as critical multicultural theory (Kincheloe & Steinberg, 1997; Mahalingham & McCarthy, 2000; Nieto, 2000) tells us, are linked to the political structures of the nation-state and the perpetuation of divisive practices in everyday politics, as well as in family and education discourses. In addition, it seems from their narratives that students are not aware of the purpose of schooling at the school they attend. Therefore, coexistence in itself at a shared school is not enough to deter students and teachers from drawing selectively from divisive discourses and practices on national identity and ethnic conflict in Cyprus.

Second, the evidence presented here shows how macro-level and micro-level sociopolitical contexts are embedded in the everyday power relationships between Greek Cypriots and Turkish Cypriots. At the macro (political)-level, there has always been a strong segregationist policy in schools and the society that essentially "prepares" children to live separately and think of the "other" as the eternal enemy (Bryant, 2004). At the micro-level of this particular school, there are oppositional views as to whether the minority (i.e. Turkish Cypriots) should be accommodated in any way as long as the Cyprus Problem is unresolved and the majority (i.e. Greek Cypriots) suffers the presence of the Turkish army. Though these oppositional views cannot be overstated, it is essential that they inform educational initiatives that are undertaken. Once again, it is shown that contact theory and social identity theory can interpret the strong emphasis on collective identity and the negative consequences of the absence of contact; however, it is critical multicultural theory that pushes things further and explains not only that mere contact between students from conflicting communities is not necessarily a guarantee of successful encounters (Bekerman, 2004, 2005), but also that education, family, and societal discourses formulate a particular ideological mission that is grounded in transmitting the values of the majority's culture (Kincheloe & Steinberg, 1997).

Finally, the evidence presented in this chapter shows that there are strong emotional tensions and challenges in negotiating the everyday reality of students' coexistence in this school. On the one hand, there is strong suspicion and resentment on the part of many Greek-Cypriot students, teachers, and parents who seem to be either utterly negative or (in the best case) apathetic toward the presence of Turkish-Cypriot students. This case study also indicates that there are incidents of concealed aggression and underlying intolerance in the school; these incidents do not seem to be acknowledged by a number of Greek-Cypriot students (and teachers) who consider this school to be "Greek" and avoid mixing with Turkish-Cypriot students. On the other hand, there is a smaller group of Greek-Cypriot students, teachers, and parents who perceive the presence of Turkish Cypriots in positive ways and form friendships with them. This (smaller) group acknowledges that there is discrimination against Turkish-Cypriot students and makes attempts to embrace these students so that they can be integrated into the school. The examples shared in this chapter suggest that there are openings available to build on the friendships created between students who come from the two communities. These openings are small yet important—such as the Greek-Cypriot student who received a pencil from a Turkish-Cypriot and was surprised about it; the Turkish-Cypriot girl who helped a Greek-Cypriot girl with her university applications and a math calculator; and the minor transformation of a Greek-Cypriot parent whose son became friends with a Turkish-Cypriot student. These small openings as well as the closures as a result of strong emotional tensions can provide critical and productive engagements with the emotional discourses and practices of negotiating the everyday reality of coexistence; *this* is precisely what critical emotional praxis is about.

In general, it is valuable to point out that the mere fact that Greek-Cypriot and Turkish-Cypriot students do not generally socialize together during breaks, hardly talk to each other in the classroom, refuse to cooperate, and refrain from attending each other's events, highlights that the issue is *not* one of personal prejudices but a matter of social and emotional practices embedded in specific power relationships. Critical multiculturalism and critical emotional praxis help us theorize stereotypes and prejudices as not simply an *individual* matter grounded in psychological characteristics or merely a *social identity* issue; rather, these ideas emphasize the emotional and political dimensions of conflict expressed through the inequalities established and perpetuated within the school and the influence of the political structures and the structures of feeling of the nation-state. One could easily find fault with the individual Greek-Cypriot teachers, students, and parents, who "had" negative stereotypes of Turkish Cypriots and expressed strong prejudiced views against the presence of this minority at the school. However, this would be the easy way out and would constitute a simplistic explanation for a rather complex set of issues. If placed anywhere, as Bekerman (2005) argues, the "blame" should be placed on social, cultural, and political structures that perpetuate divisions between "us" and "them."

Notes

1. The terms *shared* and *integrated* education are often used interchangeably; however, the term "integrated" is more accurate when there is roughly an equal balance of students who come from conflicting communities and choose to be educated together (McGlynn et al., 2004; McGlynn, Zembylas, & Bekerman, 2013). The term *shared education* is preferred in the context of Cyprus, because as it will become clear (1) there is not an equal balance of students who come from the two conflicting communities at the school that constitutes the focus of this study; and

(2) not all students at this school *choose willingly* to be educated with the "other" (see Johnson, 2007).

2. To facilitate the readers' identification of the participant's ethnicity, I have added a GC in parenthesis after the name of a Greek-Cypriot participant and a TC after the names of Turkish Cypriots.
3. The school follows the national curriculum for religious education of the Greek-Cypriot public schools and thus Turkish Cypriots are excused from attending religious education classes.

8 PEDAGOGIC STRUGGLES TO ENHANCE INCLUSION AND RECONCILIATION

Chapter 7 has focused on teachers', students', and parents' perspectives about the struggles to negotiate coexistence in a shared school in Cyprus. In this chapter I take a step further and explore the successes and failures of teachers' pedagogies and school policies to establish a culture of *inclusion* and *reconciliation*. My analysis, then, is driven by the following overarching question: Which pedagogies and policies are used to address issues of conflict and reconciliation between Greek-Cypriot and Turkish-Cypriot students and what are the implications of these pedagogies and policies? After a brief theoretical explication of the notions of inclusion and reconciliation pedagogies, I provide more empirical evidence of teachers' responses and pedagogies at this shared school, particularly in relation to efforts that promote reconciliation between Greek-Cypriot and Turkish-Cypriot students in the classroom. The evidence shows the successes and failures, the tensions and opportunities, that are created when a few teachers attempt to implement reconciliation pedagogies when most of the faculty members remain hostile or apathetic. The chapter ends with a discussion of some of the implications of this case study for peace education in divided communities, particularly in light of the emotional complexities that exist.

Teachers' Role in the Formation of Reconciliation Pedagogies

The concepts on which shared or integrated education is founded fit with the broader philosophy of "inclusive education" (Donnelly, 2004a). Based on the belief that schools can influence social values, integrated education is viewed as a manifestation of inclusive education aiming at promoting equity and justice for all children regardless of the abilities they carry with them or the community they come from. In this context, teachers play a pivotal role in the achievement of inclusion. The responsibilities placed on them to contribute to the construction of an ethos of tolerance and respect are considerable (Donnelly, 2004b). As Donnelly (2004a) has said: "To develop an inclusive ethos, teachers should not only sympathize with the values which are promoted by the inclusive school but must also actively *enact* the ethos of inclusiveness through their everyday work and through their own collegial relationships" (p. 265). For example, teachers are expected to teach equitably across the different ethnic and religious groups; they should be open to discuss issues that might cause conflict and critically analyze incidents of intolerance so that an ethos of coexistence, mutual understanding, and respect for all is established.

Particularly in the context of conflicted societies, teachers in integrated schools are in a unique social position; they can reinforce the values of the society at large (possibly those of division and hatred) or they can enact the values of reconciliation. This *enactment* is not simply manifested in the critical discussions that teachers may organize in class, questioning personal and societal taken-for-granted assumptions about conflict and the "other." Rather, it is in their everyday pedagogical practices that division and hatred might be challenged or reinforced (Bekerman & Zembylas, 2012; Zembylas, 2007a, 2008a). Thus, the decisions and choices that teachers make about how to respond to an incident of intolerance play an instrumental role in reproducing or subverting the existing ethos. Although there has not been much research investigating the role of teachers' pedagogies in integrated schools, existing research from Northern Ireland indicates the important role of teachers in sustaining or challenging societal divisions (Donnelly, 2004b; Johnson, 2001).

In the last few years, there has been a growing interest in the role of reconciliation pedagogies in conflict-ridden societies. The term *reconciliation pedagogies* emerged from an Australian-led international project that aimed at bringing into dialogue two discourse communities—"reconciliation" and "pedagogy" (Ahluwalia et al., 2012). Hattam, Atkinson, and Bishop (2012) write that the term reflects research-informed educational efforts that are grounded in multidisciplinary ideas; that aim to identify pedagogies that recognize the new complexities in these "unsettling times"; and that provide resources for reconciling ethnic, racial, and religious differences in ways that foster mutual understanding, social justice, and coexistence. In other words, reconciliation pedagogies do not only refer to the mobilization of reconciliation processes that can heal the effects of past conflict and trauma and can interrupt cycles of violence, anger, and revenge, they also include research on the pedagogical nature of these processes to engage with their global implications.

Hattam and colleagues employ an expanded version of *pedagogy*—one that locates learning not only in schools but also in public institutions within the larger society, and in the media. Reconciliation pedagogies borrow from and build on a number of pedagogical models developed around commitments to social justice, including critical pedagogy (Giroux & McLaren, 1989), critical multiculturalism (Kincheloe & Steinberg, 1997), and antiracist pedagogies (Kalantzis & Cope, 2001). What reconciliation pedagogy foregrounds is the urgent need to elaborate how people might learn to live together in societies of ever-increasing cultural complexity (Hattam & Matthews, 2012). Examples of reconciliation pedagogies are found in Australia in relation to media representations of public protests (Bishop, 2006); in South Africa in relation to classroom-based action research that engages students to investigations of the work of the Truth and Reconciliation Commission (Ferreira et al., 2012); and in Cyprus in explorations of pedagogical strategies (e.g. grounded in notions of forgiveness and reconciliation) for interrupting the ethos of conflict that perpetuates ethnic division of the island (Zembylas, 2008a, 2012c).

At the same time, Bekerman and Zembylas (2012) point out that pedagogical reconciliation-aimed practices are not enough by themselves, unless larger power relations are considered and structural changes are undertaken. Along the same lines, Johnson (2007) writes: "Stand-alone curricula and learning activities that are not part of an integrated system of the whole are bound to fail at educating for sustained peace, most especially in regions where deep-seated fears and mistrust have, over the decades, infiltrated collective ways of being" (p. 22). Therefore, educational interventions such as reconciliation pedagogies aimed at creating familiarity, acceptance, and recognition have a low level of success and a low level of critical interest if encounters ignore the existing social structures and power relations (Bekerman, 2007) such as the role of government, political parties, teacher unions, commercial enterprise, and school policies, as well as family and community.

These concerns about the meaning, prospects, and possible enactments of reconciliation pedagogies are "translated" into the following focal questions about the shared school discussed in this chapter:

1. To what extend do teachers' pedagogies address issues of conflict and promote reconciliation between Greek-Cypriot and Turkish-Cypriot students in the classroom?
2. To what extend do existing school policies and procedures support or inhibit reconciliation?

Segregation, Intolerance, and Conflict at This School

As pointed out in the previous chapter, several teachers mentioned that there was intolerance and conflict between Greek-Cypriot and Turkish Cypriot students;

sometimes, the conflict was overt, but most of the time it was hidden. Elli, for instance, referred to some "problems when it comes to the coexistence of Greek Cypriots and Turkish Cypriots," particularly when Greek Cypriots refused to work together with Turkish Cypriots on presentations or refused to sit next to each other in class. "They [Greek Cypriots] have real problems in accepting them [Turkish Cypriots] for who they are," stated Elli. Miriam, an American teacher, agreed and acknowledged that Turkish Cypriots did not integrate well in the school and they often felt excluded and isolated.

> Well, I think that many Turkish-Cypriot students do not feel accepted in the school. . . . They don't feel fully integrated in the school; they feel that it is difficult for them to form friendships. They feel that others dislike them because they are Turkish Cypriots, or that teachers prefer other students.

Classroom observations and interviews with students substantiated Elli's and Miriam's perceptions. For example, cooperation between Greek-Cypriot and Turkish-Cypriot students in the classroom was rare. The research team witnessed several incidents in which Greek-Cypriot and Turkish-Cypriot students refused to sit together; when teachers tried to mix them, the students deliberately changed seats after a while. Those who did remain in adjacent seats simply ignored each other and had no interaction whatsoever: they hardly talked to each other; declined to cooperate in team exercises; refused to share notes, books, or computers; and generally abstained from any type of contact.

Feelings of intolerance were also candidly verbalized by many children we interviewed, as shown below:

> Our class is the worst class to be in. I think they [Greek Cypriots] are the most racist people in the whole school. (Turkish-Cypriot student, female, 15 years old)
>
> They [Turkish Cypriots] are not many. . . . They are the minority and we are the majority, so they are the ones who should approach us. We will not change for them. It is they who have to change. (Greek-Cypriot student, male, 16 years old)
>
> But why should things change? Most of us do not really want the Turkish Cypriots in our school. We just put up with them. . . . and this is enough! We will never become friends with them. (Greek-Cypriot student, male, 15 years old)

Quite importantly, intolerance instances were not limited to cases of "silent" recognition of differences or mere avoidance; they occasionally escalated to expressions of hostility and aggression. Classroom observations revealed children resorting to verbal abuse by using offensive characterizations and stereotypes (particularly the Greek Cypriots toward the Turkish Cypriots), as well as threats and animosity. Notably, hostility was expressed from both communities, even though there were more noted incidences where Greek Cypriots expressed aggression toward Turkish Cypriots. In-depth interviews with students and teachers substantiated some of these aggressive attitudes:

> When we were organizing a Turkish night event, some pupils destroyed our posters. They even destroyed the sign on the door of the Turkish room. They took it off. . . . We know that we are not welcomed by some Greek-Cypriot students. (Turkish-Cypriot student, female, 14 years old)
>
> We had cases in which Turkish-Cypriot students were crying in class because they heard something offensive about them or because nobody talked to them and just ignored them. For instance, Greek-Cypriot students called some Turkish Cypriots *bromotourtzoi* [filthy Turks] in front of many other students and some teachers. (Andreas, Greek-Cypriot teacher, interview)

Andreas was very disappointed that his colleagues did not react to point out to Greek-Cypriot students that it was unacceptable to engage in racist speech. This apathetic behavior starkly demonstrates not a only lack of reconciliation pedagogies but also an implicit reinforcement of unacceptable and racist behaviors.

Teachers' Negative Reactions

Negative reactions by a number of Greek-Cypriot teachers also became an issue that seemed to create obstacles to the efforts to promote inclusion and reconciliation at this school. Monica, a Greek-Cypriot teacher, emphasized that, "It is not enough to work only with students on this issue, because the people who are against coexistence and mutual understanding are primarily the Greek-Cypriot teachers and parents." The same view was repeated by other teachers. In his interview, Andreas pointed out that, "As surprising as it may sound, there are teachers with strong racist and nationalistic views. This impedes the efforts toward integrating Turkish-Cypriot students at this school." As Miriam, an American teacher, mentioned:

> There are teachers who are totally against what we are trying to do here to help Turkish-Cypriot students integrate, and they go as far as pointing

> us out. We become stigmatized, we are labeled. Therefore, we try hard to find the courage to express our views in staff meetings, but afterwards nobody talks to us for a long time. Just visit the staff room. You will see teachers sitting in groups based on whether one is for or against reconciliation. It's really sad.

Several Greek-Cypriot students also confirmed some of the Greek-Cypriot teachers' negative reactions toward the presence of Turkish Cypriots. For instance, Danae, a 16-year-old Greek-Cypriot girl, mentioned that there was "a great deal of animosity against the presence of Turkish-Cypriot students by several Greek-Cypriot teachers." She even admitted that she was afraid to react and voice her opinion or talk to her Turkish-Cypriot classmates in public, because she would be isolated by other Greek-Cypriot students and teachers. As she stated,

> The way I see this is that if you express your opinion in this school, you run into the risk of being criticized and blacklisted. This happened to me with a Greek-Cypriot teacher. The day I expressed some positive feelings about some Turkish-Cypriot friends, he began to treat me differently. Some Greek-Cypriot students I knew of—I don't call them "friends" any more—stopped talking to me when they saw me hanging out with a Turkish-Cypriot girl.

A similar point was raised by the religion teacher, who acknowledged that even though five years had passed since the first group of Turkish-Cypriot pupils had come to the school, some Greek-Cypriot teachers and students still saw Turkish Cypriots as a "foreign" entity.

> It has been five years since the Turkish Cypriots started coming here, but the teachers' beliefs have still not changed, and in general, the conviction is that these students do not fit here. These teachers even see their Turkish-Cypriot colleagues as if they don't have a place here. The same holds for many Greek-Cypriot students; they see their Turkish-Cypriot classmates as a foreign and unwanted body.

As, Gönül, a 17-year-old Turkish-Cypriot girl, asserted: "Some teachers and students are racist in this school. And I don't think anything can be done here unless people admit this and are willing to change. People have to see us as human beings."

Teachers' Inclusive and Reconciliation Pedagogies

In spite of the fact that the hidden curriculum of the school did not reflect any inclusive and reconciliation ideals, some of the teachers we observed seized any available opportunity to introduce concepts of diversity and inclusion in their courses. For example, observations in the religious education classes (only attended by Greek Cypriots; Turkish Cypriots went to the library during this time) revealed numerous instances where discussions about tolerance and acceptance were introduced. Chris, the religion instructor, was particularly sensitized to issues of exclusion, multiculturalism, and reconciliation; he even began learning Turkish so that he could communicate with Turkish-Cypriot students. Although he did not have any Turkish-Cypriot students in his classes, Chris was often surrounded by Turkish-Cypriot students during recess time; they discussed just about everything, and he had an opportunity to practice his Turkish language skills.

In his classes Chris made frequent references to how God embraced everyone without making distinctions by ethnicity, race, or religion. As he explained:

> At the end of each class I always spend ten minutes discussing various issues that have to do with diversity because I consider these issues important for my students' interpersonal relationships. . . . We discuss the nature of Christianity as purely intercultural . . . the verb "to forgive" in Greek (συγ-χωρώ) means "I come together with others" . . . we are in a school where embracing the other is not a defeat but a step toward victory.

The courses in English literature also seemed to provide fruitful ground for challenging students' ideas on racism and diversity. Studying the work of authors from diverse cultural backgrounds allowed for many studies of diversity and racism. Although there were rare references to reconciliation in Cyprus (this issue was systematically avoided), the English literature teachers engaged students in discussions and analyses of texts that pushed them to explore alternatives to taken-for-granted assumptions about others. As Sharon explained:

> We work on a text and we go through the moments [in] which there have been exclusion or inclusion and we discuss how we, as readers, respond to these situations. Students do respond to these and I ask them to relate those situations to their personal experience. . . . Our goal is to learn how to question what is usually taken for granted. [. . .] We do no talk specifically about reconciliation in Cyprus . . . these issues are very sensitive. (Sharon, interview)

Similarly, Harry, the Geography teacher, also incorporated concepts of multiculturalism in his teaching; for example, he constantly told his students to focus on what unites us with people of different nationalities instead of looking only at what separates us.

> What we try to teach is empathy—civil and human rights—when we look at migration movements. We make students play role games in migration, in fair trade. I think these have a great impact on them, because they can, at least, begin to empathize with others.

Quite importantly, some reconciliation practices seemed to take place outside the official curriculum, such as during fieldtrips, sporting events, excursions, and games.

> In my course we have many opportunities to spend a lot of time outside class, doing fieldwork outside town, in the rivers, in the forests. Children have the opportunity to spend a whole weekend or even a whole week together. You will be surprised how well they work together on these trips. They play games together. They spend their evenings together. They eat and drink together. They stay in the same hotel. That makes wonders. (Harry, interview)
>
> During Physical Education and in their afternoon clubs . . . the students play sports together without paying attention to whether someone is Greek, Turk, or whatever, because they are united by the team spirit. I believe that games are the best practice for reconciliation. (Miriam, interview)

One particular club constituted an interesting and yet controversial initiative to bring students from the two communities together. The group was created in 2003 by a group of sensitized teachers who aimed to actively assist the integration of the Turkish-Cypriot students in the school. This club organizes various extracurricular activities (i.e. excursions and trips) aiming to provide a "safe" environment where students from different cultural backgrounds can interact and develop friendships.

> Societies like [name of the club] helped us tremendously to begin listening to each other. I am a member of this society and that's where I met my Greek-Cypriot friends. All my friends are in this society and we share the same ideas. (Turkish-Cypriot student, male, 16 years old, interview)

> Those who are members of our group would definitely GAIN something. . . . I am sure that something will change inside them, something from the lecture or the experience of traveling with the group will make them re-evaluate their opinions about each other. (Greek-Cypriot student, female, 17 years old, interview)

However, this club was fervently fought against by many Greek-Cypriot parents who accused this group of promoting "positive discrimination" in favor of Turkish Cypriots. Andreas expressed his concern and sadness that "there is so much hatred against reconciliation efforts. And this hatred spreads to the other parents and students."

Obstacles to Promoting Reconciliation Practices

Teachers acknowledged many challenges in their efforts to promote inclusive and reconciliation practices. For example, Chris referred to resistance from students.

> I took two children—one Greek Cypriot and one Turkish Cypriot—and asked them to have a "reconciliation handshake," but I realized that in real life it is much more difficult. It's difficult to make the first move. You need to educate students, cultivate the notion of reconciliation to them . . . it needs constant and persistent effort to make them take one step toward the other. [. . .] I have been struggling for three years to make them talk with some respect about each other but it is difficult . . . their ego kicks in . . . they go back to the usual historical narratives of whose fault it is and we are back to where we started from.

Interviews with students confirmed this resistance; for example, Greek-Cypriot students objected to working on projects with Turkish Cypriots.

> When they [the teachers] make us work on a common project we strongly object. There is not a good relationship between us. We will always see them [Turkish Cypriots] as enemies who occupy our country. . . . Besides, how could I accept [having] to show a passport in my own country in order to visit the occupied territories [where Turkish Cypriots live], just to collaborate with them on a project? This is ridiculous! (Greek-Cypriot student, male, 16 years old, interview)

In their efforts to promote inclusion and reconciliation, some teachers were accused by Greek-Cypriot students of engaging in positive discrimination toward Turkish Cypriots.

> Because teachers do not want to be perceived as racists, they are "pampering" the Turkish Cypriots. But teachers are racists because they are not being fair to us [the Greek Cypriots] (Greek-Cypriot student, male, 16 years old, interview)
>
> I had a heated disagreement with a Turkish-Cypriot once. He was working on the computer the whole time and wouldn't let me use it. I was very angry with him. I only touched him and he shook me strongly. But I was the one who was punished. (Greek-Cypriot student, male, 15 years old, interview)

At the same time, some of the teachers revealed that they had colleagues who held nationalistic beliefs and exhibited racist behavior; this opinion was also shared by some of the students we interviewed.

> They [these teachers] will not openly admit that anti-Turkism and racism are present also among teachers. There are teachers with intense nationalistic and racist perceptions. I do not believe that somebody who truly cares about children has such attitudes . . . (Andreas, interview). I don't think anything can be done unless people are willing to change. Some teachers are racist and very nationalist. . . . There was this incident when a Turkish-Cypriot friend was called names by Greek-Cypriot students and the Greek-Cypriot teacher who was present didn't say anything. (Turkish-Cypriot student, female, 16 years old, interview)

Finally, it is important to note that issues related to the Cyprus Problem were generally avoided as a topic of discussion in the classroom.

> Once we were punished because we started talking about the Cyprus Problem. All teachers stop these discussions. They know we are right but they do not want to show it. [. . .] What we are taught in class is generally about racism. We are forbidden to speak about the Cyprus Problem, because we have Turkish-Cypriot students in class and our teacher does not want to create any problems between us. (Greek-Cypriot student, male, 15 years old, interview)

Views on School Policies

Despite the international character of the school, there was still no official school policy in place for promoting intercultural understanding among students. The school administration was in the process of drafting such a policy, acknowledging the difficulties as a result of the political situation in Cyprus.

> We are in the process of developing such policy. It is an open issue at the moment. Obviously, since the arrival of Turkish-Cypriot students in 2003, this issue has become a more acute problem. In the past, we had been discussing it in the abstract, but now you've got reality right here. [. . .] On the other hand, we cannot ignore the sociopolitical situation in Cyprus and how this inevitably affects us. So we need to be careful. . . . (Principal, interview)

Overall, there were several practices at the whole school level that aimed at promoting intercultural understanding. For example, the school commenced the academic year by holding a fun evening where ethnically diverse students could get to know each other through games, competitions, and theatrical plays. To further help the integration of non-Greek-speaking students, Greek lessons were offered on a weekly basis. Also, some intercultural learning was offered through a course titled Personal and Social Education. For example, seminars and lectures were held by various speakers (i.e. academics, doctors, etc); these events did not concentrate on the differences between Turkish Cypriots and Greek Cypriots but provided a more encompassing and worldwide view on diversity.

> Through Personal and Social Education, children learn how to deal with conflicts, how to live in multicultural society. We try to help them develop tolerance toward difference, any kind of difference, such as race, religion, gender, age, sexual orientation etc. [...] Also, through exposing students to problems that other countries face—for example, health and famine in Africa—we want to make them think about their own problems in perspective. (Principal, interview)

The school also offered some teacher training focusing on enhancing teachers' knowledge and skills in managing racism, integration, and anti-discrimination. Despite the school's efforts to promote intercultural understanding, most teachers (and some students as well) we interviewed did not consider these efforts to be adequate for promoting mutual understanding and reconciliation.

> No official policy is in place, nor [does] there exist the will to face racist incidents against Turkish-Cypriot students. . . . [Name of academic]'s report was disregarded. [. . .] Her recommendations never materialized

> because the school board and the teachers ignored them. (Andreas, interview)
>
> Now that she [name of academic] is gone people are discussing the issues that she spotted, and they are questioning her: How did she reach these conclusions? Where did she get her evidence from? . . . They refuse to see that there is racism in the school. They do not recognize it. (Elli, interview)

In general, there seemed to be an effort to avoid discussing issues of reconciliation and admitting that there might be serious challenges for the school. Thus, various incidents (e.g. the beating of a Turkish-Cypriot student by Greek Cypriots who were not students of this school) were seen as "isolated" ones.

At the same time, various practices sent conflicting messages to the school community. For example, in an effort to find common ground after Turkish Cypriots re-joined the school, several decisions resulted in retraction of "Greek elements" from the school (e.g. with regard to national celebrations, events, and class decoration)—elements that a large group of Greek-Cypriot students valued as essential. Consequently, the elimination of these practices was perceived as discriminatory (in favor of the Turkish Cypriots), enhancing feelings of resentment, animosity, and exclusion. For instance, Greek national holidays were no longer celebrated with the same vivacity as in the past. The Greek and Cypriot flags were only raised on national holidays (four times a year) but were put down for the rest of the year. Also, the religious icons were removed from all classrooms. As Greek-Cypriot students pointed out:

> The school is trying to make the Turkish Cypriots feel better but what are we doing here? We only see our flag during the national holidays. It comes up that day and goes down the next. Our Greek identity is threatened in the name of reconciliation. (male, 15 years old, interview)
>
> Should we start forgetting our history and Greek identity because these people have a different history? This school used to be Greek and now they will make it Turkish! (female, 16 years old, interview)

At the same time, some of the school's policies were perceived as discriminatory against Turkish Cypriots. For instance, Turkish Cypriots were given the option to be excluded from Greek national celebrations; at the same time, no Muslim religious holidays (most Turkish Cypriots' religion) were celebrated as official school holidays. Turkish-Cypriot students were allowed vacation time during their religious holidays but the majority of them opt not to take the time off, as they did not want to miss out on their classes.

Further Analysis

The purpose of this chapter has been to explore how teachers' pedagogies and school policies at a shared school in Cyprus promote a culture of inclusion and reconciliation among students from two conflicting communities. The data in this and the previous chapter show two important points: First, there is generally a "culture of avoidance" when it comes to pedagogies addressing issues of conflict and reconciliation; however, evidence also shows that students feel the need to talk about these issues in light of incidents of intolerance and animosity that arise between Greek Cypriots and Turkish Cypriots. Second, there are no clear integration school policies at the systemic level; this lack of introduction of systemic policies at the whole-school level has had negative consequences for efforts to promote inclusion and reconciliation. Let's discuss each of these points individually.

First, the physical segregation of Greek-Cypriot and Turkish-Cypriot students—as seen, for example, in the classroom, during recess, on school trips, and in most social events—is indicative of the degree of social and psychological division that exists. The prevalence of this segregation contributes to the fear of teachers to address issues on conflict and reconciliation in Cyprus. Only one teacher, Chris, takes up the challenge, deliberately raises open discussions about such issues, and creates a classroom culture in which students express their opinions about the political situation on the island. Also, an extracurricular club promotes issues of reconciliation through open dialogue about intolerance and conflict. This group provides various opportunities for students to express their feelings so that empathy can be developed. In general, the existing "culture of avoidance" resonates with Johnson's (2001) research in integrated schools of Northern Ireland, where it was found that there was a tendency for teachers to avoid issues on conflict and the divide in the classroom. Similar explanations are offered in the context of he present case study; that is, teachers have difficulties dealing with issues that are politically sensitive because they think the conflict between students will be exacerbated. Rather than promoting open dialogue on students' perspectives about conflict, healing, and reconciliation in Cyprus, teachers prefer to talk generally about acceptance, tolerance, and respect. Therefore, it is up to the individual teacher whether a reconciliation pedagogy is undertaken in the classroom. For many teachers in this study, similar to Johnson's (2001) report, concerns about the potential of offending students or resistance to any efforts to promote reconciliation are enough to restrict their involvement in this direction. At the same time, it has to be acknowledged that any reconciliation efforts are embedded in a wider sociopolitical context, one where Greek Cypriots are not currently keen on supporting reconciliation before a final settlement of the Cyprus Problem. There may be some peace and reconciliation efforts at the national level, but those are in the margins and have never gained wider social status and legitimation. Schools constitute a microcosm of the wider society, and inevitably teachers' pedagogies are embedded in and influenced by the wider context. Hence, the lack of success in reconciliation attempts in the wider social structure influences the willingness of teachers' to take risks and engage in such attempts at the school level (Bekerman & Zembylas, 2012).

Students and teachers at this school appear to be divided into two groups: those who strive for the inclusion of Turkish-Cypriot students in the school and have high expectations from the school's policies to promote reconciliation; and those students and teachers who are uncomfortable with—even resentful of—the presence of Turkish-Cypriot students and consider that no special measures have to be taken to accommodate these students. The overall feedback from teachers, students, and the school principal, as well as our own observations, indicate that the school has not been very successful in promoting mutual understanding and fostering a reconciliatory culture among Greek-Cypriot and Turkish-Cypriot students. It is significant to note, however, that there are several initiatives being undertaken by teachers who struggle to promote inclusion, tolerance, and reconciliation. It is unclear what the wider impact of these initiatives is particularly beyond the school setting. This case study highlights the strengths of some of the teachers' pedagogies, particularly those that encourage open critical dialogue, multiperspectivity, and empathy; however, much more needs to be done to encourage teachers and students to engage routinely in open and critical dialogue. Pedagogical reconciliation efforts need to acknowledge these ideas, yet they also need to take into consideration identity politics—as seen for example, in the concerns of Greek-Cypriot students who fear that they will "lose" their identity. Otherwise, even well-intentioned reconciliation pedagogies may be misunderstood as offering unwelcome acculturative options that identity groups might reject for they are perceived as threatening to their collective well-being (Ahluwalia et al., 2012). Mapping reconciliatory educational options as these reflect on issues of identity politics and an integrated ethos is of utmost importance for shared schools in conflicted societies.

In general, there are two issues that create serious obstacles in promoting reconciliation pedagogies at the school in the present study: first, the hidden curriculum of the school does not reflect any of the ideals of the teachers who have taken a proactive stance; and second, the evidence suggests that some teachers might exhibit "racist" and "nationalist" behavior. To tackle these issues, it is imperative that a more clarified articulation of policy and procedures at the systemic level is undertaken so that diversity and conflict issues can be appropriately dealt with. As Johnson (2001, 2007) has suggested, this could be done as part of a whole-school approach toward collective problem solving and team building. One of the main problems in this school is that teachers seem to develop the ethos according to their own personal values (see also, Donnelly, 2004b); inevitably, this leads to inconstancies and tensions among teachers, and it is questionable whether it contributes to a culture of tolerance, mutual understanding, and reconciliation. The lessons learned from research in Northern Ireland (Johnson, 2007) and Israel (Bekerman & Maoz, 2005) are that any pedagogical and curricular initiatives need to be supported by formal structural changes, because even the best of intentions will be insufficient to sustain reconciliation pedagogies in a divided society (see also Bekerman & Zembylas, 2012). Therefore, school policies and practices need to be clearly outlined and promoted at a systemic level; school leadership and the availability of structural support appear to be important factors influencing teachers' pedagogical practices. Such leadership efforts need to include alternative options to the ones dictated in the past—such as critical consideration of the tight relationship between essentialist perspectives of identity and the larger sociopolitical context (i.e. nation-state) (Bekerman & Maoz, 2005). Special training programs targeting teachers' emotions could also be designed so that teachers who are "against" reconciliation efforts have opportunities to discuss their concerns. Such programs would add more depth and breadth in developing pedagogies of critical emotional praxis that could take into consideration the emotional complexities of coexistence with the "other."

Some Implications for the Future

In conclusion, I end this chapter with a discussion of two implications that concern structural, pedagogical, and curricular issues within this school. The first implication has to do with the notion that coexistence of students from the two conflicting communities should not be taken for granted but that every step of shared education should be carefully planned, implemented, and constantly re-evaluated. A shared school such as the one studied here could benefit from critical multicultural efforts that de-emphasize bipolar differences, yet do not neglect the power relationships involved and the impact of collective ethnic identity on people's everyday lives (Bekerman & Zembylas, 2012; Steiner-Khamsi, 2003). Working in the direction of de-emphasizing ethnicity within a sociopolitical context in which power relations and social structures are taken into consideration is not easy, yet it offers an opening that may challenge exclusionary schooling practices. It starts by restoring the concept of identity/culture to its historical sources, thus de-essentializing it (Bekerman et al., 2009; Bekerman & Zembylas, 2012). It follows by developing the skills to read/describe the world through careful observation and recording of practical activity, which in turn allows for a shift from the individual or the socializing group as the crucial analytic unit for (educational) analysis to the production of cultural and political contexts through social interaction. In the end, it leads to a new articulation of educational practices and policies that critique how particular identities/cultures are produced/constructed within particular societies. To approach the construction of identities and social structures in critical ways, then, does not necessarily mean doing away with them, but rather showing how they have come to be what we think they are. As such, critical interventions may provide a better guide for shared education than segregation, assimilation, or plural models.

Specifically, it would be helpful if policies, curricula, and teaching practices were designed to help children become aware, both at an emotional level and an intellectual level, of the shared meanings, visions, and ethical interdependence that could constrain as well as promote understanding and communal interaction. These shared meanings and visions are embodied in gestures, languages, beliefs, emotions, foods, narratives, and rituals. Within this understanding of what is important for shared schools, policies, curricula, and teaching practices designed to help students make critical choices about how they wish to relate to these shared meanings may help to redress or ameliorate the conflicted situation to some degree. What is needed, therefore, at this shared school in Cyprus (and perhaps in schools elsewhere faced with similar challenges) is to develop educational practices and policies that emphasize critical multiculturalism and leave room for competing narratives and different identities (Bekerman, 2004; Bekerman & Zembylas, 2012). Critical approaches that aim at school and social transformation offer possibilities for extending the conversation in ways that allow the production of new imaginings of civic responsibility rather than the confirmation of conflicts based on ethnicity, religion, nationality, and other social divisions. Hodgkin (2006) has suggested that students in conflicted areas should have opportunities to engage in the discussion of multiple historical understandings and narratives. She also emphasizes that students have to be encouraged to analyze and critique biased and partisan perspectives and learn to develop their own understanding of the past. At the same time, it is necessary to offer professional development for teachers who are part of this context, as well as seminars for the serving community (parents); teacher professional development and community seminars could help engage participants in the workings of critical multicultural ideas at various levels.

The second implication I discuss here has to do with the need to develop curricula and pedagogies that promote critical emotional praxis. Such curricula and pedagogies can incorporate, for example, more human rights perspectives without diminishing the importance of past traumas, emotions, and memories while abandoning essentialist and one-sided positions. These curricula and pedagogies should also create opportunities for critical dialogues so that empathy, multiperspectivity, solidarity, and social justice are nurtured. For example, Hadjipavlou (2007b) has suggested that there are five underlying principles of a shared curriculum program in Cyprus: (1) inclusion of competing narratives; (2) flexibility that recognizes shared stories of coexistence; (3) openness to dialogue that recognizes multiperspectivity and critical evaluation of social, educational, and political policies and practices; (4) mutual humanization of historical grievances, traumas, and mourning; and (5) mutual awareness of interdependence. Teachers and students at this shared school need to look beyond present curricula and the reproduction of existing knowledge and problematize the (emotional) politics of identity and culture in Cyprus. Unraveling the political aspects of identity and culture—both as analytic tools and as points of departure for cultivating individual and collective civic consciousness—creates possibilities for enriching perspectives about the implications of particular interactions that occur between individuals from conflicting communities.

Critical emotional praxis as a theoretical approach and pedagogical practice can engage teachers, students, and parents in critical dialogues in which each participant is not limited into his or her representation as a member of a specific nation or ethnicity (Bekerman et al., 2009). Freeing identity from its tight ideological connections could reinstate identity as an enriching difference (Bekerman & Zembylas, 2012). As identities become more a topic of reflection within educational theory and practice, "difference comes to be seen as a profound feature of inner life and not only a matter of encounters among diverse groups" (Burbules, 1997, p. 97). In explicating the educational consequences of what Burbules calls the "grammar of difference," he asserts that we need "to develop a language that allows us to make particular distinctions and to offer explanations without reifying our working concepts into categories or typologies" (ibid., p. 100). A form of multiculturalism limited only to the level of mere coexistence—as is now the case in this Cypriot shared school—can only encourage monoculturalism (Bekerman, 2004; Bekerman & Zembylas, 2012). It is valuable to move beyond debates about "difference" and "sameness" per se, and explore different kinds of difference and to consider their varied educational prospects (Burbules, 1997). What is needed, Burbules argues, is a critical re-examination of difference and identity and the constant questioning of the systems on which assumptions about difference and identity are grounded, and what they mean for ourselves and for other people.

9 THE VICISSITUDES OF TEACHING ABOUT/FOR EMPATHY

Yiannis: I feel sadness and bitterness. We [Greek Cypriots] lost our houses and we cannot go back. The Turks occupy half of our country. We have missing persons and dead. I feel hatred for the Turks.

Nikki: I feel sadness because there are missing persons and dead from both communities [Greek Cypriots and Turkish Cypriots] in Cyprus. I don't feel hatred for them, because some Turks are good . . . not all of them are bad. [...] Hm . . . I don't know how to feel about them, because Turkish Cypriots have suffered too. I wish I had a time machine to go back and change everything so that nobody suffered in Cyprus.

Yiannis: And why should we care if they *suffered? Did they care if* we *suffered?*

—field notes, February 18, 2011

This conversation between 11-year-old Greek-Cypriot children is part of a classroom discussion about the events that divided Cyprus in 1974. As noted in earlier chapters, in the aftermath of the Turkish invasion and the occupation of the northern part of Cyprus since 1974, the Greek-Cypriot educational system set as one of its goals educating the younger generations to remember the occupied territories and to maintain the struggle for a unified country (Christou 2006). This educational goal, which became known as *Den Xehno* (I don't forget), was integrated into the school curriculum and became part of school activities and ceremonies (see chapter 1). Research shows that the teaching of *Den Xehno* essentially transmits the grand narratives of the Greek-Cypriot community about the Turkish invasion of 1974 while it ignores the perspectives of the Turkish-Cypriot community or fails to make a distinction between Turks and Turkish Cypriots (Christou, 2007; Spyrou, 2006; Zembylas, 2008a; see also chapters 3, 5, 7, and 8). Some elements of this grand narrative are present in the introductory excerpt, specifically in Yiannis's reference to us-the-victims versus them-the-perpetrators.

Christou writes that the post-1974 curriculum of *Den Xehno* "falls short of constructing an imagination of what the future will look like in a reunified Cyprus" (2006, p. 286). Studies in peace education emphasize that to construct a unified society in the aftermath of loss and conflict, *empathy*—that is, understanding the other's perspective and imagining how the other might feel—is an important part of the peace process (Bar-Siman-Tov, 2004; McGlynn et al., 2009). But given that resistance to empathy is often powerful and the negative emotions toward the "enemy-other" are rather strong, it seems important to ask several questions: Can or should empathy have a place in primary school classrooms? What happens when primary school teachers attempt to engage children in empathetic activities that do not simply focus on one's own losses but also acknowledge the other community's losses? Does Nikki's recognition of how the other side in Cyprus might feel constitute a realistic or even a desirable pedagogical goal for children in conflicting societies?

My focus in this chapter is on the ways in which a "mainstream" fifth-grade class of Greek-Cypriot students and their teacher perceived and negotiated the meanings of empathy in the context of *Den Xehno*. Contrary to hegemonic ways of teaching about *Den Xehno*, however, this teacher and her students took as their point of departure not the grand narratives about 1974 found in Greek-Cypriot school textbooks and hegemonic public discourses. Rather, the students, with the help of their teacher, collected small narratives, *petits récits* (Lyotard, 1984), about 1974 from people in their community who had lived those events. The pedagogical goal of this approach was to uncover the emotional meanings and values that these individuals in the Greek-Cypriot community constructed about the past, themselves, and that the "other" community in Cyprus, that is, the Turkish Cypriots, constructed about their past; in other words, it enacted a form of critical emotional praxis. To show this in more detail, I focus on some classroom observations and interviews with the teacher and her students concerning their efforts to negotiate empathy during the three-month period in which *Den Xehno* was taught in this particular manner. In other words, the class lessons were essentially about both *Den Xehno* and the cultivation of empathy to reveal a more complex understanding of the two conflicting communities in Cyprus. As it will be shown, this case study exposes the "vicissitudes" (Throop, 2010) of teaching about/for empathy, that is, the complexities and unexpected (dis)connections between children's experiences and the lived experiences of those whose stories were heard.

Anthropological Perspectives on Empathy

A review of the literature by anthropologists Douglas Hollan and Jason Throop suggests that "although many anthropologists seem to presume the importance of empathy in social life and fieldwork, only a handful have been explicit about defining or invoking it or related concepts" (2008, p. 385). The definition of *empathy* remains unsettled, explain Hollan and Throop, in part because it is often not clear how empathy differs from related concepts, such as sympathy or intersubjectivity; for example, some scholars' understanding of "empathy" may be others' description of "sympathy." An exploration of the historical terrain of empathy indicates substantive differences in the use and meaning of terms used.

The word *empathy* was first used to translate the German term *Einfühlung* (lit. "feeling into"), connoting some degree of common feeling or emotional attunement between interlocutors (Throop, 2008). Halpern (2001), however, asserts that empathy is never based simply on shared feelings, like sympathy (Throop, 2010); nor is it detached insight or pure theoretical knowing of a third person observer (Hollan, 2008). Empathy is the imaginative understanding of others—both cognitive and affective—that "involves discerning aspects of a [person's] . . . experiences that might otherwise go unrecognized" (Halpern, 2001, p. 94). That is, empathy is a process that unfolds over time and is informed by the work of a person's emotions to learn more about the other's emotional states and perspectives. This process requires dialogue, imagination, and affective attunement; thus, one's emotional engagement with another through talk and storytelling helps to imagine how and why the other acts or feels the way she or he does (Halpern, 2001).

The definition of empathy as a dialogic process generates a number of interesting pedagogical questions: What enables a student to imagine well and accurately the emotional perspective of another individual, especially someone from an "enemy" community? Is it "appropriate" to teach children about/for empathy at the primary school level, particularly when a conflict is still unresolved? How does the political, cultural, and educational context shape the process of teaching about/for empathy at schools in a conflicting society? Does a student who gets to "know about" the "enemy's" life experience necessarily empathize with the "other"? All that said, it seems clear that complex personal, interpersonal, historical, and cultural influences are always at play in the process of constructing empathetic imagination (Hollan, 2008).

Therefore, empathy must always be understood in the context of particular political and cultural meanings, beliefs, practices, and values (Hollan & Throop, 2008; Throop, 2010). As Hollan wrote,: "One cannot just rely on one's own store of memories, images and experiences to imagine the plight of another, especially one from another society or culture" (2008, p. 479–480). Rather, as Geertz (1984/1974) explains, one must delve into the symbols and conceptual systems that are used by others to express themselves. Geertz warns us about the dangers of projecting one's own feelings and experiences onto others. Although Geertz's warnings are addressed primarily to anthropologists who presume to be "empathic" with their subjects of study, his idea of paying attention to people's meanings in the context in which they are embodied, felt, and experienced is pertinent not only in identifying empathy but also in teaching and learning about/for empathy.

Furthermore, Rosaldo (1989/1984) emphasizes that having homologous experiences to the experiences one attempts to understand is extremely helpful. For example, a student who is overwhelmed with grief about a family or community loss can ground his or her empathetic understanding of the other's grief in his or her own suffering. However, Wikan (1992) asserts that the greatest impediment to empathy is the lack of sufficient practical knowledge of and engagement with the other's life experience (Hollan, 2008). For example, a student's ability to empathize with someone from an "enemy" community is often overestimated because it may be grounded in limited practical knowledge of others' lives rather than on whether members from conflicting communities share common life experiences.

All in all, there seem to be many complexities and ambivalences in the process of empathy and, thus, imagining the other's perspective is rarely, if ever, unambiguous or uncontested (Hollan & Throop, 2008). What this suggests is that empathy may have variable consequences, depending on the context in which people gain knowledge of others. Gaining empathetic insight into the life of one's collective "enemy," for example, may not always be considered a positively valued practice by members of one's community (Halpern & Weinstein, 2004). Empathy may be potentially subversive of established order because the encouragement of empathetic imagination violates social and political norms (Hollan & Throop, 2008). The politics of empathy and their relation to the broader social order, then, can reinforce or undermine connectedness with others. This is one of the reasons why Kirmayer (2008) argues that to maintain empathic openness in the face of all obstacles to understanding requires also an ethical stance, not only an emotional and intellectual one.

Empathy and Peace Education

In light of the above insights and particularly of how the concept of empathy is fraught with ambiguities, it becomes clear that there is an immense challenge in any attempt to teach about/for empathy in conflicting societies. In addition to this challenge, there is often the danger of "passive empathy," as Boler (1999) argues—that is, the benign state of empathizing with the other "from a safe distance." Passive empathy runs the risk of remaining at a superficial level relational by simply acknowledging commonalities with others and putting aside difficult ethical questions, such as what one would gain by empathizing with the enemy or what the limits of empathy are (cf. Kirmayer 2008). In fact, as Boler notes, passive empathy "in and of itself may result in no measurable change or good to others or oneself" (1999, p. 178).

Teaching about/for empathy is one of the pedagogical practices often advocated in peace education. Recent research in this field of study (Bekerman & Zembylas, 2012) highlights that cultivating feelings of empathy in schools is full of endless intellectual and emotional "land mines." As has been emphasized, teaching how to empathize with the one often deemed as "perpetrator" is not simply a matter of nurturing critical objective reasoning; working through strongly held collective memories is deeply emotional and, thus, empathy is very difficult to achieve between "victims" and "perpetrators" (Jansen, 2009).

Without dismissing the numerous dangers associated with teaching about/for empathy—such as dangers from feelings of pity, voyeurism, or empty sentimentality (Boler, 1999; Zembylas, 2008a, 2012b, 2013b)—I discuss here the prospects of highlighting the reconciliatory perspective of empathy in the context of peace education efforts. This more ethically and politically focused interpretation portrays empathy as a movement that draws "victim" and "perpetrator" (those not being absolute predetermined categories though) into shared human community. In particular, this interpretation emphasizes the link between the process of rehumanization of the other and empathy (Halpern & Weinstein, 2004), that is, the process that sees the other in human terms. The major function of *reconciliatory empathy* is participating in shared reflective engagement with the other's emotional life—that is, realizing that the other is like me and that I should be engaged in a renewed relationship with the other. Finding commonality through identification with the other is perhaps the most difficult and yet profound step in his or her rehumanization. Reconciliatory empathy seems to say "I recognize the emotional injury you (or other members of your community) inflict on me and my community, but I choose to rebuild our emotional connectedness."

Reconciliatory empathy in peace education has two important qualities that make it valuable in pedagogic terms. First, reconciliatory empathy involves a genuine effort to get to know the other and his or her perspectives without insisting on placing him or her into predetermined categories. Second, reconciliatory empathy tolerates ambivalence for paradoxes as an enriching part of creating an ongoing workable relationship with the other. One such paradox is that teachers and students coping with their suffering must deal with the scenario of the other feeling "wounded" as well. To be truly critical, pedagogical spaces need to allow emotions of woundedness, no matter where they come from, to be worked through. "Woundedness," writes Gobodo-Madikizela, "is a sign of ethical responsibility toward the other. It invites reflection on the historical circumstances that divide, and continue to divide, individuals and groups who are trying to heal from a violent and hateful past" (2008, p. 344).[1]

If teachers want to encourage empathetic understanding in classrooms of conflicting societies, then, they must learn to provide pedagogical spaces in which to handle the emotional remains of historical trauma. "Only by allowing ourselves to be touched, and by reaching out to touch," write Georgis and Kennedy, "might we get closer to our losses and, therefore, to our common humanity" (2009, p. 29). This emotional encounter is rehumanizing because it recognizes the other as sufferer too, as an emotional human being; to empathize with one who wronged someone is to struggle to get over resentment, anger, and hatred (Gobodo-Madikizela, 2008). To put this more directly, teachers and students need to actively create reconciliatory empathetic spaces for this to happen in the classroom.

Undoubtedly, part of this pedagogic effort is to "navigate" through one's resistances to critique a strong emotionally held position. For this to happen, teachers have to be willing to use empathy strategically (Lindquist, 2004). That is to say, empathy should be used in ways that help students see common patterns in their emotional lives and the lives of others, and realize the implications of common humanity in establishing connectedness with others. Strategic empathy signifies a willingness to teach and learn even while coping with ambiguity, ambivalence, and paradox. To say that a teacher uses strategic empathy means that he or she encourages empathetic engagement with others even when there are seemingly intractable obstacles. This connectedness with others, without rushing to categorize them as "perpetrators," "misguided," or "evil," is precisely what avoids premature closure and sustains the possibility of constructing reconciliatory empathy in peace education settings.

The Case Study

The data for this chapter are drawn from a three-month (January–March 2011) case study in a Greek-Cypriot fifth-grade classroom according to the procedures described in chapter 1. This particular school, however, is very different from the multicultural schools described in Part I. It is located in a suburb of the capital Nicosia and has no Turkish-speaking students; it has a small percentage of students coming from other countries. The socioeconomic background of students is mixed, and the Greek-Cypriot community surrounding the school is comprised of many refugees who have relocated in this area since the division of Cyprus in 1974.

The teacher, Anna, implemented a unit on *Den Xehno*, following the "funds of knowledge" approach (González, Moll, & Amanti, 2005). "Funds of knowledge" refers to the knowledge that has existed in the community over generations, and that has secured social cohesion and community belonging. The aim of the funds of knowledge approach is to break down barriers and link schools and communities, with the purpose of influencing social change. Anna is in her late thirties and has 15 years of teaching experience. She and her 11-year-old students (ten girls and six boys) used the funds of knowledge approach to explore the traumatic past of Cyprus by collecting stories from members of the larger community. Specifically, Anna asked each student to conduct an interview with a close relative (parent, grandparent, etc.) to how that family member had experienced the events of 1974, the memories and emotions linked to these events, and his or her perspectives on Turkish Cypriots. The children prepared all the interview protocols in the classroom and were taught some skills how to conduct interviews. Each child recorded his or her interview and brought it to class for analysis. Anna also invited members of the community (e.g. poets, relatives of missing or enclaved people) to come to the school to tell their stories and respond to questions asked by the children. Anna's implementation of *Den Xehno* using the funds of knowledge approach meant, then, that community stories and feelings were tapped and became lessons on empathy, as shown in the next part of this chapter.

Den Xehno was taught three to four times a week for time periods lasting from one to two hours. Anna kept a diary with notes about everything that happened during the teaching of the *Den Xehno* unit, and I collected field note observations and conducted interviews with Anna and her students. Interviews with the children were brief and mostly informal, usually conducted during recess. Some of the interviews with Anna were formal (occasionally based on a semi-structured interview protocol), yet most of the time they were informal. For children, the questions centered on their experiences of investigating the events of 1974 and their feelings about what they had discovered, as well as their understanding of collective belonging. For Anna, the questions focused on her experiences of teaching this unit following the funds of knowledge approach, how she attempted to teach about/for empathy, and in what ways her students responded to her attempts. Also, I took photographs and collected various documents, including lesson plans, students' drawings, and documents pertinent to the curriculum of *Den Xehno*.

Finally, I should point out something about my own position as a Greek Cypriot who also experienced the school curriculum of *Den Xehno* (see also chapter 1). I too grew up with the grand narratives of us-the-victims and them-the-perpetrators. My father is a refugee and comes from a town that is still occupied by Turkish troops, so researching a topic like this is inevitably an emotional endeavor for me (see also Zembylas, 2008a). It is interesting to note, however, that engaging with this research for the past decade or so has helped me find remedies for what I had perceived rather simplistically in the past as either (un)patriotic or nationalist educational discourses and practices. My constant struggle to juggle past memories of *Den Xehno* with present concerns for research methodology and epistemology made me increasingly conscious of the importance of reflecting on the balance and continuity between the "anthropologist" and the "native" (cf. Geertz, 1984/1974). Going forward in this chapter, the reader will trace the evidence of this struggle as well as my aspirations for "compassionate objectivity" (Turner, 1978) in the account that is developed below.

What Children Know and Feel about "1974"

Children in this fifth-grade classroom quickly reminded anyone who uttered the word *1974* that the Turks invaded Cyprus and have occupied "our country ever since," and "they do not allow us to go back to our houses." Interestingly, only a third of the children came from refugee families, yet almost all of them used the collective "we" to highlight their feelings about the past: "our pain is in every corner"; "our agony and tears are everywhere"; "many of our people were tortured"; and "our refugees and missing persons are still suffering" were some of the phrases heard in classroom discussions or written in assignments and drawings.

In one of the very first lessons of *Den Xehno* in January, Anna challenged her students to create a concept map of what they knew about 1974 so that they could pose questions to be answered by the study of the coming weeks. To her disappointment, as she pointed out in a follow-up interview and also wrote in her diary, the children seemed to have difficulties responding to that challenge; when they were asked for clarifications, for example, many children retreated to repetitive claims that "in 1974 there were dead everywhere" and "everyone cries because of the war." Along similar lines, the children wrote in their notebooks that "The Turkish invaders imprisoned many of our people" and "There was a lot of blood and guns."

These 11-year-old children, like many thousands other Greek-Cypriot children and youth, were born after 1974 and spent much of their schooling learning about the Turkish-occupied territories: the names of occupied villages and mountains; the difficulties of the enclaved who lived under occupation; the peaceful life before the Turkish invasion; and the need to keep the memory alive and to struggle to free the homeland. All along, the children of this fifth-grade classroom seemed genuinely passionate when they talked about the occupied areas, yet as soon as they were challenged to become more specific, many of them quickly admitted "we don't remember much else."

Not all of the children claimed that they did not remember much, of course. Some, like Stephanie, mentioned that her parents talked to her frequently about their occupied village, because, as she explained, "they don't want me to forget how our house is like in the occupied areas." One day, to show that she remembered things, Stephanie challenged her classmates to ask about her occupied house and the things that were left inside when her parents (who were small children in 1974) had to flee to save their lives. The other children played along, and Stephanie began enumerating where the kitchen was, which trees were out in the backyard, and so on. Other children, like Loukas, however, changed the subject when they were asked to give more information about the occupied areas they had studied during five years of *Den Xehno* at school. All of the children were not so easy to categorize. As a group, they identified "1974" with the pain and suffering of their community, despite the fact that they were unable to recall much detail; their "memories" of the occupied territories were evidently unlived.

The children were also provided with opportunities to share how they felt about 1974. The majority of the feelings shared or drawn were "unpleasant" or "negative," such as "sorrow," "hatred," "agony," "anxiety," and "anger." Maria, who did not come from a refugee family, described some of these feelings in a combined writing and drawing assignment:

> My thoughts about 1974 are many. I feel sorry for those who lived the war. They must have been very scared. My feelings are anger because the Turks attacked us and sorrow because they occupy our Cyprus. I hope that one day we can get back our occupied areas. [. . .] I feel great bitterness and hatred. War is not good. I want to go back to our houses which are occupied.

Yiannis drew a tank and a helicopter, colored them red (the color of the Turkish flag), and wrote below: "I feel sadness because the [Turkish] tank destroys everything in its way. Many people run and cry, bombs are falling, and our houses are burning." Eleni drew a sun and grass representing "how it will be when we go back to our occupied villages"; half of the page in her drawing was painted black, showing "a part of my heart which is black, because our country is occupied."

All the drawings were posted on classroom walls throughout the duration of the *Den Xehno* unit.

Nikki's response to the assignment and the discussion that followed caught everyone's attention, because we all found out for the first time that she had relatives who belonged to the "other side"; that is, they were Turkish Cypriots. Many children expressed surprise mixed with confusion about how this was possible. Then Nikki explained:

> My cousins are Turkish Cypriots. Their family was forced to move out of our areas and go to the occupied territories during the events of 1974. My great-grandmother Anastasia was Greek but she got married to a Turkish Cypriot named Kemal. They had to leave because some Greek-Cypriot fanatics threatened to kill them. [. . .] I miss my cousins. I love them dearly and I would like to ask the Turks to let me go and see them, even for two minutes.

After listening to the story, the children bombarded Anna and Nikki with one question after another: Who are the Turks? Who are the Turkish Cypriots? How are they different? Who threatened to kill Nikki's great-grandparents and why? As it became evident from conversations with these children, it was the first time they had an opportunity to ask these questions in class and clarify the distinction between "Turks" and "Turkish Cypriots." Interestingly, since that day, children have been more self-conscious when they use these terms. Anna wrote in her diary that this was the first time in her career that she had experienced something like that: "I was tremendously moved. The children sat in absolute silence listening to Nikki. [. . .] I felt strange because I had never had the chance before to think about some of these issues. Today I feel that we opened a small window to our world."

"You should interview your mother and great-grandmother," suggested several children to Nikki, after what seemed to be a long discussion of her story. "Of course, I will," she responded with a smile. As the bell rang to end a remarkable day, Yiannis raised his hand and added: "(To Anna) Ma'am, about forgiveness and peace that we talked about a few weeks ago, I want you to know that I cannot forgive the Turks who conducted this war against us. I hate them. . . ."

"But We Have More Dead and Missing Persons . . ."

The following week, interviews with parents and grandparents were about to begin. Yiannis was so eager to interview his 75-year-old grandfather that he went ahead and did so without waiting for the class to finish the semistructured protocol that was being prepared. One morning he brought his MP3 player to class, announcing, "I interviewed my grandfather, and I believe you would like to listen to what he said." Anna seemed to be caught by surprise, but eventually she and the class agreed to play the recording after recess. She asked her students to take notes while they were listening to the recording; she announced that her task would be to write the main concepts or terms heard in the recording on a large piece of paper (a process that was also followed in subsequent lessons): "So . . . I'd like you to focus on three things. First, what we learn from this story about the events of 1974. Second, what thoughts or feelings you are having as you are listening to Yiannis's grandfather. And, third, what further questions you'd like to ask about this story so that we add those to the questions we have already written down when Nikki talked to us about her Turkish-Cypriot relatives."

The children were taking notes as they listened to Yiannis's grandfather, who described the days before and during the Turkish invasion: how he was imprisoned by Greek-Cypriot paramilitaries who participated in the coup against the Cyprus government, how the Greek-Cypriot army was utterly unprepared and betrayed, the chaos on the day of the Turkish invasion, the dead and the missing persons from his village, and his feelings of sorrow and pain for being a refugee for 37 years. What follows are short extracts from the recording:

> Before the war, the Greek Cypriots had Turkish-Cypriot friends. We lived together and did business together. I had a Turkish-Cypriot friend, but I haven't seen him ever since. [. . .] I don't have anything against the Turkish Cypriots. The whole thing was betrayed and Turkey invaded. [. . .] We could live together again with the Turkish Cypriots if Turkey left. Nobody wants a war. War creates wounds that are not healed. War creates hatred and evil. [. . .] I refuse to go to the occupied areas and show my passport. For me, it's unacceptable to show my passport in order to visit my own house. This pains me a lot, but we have to be patient and wait until the day the occupied areas are liberated.

When the children finished listening to the recording, they gathered their notes and questions. Androula was the first to speak: "I liked what Yiannis's grandfather said about our country . . . things we didn't know. It was as if we also felt his sadness for our occupied territories." Costas was quick to add, "I felt moved because Yiannis's grandfather talked about our occupied country. I have a million questions to ask. Who is responsible for this war? Why did the Turks invade Cyprus? Why were our people unprepared to face the Turkish invasion?" Other children added more questions: "How was life with Turkish Cypriots before the war?" "How should we feel about Turkish Cypriots?", "Why do we have to show passports to visit our houses in the occupied territories?"

Anna was busy writing on a large piece of paper everything that children were saying. The paper was divided in three columns—what we know; how we feel; what we want to ask. She checked several times that everyone in class had added their input. Eleni raised her hand somewhat hesitantly: "Ma'am, I have a question. Have the Turkish Cypriots also lost people in this war? Or is it only us? I believe I heard my father once saying that we also did wrongs against the Turkish Cypriots in the past. Is this true?" Anna said that this was an important question and suggested that it should go on the list of questions for investigation, but then added: "Would it change your perspective about Turkish Cypriots if we discovered that they also lost loved ones in this war?" Several children nodded, "Yes, maybe," but they were interrupted abruptly by Marios: "But we have more dead and missing persons! The Turkish Cypriots don't have so many. My parents told me so." A confusing situation followed in which some students were yelling, "we have more dead," while Eleni suggested: "Why don't we research this and find out?" Everyone thought it was a great idea and the dispute ended there.

When Anna and I met later, she kept asking me if she had handled the situation "well." I avoided a direct answer and instead asked her to explain the objective that was in her mind when she engaged the children in this discussion. As she pointed out, "Eleni's initial question about the Turkish Cypriots provided a powerful opportunity to introduce the recognition of the other side's perspective, a major goal of this unit, as you know. So I attempted to build on that, but I am afraid I will be in trouble with the parents who may not like what we are doing here!" Anna seemed ambivalent about teaching children to "feel" and "imagine" the perspective of the other community, and she had good reasons for it: "I believe our society is not ready for this yet. Am I doing the right thing to even raise the issue in class?" Wanting desperately to break what felt then to be an awkward moment, I jokingly suggested that she should send parents' complaints to me, and we left it at that.

"They Are Humans Too . . ."

A few days later, Nikki came to school and ran to Anna holding a piece of paper. "Ma'am, ma'am, my mother wrote the whole story of my great-grandmother Anastasia for us. Look!" Nikki explained that her grandmother had narrated the story of great-grandmother Anastasia, and Nikki's mother had typed it on a computer. After skimming the story silently, Anna smiled and went on to make copies for everyone in class. There was a sense of anticipation. A few minutes later, there was complete silence. The children began reading the story.

The story described the life of great-grandmother Anastasia spanning from the past—how she got married to her Turkish Cypriot husband Kemal, how the local society reacted, in what ways the bicommunal strife in Cyprus influenced their personal lives, the war and separation from Anastasia's (Greek-Cypriot) family—to present life in the occupied areas. What follows are two short excerpts, one from the middle of the story and the other one from its ending. Nikki's grandmother narrates:

> When the checkpoints opened [in 2003] and we all met [with grandmother Anastasia and her family from the occupied areas] for the first time, it was the happiest day of our lives. Everyone was crying, we were hugging each other and couldn't believe we were able to meet grandmother Anastasia and her middle-aged children after almost 30 years of no contact. Since then, our relatives from the other side come to visit us twice a month, except grandfather Kemal. [. . .]
>
> Grandfather Kemal has never visited the free areas since 1974. He doesn't want to visit the village in which he was born near Paphos [a town in the south part of Cyprus], because he's afraid that he will find everything in ruins. This would make him very sad so he'd rather not cross to come to our side. Grandfather Kemal is retired now and is home, helping grandmother Anastasia, who has been recently diagnosed with cancer.

After reading the story, Anna and the children followed the same process of analysis as before. They took notes and wrote on a large piece of paper what they had learned, what feelings they had after reading the story, and what questions they would like to ask for further investigation. At one point in the discussion, Christina suggested that grandfather Kemal "must be sad, after going through all these hardships in life and then finding out about his wife's health condition." Anna grasped the opportunity and asked the class how they would feel, if they were in grandfather Kemal's position.

"If I was in his position, I would feel great sorrow, because I couldn't meet my relatives for such a long time," said Georgia. "But I would feel joy, too," added Nikos, "because I would finally meet my relatives in the free areas." "I would have mixed feelings," counterpoised Louisa, "as I would be happy for being with my wife and children, but I would also feel sadness for being forced to abandon my village when some bad people threatened our lives." Gloria agreed and said, "I would lose a part of my soul, if I had to leave my home. I feel pain in my soul for all the people who lost their homes in Cyprus and fear for their lives. It doesn't matter if it's Greek Cypriots or Turkish Cypriots. They [Turkish Cypriots] are humans too. . . . They carry wounds and traumas from the war. Their loved ones get cancer too. . . ." Anna told the children that she found their thoughts to be "remarkable" and added:

> I like what you said about pain not distinguishing between Greek Cypriots and Turkish Cypriots. I also like what you said about the feelings you would experience if you were in grandfather Kemal's position. This is called *empathy* [*ensynaisthisi, ενσυναίσθηση*]. Empathy is the ability to imagine that you are in the other's position and you understand how he would feel.

This was the first time that Anna used the word *empathy* in the classroom. Yiannis responded immediately saying that "empathy with our enemies" was very hard because "the Turks are evil and they occupy our country." Nikki replied that they were not talking about the Turks but, rather, about the Turkish Cypriots "who are also Cypriots." The introductory excerpt of this chapter was part of the discussion that followed. A few other children agreed with Yiannis and asked, "why are the Turks so evil?" Costas also wondered, "Why didn't they [Turks] come to Cyprus only for a visit, just like tourists do, and instead occupied half of our country? We wouldn't have a problem with them if they came as visitors. . . . I don't understand why they occupy our homes." Anna reiterated that empathy was very difficult indeed and often impossible, but it was worthwhile to explore its difficulties in their *Den Xehno* unit.

A few days later, Nikki's mother visited the class. The children had the opportunity to ask questions about grandfather Kemal and grandmother Anastasia. Yiannis asked whether sharing her family story made her sad. Nikki's mother assured the children that "to share your heart with others helps you process your feelings and thoughts, even if it sometimes makes you sad." At some point of the conversation, Androula asked about grandmother Anastasia's health. "Unfortunately, grandmother Anastasia is at the hospital these days. She's not very well," said Nikki's mother. Eleni suggested that the class should write cards and send them to grandmother Anastasia at the hospital in the occupied areas. Everyone thought it was a great idea.

On the following day, the children prepared their cards for grandmother Anastasia. Below are some excerpts from those cards:

> The whole class wishes you well. We found out the hardships you and your family went through in the war of 1974. But you were saved and so I am sure you will get well now too. Thank you for teaching us so many things about our history. I feel sad that grandfather Kemal cannot cross the borders. [Georgia]

> I feel joy that you are fighting for your life. I hope that these cards will make you feel better and encourage you to keep fighting for your life. Thank you because your life teaches us so many things about Greek Cypriots and Turkish Cypriots. Some events were sad in your life, but I will remember the happy events. I wish you got well soon. [Eleni]
>
> My beloved grandmother, we don't know each other very well but I want you to know that I love you very much. I am sad for your illness but I know you will get well because you've gone through difficult times in your life before and you won. With love, your granddaughter, Nikki.

A few weeks later, the class received a message from great-grandmother Anastasia (still at the hospital then) that said how deeply moved she had felt when she received their cards. Her message was placed on the classroom wall next to their drawings.

"Who Can Really Stand so Much Pain?"

In the following weeks the students brought in numerous interviews that had been recorded at home with parents, grandparents, uncles, and aunts. Relatives and community members like poets and writers were also invited into the classroom; they recited their poems, narrated or read their stories, and discussed with the children the conflict that kept Cyprus divided. Floating through this classroom all this time was an array of ambivalent emotions; the varied feelings were the result of a journey taken by these young children through which they began to experience in depth the complexities of the past and the lasting memories: feelings of hatred and anger for the ongoing Turkish occupation alongside feelings of caring and humanity between members of the two conflicting communities; the unimaginable pain and suffering of people from both communities; and the joy of learning about less known stories of collaboration and respect between members of the two communities. The events taking place in this classroom were too many to recount them all here, and the struggles to negotiate empathy were too complicated to cover all of the nuances in a single chapter. Instead, I share two more events, because they highlight perhaps more profoundly the unending ambivalences on the part of children to engage with empathetic activities and imagine the perspective of the "other side."

The unit on *Den Xehno* was in its ninth week. On this particular day, Greek-Cypriot schools commemorated the death of a famous national hero, named Gregoris Afxentiou, who sacrificed his life in the 1955–59 guerilla fight against the British. The school organized commemorations both in each classroom and outside in the schoolyard where all students and teachers of the school were present. Class time in Anna's fifth-grade classroom was allotted for reciting poems about the heroic sacrifice of Afxentiou to liberate Cyprus from the British colonial forces. After reading a story about how the hero was killed by the British who surrounded him and eventually burned him alive, Anna asked her students to discuss the question, "What do you think is the relationship between the things we have been studying in the *Den Xehno* unit and the commemoration of Afxentiou's sacrifice?"

"Both are relevant to war and death, their terrible consequences on people and the negative emotions we feel about these events," answered Costas. "We have mixed feelings about both events," added Maria, who continued: "On one hand, we feel uncertainty about what will happen to our Cyprus and on the other hand, we feel pride for the sacrifice of this hero." Yiannis counterpoised that "This hero is an example to us. If we also need to die for our country, like many of our own people did in the war of 1974, we will die for our country." Anna repeated what Yiannis said and asked if the rest of the class shared Yiannis's feelings. Three quarters of the students raised their hands. "Aren't you afraid to die for your country?", Anna asked back. "No, ma'am!" answered Nikos and several others. "If we need to throw the Turks out of Cyprus, we'll do it!" added Loukas.

Several girls disagreed and reiterated that the war would bring more death and suffering. "If we place ourselves more frequently in each other's position, just as empathy teaches us, then maybe we won't need to have more wars," suggested Georgia. Nikki also pointed out that "If we live in peace with each other, like we used to do with Turkish Cypriots, maybe the Turks can also live in peace with us." "No way, it's not going to happen!" replied Yiannis immediately. "Why don't they [Turks] leave us alone. We don't want them here," added Marios.

A few days later, Anna brought in a photograph showing a young boy holding the picture of a missing person and next to him a group of men digging. A discussion followed on who this boy might be, what he did there, and how he might feel. Initially, everyone assumed that this boy was Greek Cypriot and held the picture of his missing father. The children shared once again their feelings of sadness, agony, and anger about the emotional pain of this boy and the Greek Cypriot community as a whole for its suffering in the war of 1974. They talked about the missing persons and the feelings of their loved ones who stayed behind, waiting for them. Then Nikki suggested that the boy might also be a Turkish Cypriot because from the previous interviews they had analyzed in class, they had discovered that there were Turkish-Cypriot missing persons, too. Other children confirmed Nikki's observation and remembered the story of the poet who had visited their classroom and mentioned this as well. Anna asked them then: "If I told you that this boy's name was Ahmet and indeed this was a Turkish-Cypriot boy, would anything change? How would you feel if you were in Ahmet's position?" Many children reiterated that Turkish Cypriots also lost loved ones and so their feelings of sadness would not change. Some of their responses were the following:

> If I was Ahmet, I would feel deep pain and sorrow for losing my father. [Louisa]
>
> I would lose all hope and I would feel fear, if my parents were killed in the war of 1974. A part of my soul would be gone. [Yiannis]
>
> I am thinking about this child, Ahmet. Who can really stand so much pain? At the end, his heart will break. This is what happened with all Cypriots who lost their houses and their loved ones. [Panayiotis]

Anna then asked: "How could someone overcome so much pain?", to which Georgia responded, "by looking forward and seeing our future living in peace with each other." Other children shared similar views and Anna asked further: "How do you think a Turkish Cypriot like Ahmet would feel about Greek Cypriots?" The class seemed divided between those who said that "Ahmet would hate us for what we did to his father" and others arguing that "He would forgive us, because not all of us did wrong to his family." Loukas suggested that "Perhaps we should forget the past and move forward," but other children disagreed and argued that it was hard to forget; yet, "we should find a peaceful solution to our problem in Cyprus, love and respect each other and become friends with Turkish Cypriots," asserted Eleni. The class meeting ended with an activity in which each child was asked to imagine that he or she was in Ahmet's position and that he or she was writing a letter to Greek Cypriots. Almost all of the children shared their feelings of sadness and how war brought pain and suffering. The following excerpts from two letters show children's emotional ambivalence.

> [. . .] I know you Greek Cypriots killed my father and normally I should feel hatred for you. But I don't, because I don't want another war. [. . .] I feel relief that my father's remains were found in a mass grave. I cannot forget him. I cannot stop thinking about my father. [Stephanie]
>
> I feel angry at Greek Cypriots but I don't hate them. It is not everyone's fault for what happened to my father, just like it is not the fault of all Turkish Cypriots for what happened to Greek Cypriots. [. . .] I know you experienced similar pain, so we should learn to live together in peace. [Yiannis]

"These children have come a long way," Anna told me in one of our last meetings. "I didn't expect that some day they would have been able to express their empathy about others with so much care and precision. A few months ago, this unit would have been impossible to teach. Now at least they have begun to pay attention to others' feelings and perspectives, especially those of the other side. If you consider that when our generation went to school this would never have happened, maybe we are making some progress here!"

On the last day of my observations, the children were given a "dilemma" scenario that went like this: "If a Turkish Cypriot who fought against me in 1974 and tried to kill me, comes in front of me and asks for food because he's hungry, would I let him die or give him food?" A few children were not sure what they would do and shared their arguments for and against. Most children, however, responded almost right away that they would not let this person die because "above all he's a human being."

Final Thoughts

In this chapter I have made an attempt to describe the efforts of one teacher to cultivate empathy in a classroom situated within a conflicted society with an unresolved political problem. This teacher employed the "funds of knowledge" approach and analyzed with her students how community stories and feelings tie in with empathy. The multifaceted complexities of this account point to the emotional ambivalences on the part of "children-empathizers" to perceive and negotiate empathetic acts for the "enemy-other." Throop's (2010) conclusion about the vicissitudes of empathy in the context of the island of Yap, Micronesia, is equally pertinent in the case of children's engagement with empathy in this Greek-Cypriot classroom; that is, empathy is "very seldom, if ever, an all or nothing affair. Nor is it unambiguously valued" (ibid., p. 780). The findings suggest that the process of engaging with empathy in a primary classroom of a conflicting society is full of fractures and failures, possibilities and impossibilities, connections and disconnections. These (dis)connections, writes Throop, often range "from feelings of mutual understanding, attunement, and compassion to feelings of confusion, misalignment, and singularity when confronting the, at times, impenetrability of others' and our own subjective lives" (2010, p. 771).

One might argue that this class attempted to do something too complex for the age or the maturity level of these children; that the notion of "empathy" and its relevance to the everyday life of children clearly needed further clarifications, and that the society in Cyprus was still so torn and divided that the educational object of "reconciliatory empathy" for the "enemy-other" was audacious, utopian, or, perhaps, dangerous. And, yet, children's responses indicate that there were indeed some unexpected transformations taking place in this classroom, even if initially it seemed impossible to imagine engaging in empathetic activities involving the "other." Despite these transformations and the obvious uncertainty about whether they would last into the future, it also became clear that children's ambivalences were embedded in powerful emotional forces politicizing any form of connectedness with the other community (Christou, 2007; Zembylas, 2008a). In fact, it was the acknowledgment of these ambivalences that made the teaching of *Den Xehno* more enriching, strategic, and multiperspectival (see Lindquist, 2004) in this classroom compared to the "traditional" teaching of this subject in the past. In a context rife with intense emotions about the ongoing occupation of half of their country, Anna and her students found in the "funds of knowledge" approach an opportunity not to feel better or simply reiterate their feelings of sorrow, agony, and anger, but rather a chance to engage with the "difficult" emotions of decentering the "national self" from its own historically situated experience and begin to imagine the perspective of another (see Boler, 1999; Jansen, 2009). Anna did not adopt depoliticized or romanticized language about *Den Xehno* in order to confirm hegemonic feeling norms. Instead, she encouraged children to engage with emotional reflexivity both about their own and the other's suffering and pain. That said, even in those moments in which empathy clearly failed, differing modes of engagement with the other still were explored that did not foreclose possibilities for new moments of empathetic connection in subsequent lessons (cf. Throop, 2010). It is, therefore, important to remind ourselves that some of the most significant insights regarding the (im)possibility of teaching about/for empathy in conflicted societies arise in moments in which there is loss of empathy (cf. Hollan & Throop, 2008).

Note

1. In recent years, the notion of "forgiveness" has been considered in educational literature as a possible response to "woundedness" (e.g., see Papastephanou, 2003; White, 2002). Although the reconciliatory dimensions of teaching empathy could have been significantly enriched by the notion of forgiveness, I chose not to discuss forgiveness in this chapter, because the notion of forgiveness did not come up much in classroom conversations between the teacher and the students. However, the entanglement between forgiveness and reconciliation in education is explored further in some of my other work (e.g., see Zembylas, 2011, 2012c; Zembylas & Michaelidou, 2011).

IV EMOTIONAL TENSIONS AND CRITICAL RESPONSES TO PEACE EDUCATION EFFORTS

He really had been through death, but he had returned because he could not bear the solitude.

—GABRIEL GARCÍA MÁRQUEZ, *One Hundred Years of Solitude*

If he loves justice at least, the "scholar" of the future, the "Intellectual" of tomorrow should learn it and from the ghost. He should learn to live by learning . . . how to talk with him, with her, how to let them speak or how to give them back speech, even if it is in oneself, in the other, in the other in oneself: they are always there, *specters, even if they do not exist, even if they are no longer, even if they are not yet.*

—JACQUES DERRIDA, *Spectres of Marx*

I'm a pessimist because of intelligence,
but an optimist because of will.

—ANTONIO GRAMSCI, *Letters from Prison*

10 REFUGEES, EMOTIONS, AND CRITICAL PEACE EDUCATION

I have been a refugee since 1974. I cannot even imagine engaging in teaching the educational objective of peaceful coexistence that was recently announced [by the Ministry of Education and Culture], unless there is a solution to the Cyprus Problem and the Turkish occupying forces leave my country so that I can return home. Until then, I feel that any one-sided peace education efforts by our side are insulting to me and disrespectful to what my family is still going through.

—MARIA, *refugee Greek-Cypriot teacher*

In the previous two parts of this book, the emphasis has been on providing empirical data from schools on the emotional spaces of racism and nationalism in schools and the emotional complexities of coexisting with the "enemy-other." In societies that are still suffering from the aftermath of war and traumatic conflict, there are some experiences that heighten the emotional tensions and dilemmas that derive from having to coexist with the "other." One of these experiences is "the refugee experience." It and its impact on teachers', parents', and students' emotional (un)willingness to be involved in peace education efforts have been explored in several chapters (e.g. 3, 4, 5, 7, and 8). As the preamble statement by Maria (a Greek-Cypriot refugee teacher) indicates, there are strong negative emotions toward peace education initiatives for a variety of reasons. Most notably, the infusion of emotions—such as fear, anxiety, depression, vulnerability, helplessness, resentment, and bitterness (Das et al., 2000)—into public and school discourses seems to raise concerns about the "appropriateness" of peace education initiatives, when a sensitive issue (e.g. being a refugee) remains unresolved in the aftermath of traumatic conflict. The role of sensitive issues in peace education initiatives is fairly well understood from previous research (e.g. see Bekerman & Zembylas, 2012; Davies, 2004; Gallagher, 2004; McGlynn et al.,

2009). However, what has not been widely explored so far is the role of emotion in the experience of being a refugee and especially how this experience is represented in society and schools. In this chapter, then, I undertake this exploration by taking a step back from the empirical data provided in previous chapters and making an attempt to further analyze the emotional experience of being a refugee and its implications in peace education efforts.

Drawing on the discussion of the politicization of emotions in chapter 2, this chapter covers some of the processes and strategies by which educational policies and pedagogical practices "emotionalize" (Holmes, 2010) the representation of refugees. This discussion has two main objectives: first, it aims to refine our understanding of how emotions affect the ways in which educational policies and practices reproduce self–other dichotomies through certain representations, such as that of the refugee experience; it is argued that these dichotomies are relevant to emotional reactions against peace education initiatives. Second, this chapter examines alternative possibilities of promoting peace education, taking into consideration the affective (re)production of refugee representations without undermining the sensitivity of the refugee experience. A better understanding of how emotion is involved in such representations will help educational policy makers and teachers in conflicted societies to take into account the hitherto poorly developed aspects of the ways in which emotions, sensitive issues, and peace education are inextricably intertwined.

Revisiting Some Ideas about Emotions

As a brief reminder of my approach on emotion (chapter 2), it is sufficient to emphasize here two important ideas: the involvement of discourses in emotional processes (Harré, 1986; Svašek, 2010) and the politicization of emotions (Ahmed, 2004; Svašek, 2008). First, the perspective of emotion-as-discourse outlines how cultural categories of emotions produce knowledge about the world and the self in ways that are historically specific and group-specific. In other words, it is maintained that cultural, discursive, and social phenomena are constitutive of emotions and that they affect the ways in which people feel, perceive, and conceptualize life events (e.g. Denzin, 1984; Lutz & Abu-Lughod, 1990; Svašek, 2010).

According to the perspective of emotion-as-discourse, emotions are public, not exclusively private, objects of inquiry that are interactively embedded in power relations. This view brings me to the second idea, that is, how emotions are historicized and politicized in the ways in which they are constituted, in their organization into discourses and technologies of power, and in their importance as a site of social and political control through surveillance and self-policing

(Ahmed, 2004; Barbalet, 1998; Lupton, 1998). Thus the interrelation between emotion and politics acknowledges the cultural and historical norms of emotion with respect to which emotions are expressed and how, who gets to express them and under what circumstances. As Reddy (1997) explains, this entails the process of determining "who must repress as illegitimate, who must foreground as valuable, the feelings and desires that come up for them in given contexts and relationships" (p. 335).

Drawing from Ahmed (2004), it is also understood that emotional encounters with others create boundaries or deconstruct such boundaries. That is, emotions play a crucial role in the ways that individuals come together, move *toward* or *away* in relation to others, and constitute collective bodies. The constitution and reiteration of selves, collectives, and self–other relations create "repositories of emotion" that structure the boundaries of the possible in policies and practices. "By *repositories of emotion*," writes Leep (2010), "it is taken to mean that Others become the cause of the Self's emotions towards the Other through attributing the causes of emotions to Others" (p. 335). For example, in a discourse in which country x is perceived to cause "resentment" in country y, country x is said to become a repository of country y's resentment. This process renders the others a repository of emotions, transforming them into "objects of feeling" (Ahmed, 2004).

But let's contextualize these ideas by referring specifically to the representation of refugees in public discourses. If emotions shape and are shaped by certain representations of refugees, then it is interesting to investigate how particular emotions—e.g. resentment or hatred—"stick" to those considered responsible for the historical events that created refugees. In previous chapters, for example, intense emotions of resentment and hatred were expressed by many Greek Cypriots toward anyone with Turkish origin. The "self" and the "enemy–other" in these emotion discourses are produced affectively through normalized discourses, shaping how "we" may feel about others and subsequently the prospects of reconciling with "them," especially if we consider them responsible for our displacement. The effectiveness of these emotion discourses relies precisely on their capacity to normalize ways of thinking, feeling, and acting about self and others.

Emotions, therefore, become attributes of collectives, a process that, through repetition, blocks new meanings that may exist alongside not-hateful others (Ahmed, 2004). Thus resentment and hatred are not viewed as isolated, individual emotions but exist relationally within particular historical conditions that call attention to the nature of discourses and practices that constitute feelings of resentment and hate under such conditions (see Card, 2002; Eisenstein, 1996; Scheff, 1994). Scheff (1992, 1994; Scheff & Retzinger, 1991) and Retzinger (1991) use social and political theories of emotion to explain ethnic conflict and ethno-nationalism. Scheff explains that the construction of resentment and hatred of others via the media and educational and political discourses is the most powerful way of forming an us-and-them mentality, idealizing one's own group while demonizing the other. These ideas urge us to consider how emotions organize social and physical space (e.g. in schools), creating a powerful border that prevents reconciliation with the other. As Leep (2010) further explains, it is emotion discourses and practices that initiate and sustain normative structures of feeling on which basis the self acts toward others according to the appropriate feelings. Inscribing identities with affects not only moderates possibilities of engagement toward these identities but also authorizes motivation to act.

Examining how emotions affect the ways in which educational policies and practices produce a self–other attitude toward relationship entails looking at how those policies and practices "emotionalize" certain representations of traumatic conflict, such as those of refugees. The following sections of this chapter situate the largely theoretical discussion by showing some of the processes and strategies through which the representations of Greek-Cypriot refugees are emotionalized, both by looking at public discourses in the Greek-Cypriot community and studying empirical evidence emerging from previous chapters.

Emotions, Public Discourses, and Representations of Greek-Cypriot Refugees

The starting point of my analysis is the long-term work by anthropologist Peter Loizos on Greek Cypriots who have been refugees since 1974. Loizos's two monographs, *The heart grown bitter: A chronicle of Cypriot war refugees* (based on fieldwork conducted right after the 1974 displacement), and *Iron in the soul: Displacement, livelihood and health in Cyprus* (based on fieldwork conducted thirty years after 1974) provide deep insights into the emotional lives of Greek-Cypriot refugees over a span of almost four decades. Although these accounts do not focus on the emotions of refugees per se, there is a solid and deep analysis of the emotions involved in the loss and trauma of displacement and its consequences (emotional, physical, material, etc.) for refugees' lives over the years.

The social implications of emotions such as fear, anxiety, depression, vulnerability, helplessness, resentment, and bitterness are at the heart of Loizos's anthropological work. His discussion of how refugees cope emotionally with their displacement and its consequences provides a rich base for understanding how the identity label *prosfyghas* (Greek for "refugee") carries a submerged sense of grievance and bitterness that marks the lives of Greek-Cypriot refugees decades after their displacement. Refugees suffer not only because they have lost their possessions and homes but also because they have lost their way of life, their social networks, and a pattern that gave them purpose and meaning in life.

A small study by Evdokas (1978) specifically addresses the emotional factors used to promote partition in Cyprus and discusses the psychopolitical role of Greek-Cypriot refugees, stating that refugees could act as pressure groups in the case of a solution to the Cyprus Problem that is perceived to be unjust and non-viable. Evdokas also recognizes the possibility that the emotional vulnerability of refugees might be exploited by political rhetoric, a theme that is taken up in another landmark ethnographic study by Sant Cassia (2005).

Sant Cassia, also an anthropologist, has focused on missing persons in Cyprus and discussed the strategies and mechanisms through which political rhetoric has constructed and used particular representations of conflict and trauma over the years. In particular, he has shown how the memorialization and emotionalization of loss and trauma promoted by the state, politicians, and other social and political groups have not necessarily focused on bereavement. Rather, the emphasis has been on the social and political gains in relation to how the past should be remembered and what individual and collective emotions should be harnessed to maintain the desire for return. Narratives of loss and trauma, then, and the emotional rhetoric that characterizes them are central to how collective memories are interpreted (Connolly, 2002).

Particular policies and practices provide important mechanisms that sustain the collective memory of loss and the solidarity of Greek Cypriots. These include refugee associations (constituted by the populations of former towns, villages, and districts); retention of electoral constituencies in the north, and old telephone numbers in current directories; exhibitions of photographs of now occupied villages; documentation of folk history, music, dancing, and other traditions; powerfully expressive poetry and stories; school ceremonies; church liturgies; and television and radio shows, among other cultural factors (Zetter, 1994). Embedded in these practices, argues Zetter, are the feelings and beliefs that refugees will one day return to their villages and homes.

It is therefore important to pay attention to how policies and practices evoke particular feelings toward Greek-Cypriot refugees and their displacement. For example, bitterness and resentment become part of a discursive logic of feeling in political life that constitutes Greek Cypriots as eternal "victims" of Turkish expansionism (Papadakis, 2005); these feelings become integral and "stuck" to Greek-Cypriot consciousness, as has been evident in many statements by Greek-Cypriot teachers, students, and parents quoted in previous chapters. This "stickiness" works through discursive rituals to render bitterness a justifiable emotional response as a result of trauma, loss, and perceived injustice.

The commitment to the idea of returning to the land now occupied by Turkish troops, then, is galvanized by a range of feelings about displacement (see Loizos, 1981, 2008; Zetter, 1991, 1999).

Return, in particular, as a slogan, has dominated the domestic and international political agendas of Greek Cypriots. As Zetter (1999) wrote: "Frustration and even disbelief are exacerbated by protracted exile of the Greek Cypriots, but the intention, aspiration and the right to reclaim what has been lost is never disputed" (p. 6). However, a myth has been constructed around return, as he argues. What is mythologized and idealized is the extent to which the physical and symbolic past can ever be reclaimed. It is crucially important, then, for educational policy makers and teachers who may wish to promote peaceful coexistence in Cyprus to appreciate the emotional dynamics involved in Greek-Cypriot narratives of loss and trauma, as well as refugees' desire for return.

The Emotionalization of Refugee Representations in Family and School Contexts

While so far the stage has been the wider social and political context of emotions in relation to the refugee experience of Greek Cypriots, here I focus on the emotionalization of refugee representations within the micropolitical context of family and school. The point of departure for this analysis is Hadjiyanni's (2002) research (conducted in 1994) as presented in *The making of a refugee: Children adopting refugee identity in Cyprus*. Hadjiyanni's work reveals that members of the first generation of refugees transfer their traumatic experiences of displacement so that their children will know their predicament, remember it, and continue to struggle for return. For this reason, Hadjiyanni makes an important conceptual differentiation between refugees who experienced displacement and their descendants. On the basis of this distinction, she names the refugee identity of generations born after dislocation "refugee consciousness" instead of "refugee identity."[1] *Refugee consciousness*, therefore, refers to the secondary experience of trauma that is transferred from the first generation.

The process of developing refugee consciousness appears to take place in four different stages, according to Hadjiyanni; the stages range from the parent experiencing the trauma of becoming a refugee to the projection of its effects, the transfer of memory, and the adoption of the refugee identity by the child. Although Hadjiyanni does not engage in an explicit analysis of the emotions involved in these stages, emotions are clearly present in creating, recognizing, reinforcing, and mobilizing collective memory about the refugee experience. According to Hadjiyanni, family members, and especially women as mothers and grandmothers, are the primary transmitters and supporters of refugee consciousness; their role is instrumental in reinforcing the loss instead of de-emphasizing it. The strong emotional bond of refugee mothers with the lost places and the recognition of their role as safe-keepers of the refugee identity are powerful elements in the construction of refugee consciousness. Other sources from which children learn about the past and develop refugee consciousness are the school, other refugees, the media, books, social ceremonies, and refugee associations.

Besides the family level, where children are taught about the past, there has been a powerful educational policy through which collective memory is strengthened; the policy of *Den Xehno* (I don't forget). Bowman (2006) describes how the *Den Xehno* policy, especially a few years after the events of 1974, has come to permeate all facets of the Greek-Cypriot society over the years:

> "I Don't Forget." These words were a symbol found everywhere in Cyprus. They were on school exercise books and on photos of villages under occupation. Children saw them every day they went to school, every time they had to write. Every night, before the main evening news, the photo of an occupied village was shown with the caption "I Don't Forget" beneath. What should not be forgotten was so clear that there was no need to say more. "The memories of our occupied villages, our ancestral hearths, our graveyards, our occupied churches, our occupied homes, our gardens, our orchards" (Bowman 2006, p. 122).

As a permanent goal at all levels of Greek-Cypriot public education after 1974, "I know, I don't forget, and I struggle" [*Gnorizo, Den Xehno, kai Agonizomai;* henceforth *Den Xehno*] involves both cognitive and emotional objectives (see chapter 1). The cognitive part of this goal ("knowing" and "remembering"), however, is inseparable from its other part, which aims to develop the emotional strength that keeps "struggling" for return. Knowledge and remembrance are seen as important ways to help the younger (post-1974) generations maintain the necessary "militancy" for "fighting" to reclaim the occupied territories.

In the empirical data presented in the previous chapters, it is shown how the *Den Xehno* policy has been used as a potent vehicle for actually promoting the emotionalization of loss and trauma in order to reproduce the Greek-Cypriot collective narrative about conflict; that is, how Greek Cypriots are the eternal "victims" of the other side's perpetration. In examining the emotional structure of this policy, my focus here is on how *Den Xehno* bonds the "appropriate" emotions about refugees with Greek-Cypriot collective identity through school curricula and pedagogical practices. Children in schools are turned into *emotionalized subjects*—that is, elicitors and repositories of emotions—who need to "perform" the emotions that demonstrate *Den Xehno*. Two examples, one from the school curriculum and the other from particular pedagogical practices, show how *Den Xehno* aims to *nationalize* children's and teachers' emotions about refugees.

The first example is a series of excerpts from the 1996 *Den Xehno* curriculum:

> [The students need] to mention and justify the elements that keep refugees and generally the [Greek-Cypriot] people emotionally tied to their land [. . .]; to become emotionally moved through experiencing customs and traditions of our occupied land [. . .]; to learn about the living of the inhabitants of occupied Cyprus before and after the invasion, and to collect information that shows nostalgia for return from those who were uprooted (Ministry of Education and Culture, 1996, p. 96).

These excerpts show clearly and emphatically the goal to "move" students "emotionally" through memories of occupied Cyprus. This "nationalization" of emotions aims to invest students and teachers with specific norms that reify particular perceptions (e.g. the Greekness of the land; the emotional ties of refugees to their land; the need to be emotionally moved and committed to the struggle for liberating Cyprus, and so on).

In the empirical evidence from previous chapters it is illustrated how pedagogical practices and discourses are entangled with emotions about the "enemy-other" and the continued partition of Cyprus. More specifically, it is shown how classrooms and schools set up emotional spaces that formulate and maintain particular racialization and ethnicization processes; that is, children are encouraged to "perform" certain emotions about the continued partition of Cyprus. For example, in chapters 3, 4 and 5 it is shown how emotional geographies of proximity and distance with Turkish-speaking children are very much relevant to traumatic conflict and *Den Xehno*. As it is evident from those chapters, it is expected that Greek-Cypriot children—children of refugees and non-refugees alike—demonstrate an essentialized perspective of "us" versus "them" (see also Spyrou, 2002, 2006). When they are not exhibiting the expected self-categorizations, children are directly or indirectly urged to do so. The "us-versus-them" frame of reference is linked to a number of emotions: "pride" for being Greek; feelings of obligation to struggle for the liberation of Cyprus; "empathy" for refugees and the relatives of missing persons; and "resentment" and "bitterness" for being victims of injustice. Also, in chapters 7 and 8, it is shown how hegemonic narratives about 1974 are emotionally grounded in feelings of suffering, resentment, and victimhood. As one of the students pointed out: "My mother is a refugee. At home, she talks about the home she once had and lost because of them. Living with the Turks is impossible." Another one reiterated: "We cannot be friends with Turkish Cypriots, because at school we learned to say 'Den Xehno.'"

This evidence reveals how Greek-Cypriot children's identities become reproduced through the emotions to which they are discursively linked. It shows how specific educational policies and pedagogical practices follow a particular logic that aims to nationalize emotions and to reproduce normalized identities. Certain refugee representations need to be continuously reinforced because it is assumed that if younger generations stop "feeling" like refugees or "knowing" about the refugee experience, then the dream of return will be compromised and the political struggle will be eroded (Zetter, 1999). Therefore, families and schools engage in emotion discourses and practices that promote the development of us-and-them dichotomies, because the sense of collective emotional connection grounded in loss and trauma provides a powerful idiom for remembrance and for the struggle to return.

Reconceptualizing the Role of Emotion in Critical Peace Education

After the permission was granted by the Turkish-Cypriot side for unfettered access across the Green Line in Cyprus in 2003, the *Den Xehno* objective was somewhat loosened in Greek-Cypriot education (see Christou, 2007; Zembylas et al., 2011). In August 2008, the new Minister of Education and Culture released a circular to all primary and secondary schools (Ministry of Education and Culture, 2008), announcing the introduction of a policy initiative to promote "peaceful coexistence." The new initiative set peaceful coexistence as the primary educational objective of the school year 2008–09, emphasizing that education "must cultivate those elements that unite us and characterize us as one people [. . .] [preparing] children and youths for peaceful coexistence and collaboration between Greek Cypriots and Turkish Cypriots" (Ministry of Education and Culture, 2008, pp. 1–2).

This circular generated considerable debate and controversy, not only in schools but also in the media and the press, in Parliament, and in society more generally. Most reactions criticized the "appropriateness" and "timeliness" of an objective for peaceful coexistence while a large part of Cyprus is still under Turkish occupation and the dream of return remains unfulfilled. As a matter of fact, a few months after the Minister's circular was distributed, the primary teachers' trade union (POED) issued its own circular (4 February 2009), stating its strong disagreement with the suggestion that exchange visits be allowed between Greek Cypriots and Turkish Cypriots, and announcing its refusal to accept any kind of institutional control of teachers' classroom practices (POED, 2009). It is against this objective that the refugee teacher Maria expresses her emotions in the opening statement of this chapter.

The case of Cyprus provides a fascinating illustration of how educational battles are easily transformed into highly emotional ones, significantly complicating peace education initiatives. The obvious question, therefore, is: When and how can peace education be promoted in schools while teachers and/or the public have strong emotions and feel that it is inappropriate to talk about peace education in a divided society in which fundamental human rights (e.g. the right of return to one's property and house) are violated? Or, as Lindner (2009b) has put it, "When and in what ways are emotions (feelings of suffering and rage, humiliation, or love and caring) part of a "conflict" that calls for reconciliation and resolution? And when are they not? Who decides?" (p. 163). The short answer is that emotions and their consequences *are* part of peace education efforts, either we recognize this or not. The long answer is provided in chapters that follow, in which I sketch a number of different ideas that highlight the role of emotions in critical peace education, especially when there are serious emotional tensions, dilemmas, and complexities around those initiatives. In the remaining pages of this chapter, I begin to outline some of these ideas that are further discussed in the succeeding chapters.

First, as has been shown in Parts II and III of this book, emotions are integral to public and educational efforts around issues of traumatic conflict, healing, and reconciliation. The interrogation of one's emotional investments in particular self–other ideologies is an important component of peace education efforts involving teachers and students in conflicted societies (Bekerman & Zembylas, 2012). A peace education approach that focuses not only on one's own emotions (e.g. of being a refugee) but also on others' emotions (e.g. recognizing that others are also refugees) often requires engagement in discomforting learning experiences. Such an approach in peace education—for teachers and students alike—includes examination of one's own emotional experiences, values, and perspectives about peace, conflict, justice, human rights, and diversity. Unavoidably, this examination can threaten one's core beliefs and create powerful negative feelings, such as anger, shame, or resentment, that may inhibit or support peace education interventions (Zembylas, 2008a).

In particular, for critical emotional praxis to be promoted in peace education initiatives, emotional and organizational support should move in the direction of systematic and systemic initiatives (Abu-Nimer, 2004) that use teachers' negative perceptions and emotions in constructive ways—e.g. teacher education workshops, curriculum development sessions, school leadership seminars, and action research projects. As the empirical data in previous chapters show, radical and largely unplanned policy initiatives are unlikely to permeate schools. Such initiatives should adopt a holistic approach to curriculum development, school leadership, and culture (Salomon & Nevo, 2002) and not refrain from dealing with the tough emotional issues. For example, a multiperspective analysis on the emotions of the refugee experience and the gains and losses from one's involvement in peace education efforts can be helpful. Although this task of performing such an analysis is undoubtedly challenging, the confrontation and critical engagement with troubled knowledge (e.g. chapters 7 and 8) appears to be an important way forward toward addressing explicit concerns about education for peaceful coexistence.

Once teachers and students begin to have a multiperspective understanding of the emotional complexities involved in a conflict, they may become able to see the "humane connections" between "victims" and "perpetrators," including the frequent reversal of roles. Thus teachers and students in conflicted societies need to find pedagogical ways of working through the differences that keep traumatized and conflicted societies apart. The re-humanization of both victim and perpetrator is an important pedagogical goal, and the exploration of the ambivalent emotions involved in the process offers a unique opportunity in the classroom to break down the absolutist polarities between self–other and victim–perpetrator. A pedagogical approach that acknowledges both positive and negative emotions in such difficult experiences as being a refugee in a conflicted country allows teachers and students to critically unpack the feelings and perceptions that accompany traumatic experiences. If schools are to become places of healing and reconciliation, then members of the school community need to draw more actively upon those feelings, including feelings of empathy and common humanity (see chapters 9 and 11).

Rosenblum (2002) has asserted that the role of peace educator is to expose the students to unresolved dilemmas and tensions and to analyze the resulting implications: "The purpose is to train students to be 'ambivalent advocates'—committed to action, but alert to the multiple consequences; to make them more sympathetic to the plight of people trying to do good, while at the same time more critical of those who do it without reflecting on the possible negative consequences" (ibid., pp. 304–305). Therefore, he suggests that we adopt an attitude of "ambivalent activism" in our pedagogical approaches to peace education, acknowledging the complexities in interpretations of trauma and victimhood and exposing both of the transformative possibilities that are available.

One has to recognize that teachers like Maria are legitimately concerned that peace education may have no meaning at all without a political settlement that addresses human rights violations, refugee claims, and other unresolved issues. The choice to adopt ambivalent activism might be initially experienced by some of these teachers as discomforting. However, it is valuable to situate these concerns in the context of critical pedagogical praxis: First, this pedagogical praxis does not simply affirm any representations (e.g. refugee representations) uncritically but engages in a serious political analysis that recognizes and respects the emotional dilemmas and tensions involved. Second, this pedagogical praxis does not only focus on the "negative" side of things (e.g. trauma and human rights violations) but also unveils possibilities for solidarity and acknowledgment of common suffering with the other, as well as emotions of humiliation and powerlessness that often accompany the reception of trauma narratives.

The task of teachers in conflicted societies, then, is—or at least ought to be—to create emotional spaces where grievances can be freely expressed along with the exploration of the potential to offer recognition not only of one's own pain and suffering but also to the other's pain and suffering. The potential for recognition is linked to the pedagogical need to open lines of communication toward moving beyond, at least at some level, the negative emotional aspects that dominate public and educational discourses and practices. The major challenge lies in shifting the dominance of resentment, bitterness, and hatred to pedagogical practices that strive to affirm common humanity, but without necessarily denying one's own grievances. Rather than constructing policies and practices around negative feelings alone, an alternative pedagogy could be encouraged by feelings of common vulnerability with the other as the ground of promoting deeper understanding and solidarity.

Note

1. Hadjiyanni argues that refugee consciousness is an identity that develops over a long period of time. "Refugee-ness," in other words, is grounded in the identity paradigm and is described as a process in the making.

11 TOWARD CRITICAL PEDAGOGIES OF COMPASSION AND SHARED FATE

Ben-Porath (2006) has argued that a protracted conflict reconfigures the horizontal and vertical relationship between citizens and their state. She uses the concept of "belligerent citizenship" to highlight the dangers posed by conflict (e.g. war with another country; ethnic conflict within a country), when citizenship is deeply rooted in conceptions about a rigid, monological, and static national identity. These dangers include such things as directed and mandated civic participation, suppression of deliberation, and moral scrutiny regarding one's patriotism. In arguing for "expansive education," Ben Porath (2011) argues that citizenship education in times of conflict should promote an alternative vision of citizenship as "shared fate" (Williams, 2003). The concept of *shared fate* recognizes relationality and multicultural commitment to diversity and change compared to the monological root of national affiliation. Such a conception of citizenship, asserts Ben-Porath, is better because it can address the complex relations of citizens, the state and their inter-relations, both during conflict and in other times.

There is hardly any disagreement with a vision of citizenship education that is "expansive" and includes not only a critique of monological national narratives (see Gallagher, 2004; McGlynn et al., 2009), but also promotes the values of shared fate, relationality, compassion, and recognition of diversity and human rights (see Banks, 2004; Osler & Starkey, 2005). However, there are two problems that need to be seriously considered in propositions that entail the promotion of certain values in citizenship education. The first problem has to do with the emphasis on preparing children and young people to learn the values underlying citizenship, and a reduction of citizenship education to a form of socialization aimed at the reproduction of the existing sociopolitical order; this view, which has been referred to as a "psychological" or "instrumental" view of citizenship education (see Biesta, 2007, 2009, 2010, 2011), conceives the role of citizenship education as that of producing individuals with a particular set of moral qualities and values. The second problem has to do with the lack of attention to the role of affect and emotion in citizenship education (see Ruitenberg, 2009, 2010; Zembylas, 2008a, 2014a); this view raises questions about the education of political emotions and the kind of affective relationality that is required to enact values such as shared fate. Especially in sites suffering from normative ethnic divisions, there are important implications for citizenship education in terms of how to develop new affective relationalities on the basis of shared fate while paying attention to human rights demands.[1] Both of these problems are closely connected because the role of affect and emotion cannot be disassociated from the vision that is formulated for citizenship education.

In light of these problems, there are three philosophical issues that merit attention and constitute the focus of this chapter: first, the requirements of affective relationality in the notion of citizenship-as-shared fate; second, the tensions between the values of human rights and shared fate in conflicted societies; and third, the ways in which citizenship education might overcome these tensions without falling into the trap of psychologization and instrumentalization, but rather focusing on providing opportunities for social and school practices that manifest shared fate and compassion in critical ways. What teachers and schools should try to do, therefore, is to make practices of shared fate and compassion possible through creating conditions for children and young people to experience what it means to enact such practices in conflicted societies.[2] It is also argued that teachers and schools in conflicted societies cannot produce "new" citizens on the basis of any values, no matter how "noble" these values may be. The most that can be done is to help children and young people to critically reflect on the conditions under which people in conflicted societies can act on the basis of shared fate and compassion and provide support so that these possibilities can become realistic. In this chapter, then, I sketch a response to some of the questions raised in earlier chapters regarding the prospects of teaching for/about empathy, compassion and shared fate, and the connection between these issues and citizenship, when a traumatic conflict is still considered unresolved.

Citizenship, Shared Fate, and Affective Relationality

Citizenship and citizenship education are debated around the world on the basis of a number of historical, political, social, and cultural developments such as increasing diversity, immigration, globalization, and war/conflict (Arnot & Dillabough, 2000; Banks, 2004; Gutmann, 2004; Knight Abowitz & Harnish, 2006; Kymlicka, 2001; Osler & Starkey, 2005; Soysal, 1994). These debates have attempted to reconceptualize citizenship and citizenship education in ways that address these developments. Generally speaking, citizenship entails membership, identity, shared values, and rights of participation at the individual and community levels (Kymlicka, 2001). "National" citizenship, for example, associates citizenship with ethnic groups, as in the legal principle of jus sanguinis (the right of blood); this conception is grounded on understanding the nation as a stable, well-defined group whose members have blood ties. Citizenship education programs, especially in conflicted societies, are often grounded in such conceptions of citizenship and thus contribute to perpetuating existing sociopolitical order (see Biesta, 2007, 2010).

Particularly in times of war and conflict, there are shifting conceptions of citizenship; tolerance of diversity is diminished and dichotomies between "us" and "them" on the basis of ethnic terms are further accentuated (Davies, 2008; McGlynn et al., 2009). "Belligerent citizenship" is a form of citizenship that reinterprets key components of democratic citizenship—e.g. deliberation, unity, solidarity—in times of conflict, so that citizens' patriotism and devotion to their country are demanded (Ben-Porath, 2006). Security issues, national survival, and patriotic duty are at the forefront of public debates; diversity is contained for the perceived sake of national survival, deliberation is suppressed, and a strong national unity is mandated. Working to preserve rather than contain diversity, argues Ben-Porath (2011), is an important educational aim that could better be met through the concept of citizenship as shared fate.

Citizenship of shared fate (Williams, 2003) is grounded in the notion that we find ourselves in webs of relationships with other human beings that profoundly shape our lives. In particular, the notion of citizenship as shared fate "is based not on interpretations of identity, but rather on *ties* among the members of the community and the mutual effects of their political choices" (Ben-Porath, 2011, p. 320, emphasis added). These ties may be historical, institutional, or territorial, in ways that "encompass multiplicity and diversity in all of these aspects" (ibid.) and reinterpret nationality on the basis of the view that it is shared. Conceptualizing citizenship as shared fate, explains Ben-Porath,

> offers a more persuasive understanding of citizenship as well as a more valuable educational endeavor. Citizenship as shared fate can be based on a shared cultural identity (much like identity citizenship), but its foundations incorporate a host of other features, among them *institutional linkages* (such as representative government), *material linkages* and "seeing our own narratives as entwined with those of others" (Williams, 2003, p. 231).

In other words, the conceptualization of citizenship as shared fate entails an argument that is grounded on *relationality* rather than on identity-based conceptions. It is common objectives and interests with others that turn us into compatriots and establish ties and linkages with them.

The language of "fate" undoubtedly has its pitfalls (Williams, 2009); however, it "captures this sense that the condition of political action is a world that has been shaped by forces other than our intentional agency" (p. 44). Furthermore, Williams argues that the emphasis on fate does not imply fatalism or destiny; on the contrary, the identification of a particular web of relationships on the basis of shared fate is a pragmatic step toward exerting political agency.

Not surprisingly, some interpret the shared fate argument as having a communitarian "flavor"; therefore, there are critiques similar to those directed against communitarianism—e.g. the idea that any sort of belonging to a group stands in the way of critical thinking. However, Ben-Porath clarifies that "shared fate does not describe social membership as 'evident' but rather as an individual and communal interpretive project that is a central aspect of civic life" (2011, p. 321). That is to say, communal affiliation is not taken for granted but rather it is considered open, flexible, and contingent. The most important aspect of this conceptualization of citizenship is its continual, institutional commitment to diversity and deliberation.

Conceptualizing citizenship as shared fate, continues Ben-Porath, offers some important advantages compared to identity-based definitions of citizenship, especially during times of conflict. First, citizenship as shared fate does not subscribe to a thick but rather a thin layer of identity that promotes trust among a wide variety of subgroups. Therefore, there is a "continual process of shaping the meaning and implications of membership" (Ben-Porath, 2011, p. 321). This claim encourages the view of identity as dynamic, constructed, and ever-changing, and therefore opens spaces for a version of citizenship education that re-conceptualizes identity as a non-dividing construct. These spaces may create opportunities for understandings of identity that are not bounded in the limitations imposed by the nation-state (Bekerman & Zembylas, 2012).

Second, citizenship as shared fate does not presuppose that all groups understand their place or identity in the same manner as others do. It is the relationships among human beings that are more important; although these relationships are not all of conscious choosing, there is common interest in belonging to the same polity. These relationships bind individuals and groups together and are constituted by a variety of bonds that are not necessarily based on culture, language, or religion. This claim suggests that there are different ways in which people can come together and formulate shared goals to promote social harmony and cohesion. It is through actions that are beneficial to the whole society (e.g. a future without war) that shared fate is constituted—not through strengthening ethnic identities.

Despite these advantages, however, the notion of citizenship as shared fate has been theorized so far in ways that fail to recognize the requirements for *affective* relationality. In particular, there are two issues that merit attention: first, whether the notion of citizenship as shared fate entails particular formations of connectedness that are not only rationally based but also affectively grounded; and second, the kind of affective relationality that might be required to ground perceptions of shared fate in the first place, especially in conflicted societies. As already noted, affectivity constitutes an important site of political belonging and of political change in society (Ahmed, 2004), as well as in schools (Zembylas, 2008a). After all, relationships and connectedness are fundamentally about affects and emotions (Ruitenberg, 2009). I want to invoke, therefore, that affective relationality ought to be taken seriously in discussions about shared fate in citizenship and citizenship education.

Affectivity is not simply a state but rather a set of affective exchanges and expresses the potentiality that exists in people to relate to one another (Venn, 2010). Relationality is fundamentally affective and action-based because it has the potential to transform people and their communities. This view of relationality as affective and transformational entails an ontology, asserts Venn, that concerns elements that are constituted in the course of the relation, but they are not pre-existing to the relational act. Shared fate as relational and affective is firmly located to the contingency of all people and groups as beings who are constantly becoming. This idea highlights that despite historical narratives that form normative divisions between ethnic groups, it is possible to interrupt this form of relationality and constitute new relationalities, *if* new emotional attachments are created—e.g. on the basis of common humanity, compassion, and vulnerability (Butler, 2004). The idea of shared fate implies that individuals create affective relations with others in some way; it does not require that these affective relations are the same for everyone.

Recent political and social theories explain how emotions contribute to the formation of political identity and citizenship (Clarke, Hoggett, & Thompson, 2006; Goodwin, Jasper, & Poletta, 2001; Marcus, Neuman, & MacKuen, 2000). A key idea of these theories is that emotions not only contribute to forming communities of feeling or collective bodies but also are mobilized for the polity to uphold firm emotional commitment to particular values such as patriotism and citizenship (Ahmed, 2004; Berezin, 2001; Svašek, 2008). Shared fate, then, may manifest in different ways that range from empty sentimentalism to more critical forms of affective relationality (see Zembylas, 2008b). Therefore, it is important to examine the emotional dimensions of citizenship as shared fate, especially in conflicted societies in which shared fate may be *felt* differently by conflicting ethnic groups.

In the next part of this chapter, I take an example that is often debated in human rights literature, namely, how feeling differently about the violation of "our" community's human rights compared to the violation of "their" community's human rights—an issue that has also come up in several chapters of this book—endangers the prospects of citizenship as shared fate. The purpose of discussing this example is twofold: First, I show how shared fate might be felt differently by conflicting ethnic groups. Second, I analyze how certain entanglements of values—e.g. shared fate and human rights—entail tensions that create serious obstacles for critical citizenship education in conflicted societies.

Tensions Between Human Rights and Citizenship as Shared Fate in Conflicted Societies

Human rights discourses are increasingly being coupled to discourses on citizenship and citizenship education (Kiwan, 2005). However, as Kiwan rightly observes, there is often no engagement with the conceptual distinction between "human rights" and "citizenship rights." As she explains:

> Whilst, in practical terms, human rights are clearly exercised within a political community, in conceptual terms, human rights discourses are located within the universalistic approach, where there is the notion of common humanity based on ethical conceptualizations of the individual. This contrasts with citizenship rights, which are defined in relation to a political community, based on political conceptualizations of the individual. (2005, p. 37)

An important issue, therefore, emanating from this clarification is how to integrate, on one hand, the differential ways in which human rights appeal to individuals and groups, and on the other, the efforts to formulate citizenship on the basis of shared fate. That is, there seems to be a tension between citizenship as shared fate and human rights discourse; the former is located within particularist discourses, while the latter is conceptualized in universalist terms (see Laclau, 1995).[3]

For example, one such tension is manifest in the way that ethnic groups, which struggle to formulate shared fate in a conflicting society, "nationalize" their claims about human rights; that is, they represent themselves as a homogeneous bloc and conceptualize violations of human rights through a narrow national(ist) lens.[4] Such a tension threatens the process of constructing new affective relationalities on the basis of common objectives (e.g. shared fate). Needless to say, there is no simple or obvious way to analyze the dense entanglements between human rights discourse and discourse about citizenship, especially in conflicted societies. The aim at this point is not to analyze all of these multifaceted entanglements but rather to focus on how it is possible to integrate human rights concerns within a citizenship education approach that is grounded in the values of shared fate.

Generally speaking, human rights are conceptualized within a universal frame of reference that applies to all human beings, without distinction of any kind (race, color, language, religion, etc.) (Tibbitts, 2002). Mutua (2002) argues, however, that interpretations of human rights are not neutral but very much embedded in cultural and political assumptions, explaining that, "The grand narrative of human rights contains a subtext which depicts an epochal contest pitting savages, on the one hand, against victims and saviors, on the other" (p. 10). Given that we live in a world divided into territorial states, with laws, legislatures, courts, and the like, it is not surprising that the dominant grounding of human rights during the last fifty years has been law and politics (Ignatieff, 2001). An implication of these concerns is the need to constantly re-examine whether current versions of human rights are really what we want them to be, especially in relation to citizenship discourses.

By *mis*representing human rights as being rooted in a humanist idolatry or within nation-state structures, an ethnic group in a conflicted society creates an image that any violation of its human rights by a rival ethnic group is simultaneously a threat to its physical and national survival (e.g. see Eckmann, 2010), while there is less or no concern for the violation of the other group's human rights. Thus, the hijacking of the human rights discourse by the nation-state ideology sustains the view that social membership is pre-given rather than contingent, as the notion of citizenship as shared fate suggests. In particular, when a group interprets human rights by promoting an image whereby it is grounded within a more nationalistically defined human rights discourse (i.e. "we" are the victims; "they" are the perpetrators), then one wonders whether there is any space to establish any discourses or practices of citizenship as shared fate.

In her analysis, Kiwan (2005) has responded that regardless of how citizenship is conceptualized, human rights discourse cannot be the theoretical underpinning of citizenship. This is because, she has written, "citizenship is always defined in terms of membership within a political community, in contrast to human rights, which are based on membership of common humanity, or in other words, an ethical community" (p. 47). Although Kiwan makes a valid argument about the fact that human rights discourses and discourses on citizenship should not be treated as synonymous, a more far-reaching concern, in my view, is how national *identification* might be weakened and in what ways a *subjectification*—based on shared fate—could be re-claimed and sustained.[5] In other words, it is important to find ways in which human rights claims are neither nationalized nor simply universalized in an abstract manner. Rather, what is needed is the formation of a political imagery that does not erase this tension but articulates it on the basis of shared objectives and visions. A citizenship education approach that provides opportunities for social and school practices that manifest shared fate is valuable, because it encourages subjectification—a process in and through which the emphasis is not on identification with national identity, but rather one in which new ways of achieving affective relationality come into existence.

For example, there are important questions to be asked that further clarify this tension so that it does not concede shared fate to ethnicity or culture but rather problematizes the superiority that some individuals and groups claim for their sense of belonging: Can human rights be interpreted in ways that weaken national identification so that individuals and groups learn to become tolerant of different historical narratives?Should this be done merely according to strict legalistic models of human rights or through recognition of different violations of human rights and witnessing of a variety of trauma narratives on the basis of solidarity, compassion, and shared fate values? In which ways can educators in conflicting societies be convinced that not all educational practices of citizenship as shared fate undermine human rights? That is, how can citizenship education provide opportunities to support shared fate, while acknowledging that there are varied interpretations of human rights, politics, and conflict?

The relationship between human rights and citizenship is still an issue of debate in the literature and will not be easily settled (Bajaj, 2011). However, it will be valuable for citizenship education and human rights education to broaden the discourse and discuss in greater depth how to reclaim a critical stance over the different meanings and levels of rights, as well as their relationships, particularly within a political framework of shared fate. The issue is not simply to claim that human rights ought to have priority over citizenship rights. Rather, the main concern, in my view, is how to engage critically with competing discourses in order to articulate their educational implications so that action on the basis of shared fate is made possible.

In the next part of this chapter, I discuss ways in which citizenship education might overcome the aforementioned tensions without falling into the trap of psychologization and instrumentalization, but rather focusing on providing opportunities for social and school practices that manifest shared fate in critical ways. The discussion addresses the conditions needed for children and young people to experience a different *habitus*—a habitus that comes to existence through new ways of *doing* and *feeling* shared fate. This effort should not be a process of moral socialization that prepares children and young people for their future participation in political life; rather, it should emphasize modes of political action and civic learning (see Biesta, 2010, 2011) that embody a commitment to a more critical and political form of shared fate.[6]

Creating Conditions for a Different Habitus

Habitus is understood as a socially constituted system of dispositions that provides the link among emotions, affect, and embodiment (Probyn, 2004). Dispositions include a spectrum of cognitive and affective factors, and thus the concept of habitus explains how objective structures and subjective perceptions affect actions (see also Bourdieu, 1990, 2000; Bourdieu & Wacquant, 1992). The habitus makes up our habitual patterns of understanding and inhabiting the world (McNay, 1999), producing embodied experiences that coincide with objective structures (see Bourdieu, 1990). As McNay explains, affects are filtered through habitus into emotions (as self-perceived) and emotional performances (as displayed by enculturated social actors); in this model, emotions and emotional performances may be redirected by readjusting our habitus (1999). Habitus may be seen, then, as a set of embodied practices that are, to some extent, a product of prior experiences—not in the sense of a cluster of dispositions that are static and unavoidable, but rather as embodied practices that are strongly influenced by historical, social, and cultural contexts (Zembylas, 2007a).

In light of its generative view, habitus constitutes a site of transformative emotional practices (Hoy, 2004; McNay, 1999; Probyn, 2004). Take, for instance, citizenship education: While someone may be predisposed to act negatively toward "non-citizens," the potentiality for new affective relationalities with them is not foreclosed (Emirbayer & Goldberg, 2005). Undoubtedly, kinship dispositions among members of the same ethnic group predispose individuals to select particular forms of conduct with "others" (e.g. excluding them from certain social and political practices). However, this set of dispositions can be adjusted according to new social structures and available resources that may eventually modify previous dispositions.

For example, if shared fate becomes a valued commitment and emotional resource in the context of an ethnically divided society, then social and pedagogical spaces might be created to experience different ways of inhabiting the world. This potentiality is manifest in the different affective relationalities in which children and young people begin to engage in schools—e.g. friendship, compassion, and conviviality. Citizenship education that provides children and young people with opportunities to experience a different habitus—e.g. a habitus of shared fate—makes possible the creation of openings for a potentially different future with individuals and groups with whom there is pending conflict.

The focus is not on the preparation of individuals—by equipping them with the "right" set of dispositions and values of shared fate—but rather on supporting actions that develop shared-fate practices. A habitus of shared fate, then, is developed through engagement in actions with the "experiment" of shared fate; also, this creates a political rather than a moral kind of subjectivity in that citizenship-as-shared-fate is seen as a political "project."

As already noted, the aim here is not to erase the tensions identified earlier, but rather to use them constructively to identify insights that evoke critical perspectives of citizenship coupled with recognition of the politics rather than the morality of shared fate. The broad name "critical" includes theoretical views from feminist, reconstructionist, cultural, and transnational discourses of citizenship (Knight Abowitz & Harnish, 2006). Critical perspectives have developed, as Knight Abowitz and Harnish have explained, as a result of the unfulfilled promises of the civic republican and liberal discourses and challenge normative meanings of identity and membership. Unfortunately, "the current formal, taught curriculum of citizenship produces a relatively narrow scope and set of meanings for what citizenship is and can be" (Knight Abowitz & Harnish, 2006, p. 657). I want to consider, therefore, how critical perspectives of citizenship education can expand the set of interpretations around citizenship as shared fate, taking into consideration the importance of creating opportunities in schools that provide new affective relationalities and a habitus grounded in shared fate (see also Zembylas, 2014a).

First, it is important to clarify that the term *critical citizenship education* refers to a framework that aims to provide the conditions for collective social change through a combined focus on knowledge and participation (DeJaeghere & Tudball, 2007; DeJaeghere, 2009; Johnson & Morris, 2010). Critical citizenship education is grounded in ideas of critical pedagogy, human rights education, and critical multiculturalism. In addition, I argue that critical citizenship education approaches need to problematize the role of emotion practices in democratic citizenship in ways that address emotional exclusion and its civic realities (see Zembylas, 2014a). To return to the tension identified earlier and phrase it in terms of its implications for citizenship education, I pose the following questions: Should the focus be on preparing children and young people for their future citizenship responsibilities through practices of identification on the basis of ethnic kinship? Or, should the emphasis be on providing opportunities for subjectification so that children and young people can open up themselves and move experientially toward others with whom there is a shared fate, regardless of who these others may be?

To show the implications of choosing one answer over the other, I go back to some of the empirical evidence presented in earlier chapters. As shown, there are intense emotional challenges in educating Greek-Cypriot children and young people to open themselves to move toward those they consider the "enemy." The politics of emotions (e.g. fear, hatred, resentment) formulate particular dispositions, values, and emotional geographies about belonging, identification, and citizenship among students and their teachers (e.g. distinctions between "us" and "them"), and so it becomes very difficult to encourage new affective relationalities. The mechanisms that are exposed through institutional and everyday (school) practices indicate how the "enemy-other" is utterly excluded from visions of shared fate on the basis of arguments such as the one emphasizing that the "enemy-other" has a perennial history of violating human rights. The emotional geographies that are nurtured in schools, as shown in chapters 3 and 4, work to formulate a habitus of citizenship that would certainly define shared fate with the "enemy-other" as a dangerous, if not absurd, endeavor.

In contrast, there is also evidence suggesting that the habitus contains important uncertainty and tension, which students and teachers must negotiate. For example, as shown in chapters 7, 8, and 9, feelings of resentment or fear are often full of ambivalence; that is, reflecting on the possibilities of shared fate with the "enemy" is not always clearly demarcated as "impossible." This emotional ambivalence leaves some space for the development of new habits of the mind, attitudes and dispositions such as friendship, compassion, and conviviality. Thus, there are real examples in which "pockets" within schools formulate an alternative habitus on the basis of shared fate and compassion; in these spaces, the teachers offer practical opportunities for students to open themselves to meet the "enemy-other" and experience in action the consequences of living with compassion rather than perpetuating hatred and resentment.[7]

The insights from research such as that presented in this book show the importance of paying attention to the politics of emotion in citizenship education programs. In particular, critical citizenship education practices that problematize emotions include a commitment to systematic analysis of how a particular habitus that does not condone shared fate is socially, historically, culturally, and politically constituted. Such a "genealogical" analysis of habitus in schools enables teachers and students to explore how and why emotional investments in certain ideals (the nation-state; national identity; religion etc.) are experienced, expressed, circulated, and sustained. It is the careful analysis of political structures and their entanglements with emotional realities that creates openings for compassion and practices of shared fate, such as acknowledging past wrongs, recognizing shifting differences within and across ethnic groups, and learning to live in peace with others. The objective is not to develop compatible historical narratives between members of conflicting ethnic groups that erase past trauma and grievances. Rather, the focus on creating openings for compassion and shared fate emphasizes the importance of transforming perceptions of others as the moral enemy and approach them instead in political terms.

A critical approach of citizenship in relation to human rights issues, for example, has a different point of departure and purpose than citizenship education that simply focuses on preparing students to learn about all the human rights violations by the "enemy." A critical citizenship education exposes the emotional dilemmas, tensions and divergent viewpoints that exist between citizenship and human rights and does not seek to impose homogenization and standardization. It also examines how children and young people construct emotional meanings of citizenship and human rights in conflicted societies, and how they (and others, who may belong to a rival community) understand justice, rights, and shared fate in relation to others. All of these understandings need to be constantly interrogated by explicitly addressing the emotions arising in practice and by engaging in action that engages with new affective relationalities such as compassion and shared fate, rather than dismissing them from the beginning. The final part of this chapter explores how these understandings may be translated into critical pedagogies that benefit children and young people in educational sites of conflicted societies.

Toward Critical Pedagogies of Compassion and Shared Fate

So far, it has been argued that it is valuable to create citizenship education practices that critically examine students' and teachers' emotional attachments to ethnic identities and national symbols. The goal of this effort is not to formulate another moralization of the political space (Mouffe, 2005), albeit in a classroom context this time. Rather, the aim is to examine the conditions in which citizenship as shared fate can be translated into action to form new affective relationalities that are grounded in what may be called *critical pedagogies of compassion and shared fate*. The aim of these critical pedagogies is to interrogate moralistic discourses of citizenship (e.g. blind patriotism) that often prevent the enactment of compassion and shared fate. Therefore, critical pedagogies of compassion and shared fate should be seen as practices that envision the radicalization of solidarity and affective relationality with those with whom we are in conflict.

First, it is important to clarify that the notion of *compassion* has diverse meanings, and many philosophers from ancient to modern times have engaged with a long-standing debate about its nature as an emotion and as a moral and political practice (Pinson, Arnot, & Candappa, 2010; Zembylas, 2013b). "In compassion," writes Hoggett, "the other is tolerated in his or her otherness—someone with flaws, lacking in some or many virtues, willful but also still suffering, still to some extent a victim of fate or injustice" (2006, p. 156). In addition, compassion is action-oriented and demands not only feeling pain for the other's suffering but also understanding the experience of suffering and its consequences and taking action to alleviate suffering (Woodward, 2004). Compassion, then, is important for the development of shared fate because it leads to the recognition that each one of us is vulnerable. The recognition of one's own vulnerability can constitute a powerful point of departure for developing compassion and solidarity with others (Butler, 2004).

Particularly in conflicted societies, Butler's notion of "common vulnerability" enables teachers and students to explore how they might move beyond "us" and "them" dichotomies that single out the self and the other as "victims" and "perpetrators," respectively. The idea of common vulnerability puts in perspective the notion of all of "us" as vulnerable. This manifestation of compassion addresses the concerns of those who may be stuck in self-victimization claims and refuse to acknowledge that others also suffer. Although the idea of common vulnerability does not guarantee any transformation, it opens up some space to question moralistic identifications and therefore may entail shared fate as a more pragmatic possibility. Shared fate, then, does not imply the same vulnerability but rather the recognition that despite having caused pain to each other, there is commitment to envision a shared future without further suffering.

Therefore, attentiveness to common human vulnerability is an important component of citizenship as shared fate. To pay attention to common human vulnerability means to begin by identifying how we all suffer sometimes as fragile, vulnerable humans. The acknowledgment of common human vulnerability is an admission of one's own weakness. Children and young people in schools are enabled to do this when they begin to question and challenge arguments based on binaries like we/they, allies/enemies, and good/evil. For example, children and young people will learn about/with compassion when they begin asking questions and engaging in action to challenge the stereotypes about "evil enemies": If all of us have human rights and if all of us are vulnerable, why do "we" think that only "our" human rights are violated? What does it take to accept that "we" may be involved in the violation of others' human rights? What are the conditions needed to construct a particular mode of togetherness with these others on the basis of shared fate?

The goal of critical pedagogies of compassion and shared fate is to initiate children and young people into a discourse of critique and multiperspectival analysis that purposely politicizes and historicizes suffering and incites "compassionate resistance" (Sharoni, 2006). Sharoni's notion of compassionate resistance emphasizes "the transformative potential that lies in blending the two concepts [compassion and resistance] and utilizing them to inspire social and political struggles" (2006, p. 289). Compassionate resistance suggests that children and young people learn to resist the policies and practices that are inhumane and simultaneously show solidarity with those who need it; so, there is resistance against oppressive systems and policies and at the same time compassion for those who suffer. Furthermore, compassionate resistance, argues Sharoni, seeks to humanize a conflict without overlooking its history, root causes, and the unjust and inhumane systems that have made it seem intractable. Compassionate resistance includes, for example, the analysis of how particular ideologies (e.g. nationalism, racism) are accompanied by certain emotional investments that might prevent identification with the other who suffers or encourage identification only with those people who are perceived as "similar." In conflicted societies (e.g. Israel, Cyprus, Bosnia-Herzegovina), for instance, one cannot speak about compassion between conflicting sides without explicit reference to the refugees and the missing persons of all communities and to such oppressive practices as dividing lines, checkpoints, demolitions of monuments and houses, and occupation of land. Hearing about the suffering of someone from the other community might offer a unique educational experience and opportunity to identify with some parts of their story while reiterating the uniqueness and asymmetry of each story of suffering.

Furthermore, critical pedagogies of compassion and shared fate suggest alternative ways of infusing human rights into citizenship education without remaining stuck in nationalized views of human rights. Such pedagogies open up conceptual and action-oriented spaces so that human rights experiences (e.g. the experience of both sides in a conflict) become human rights instruments in themselves (Keet, 2010). It is important to clarify, once again, that the issue is not about contextualizing human rights universals and nationalizing them. Rather, teachers need to create conditions in which students can begin to explore how human rights speak directly to human suffering. Viewing human rights as a political project rather than as a moral ideology means learning to be open to the multitude of human rights constructions (Arslan, 1999). This conceptualization of human rights privileges the acknowledgment of human suffering and encourages praxis that provides both ethical and political responses to suffering.

Finally, we are reminded once again of Rosenblum's (2002) assertion that children and young people should be educated to become 'ambivalent advocates' (see chapter 10). Therefore, teachers could encourage students to adopt an attitude of "ambivalent activism" in human rights and citizenship education, acknowledging the complexities in human rights and citizenship interpretations and exposing both the transformative and conservative nature of human rights and citizenship rights in conflicting situations. The aforementioned pedagogical approach does not simply affirm human rights or citizenship rights uncritically but engages in a serious political analysis that recognizes the dilemmas and tensions involved.

Moving A Step Forward . . .

In this chapter I have discussed three interrelated issues and their consequences for the formulation of citizenship as shared fate: first, the requirements of affective relationality in the notion of citizenship-as-shared fate; second, the tensions between the values of human rights and shared fate in conflicted societies; and third, the ways in which citizenship education might overcome these tensions without falling into the trap of psychologization and instrumentalization, but rather focusing on providing opportunities for social and school practices that manifest shared fate and compassion in critical ways.

Critical pedagogies of compassion and shared fate involve interrogation of the ways in which the explicit mobilization of compassion and common vulnerability produces inclusive definitions of citizenship as shared fate. Needless to say, teachers and students need to constantly question whether the mobilization of compassion and common vulnerability creates indeed new affective relationalities with others. The question, writes McCormack (2003), "is not only 'how far can we care,' but also becomes one of cultivating a commitment to those relations that may increase the intensity of attachment and connectivity" (p. 503). Critical pedagogies of shared fate and compassion in citizenship education emphasize the need to identify how emotion discourses and practices are embodied in the day-to-day routines of school life. Such forms of citizenship education include the development of a mode of critique that comprehends the habitus of citizenship and its effects on students' and teachers' lives. It is realized, therefore, that the emotional histories brought by students and teachers need to be constantly examined. Critical pedagogies of shared fate and compassion offer opportunities to interrupt policies and practices that exclude and dehumanize individuals and communities of fate.

Admittedly, this chapter has only sketched out the requirements of the affective relationalities that need to be built in order to formulate shared fate. Yet, I hope that I have made clear that shared fate, solidarity, deliberation, and compassionate resistance offer some valuable pedagogical openings for creating a different habitus in schools—a task that is by no means easy. Recognizing the importance of affective relationality in citizenship as shared fate is the first and most important step; the real challenge is developing pedagogies that restore common humanity and the ability to live and act in conflicted societies with an open heart rather than with resentment.

Notes

1. The challenges in these sites are further complicated when citizens have to live together under a common statehood, yet pragmatically the society is divided in ethnic groups whose members have little or no cross-group interactions in everyday life (e.g. Cyprus, Israel, Bosnia-Herzegovina).
2. For example, this is what some teachers attempt to do in the context of the school discussed in chapter 8; similarly, the efforts of the teacher in chapter 9 focus on enacting practices of compassion and empathy.
3. *Particularism* is the claim that ethnicity, race and nationality are unique; *universalism* refers to the fact that some principles apply to all, regardless of particular claims.
4. The reader is reminded that in several chapters of Parts II and III, there are examples of claims about the violation of "our" human rights or "our" suffering as being hierarchically more important than the violation of "their" human rights or "their" suffering. For example, this is evident in some Greek-Cypriot students' statements in chapters 7 and 8 as well as in Yiannis's claim in chapter 9, "And why should we care if *they* suffered? Did they care, if *we* suffered?"
5. Drawing on Rancière, Biesta (2011) discusses an important distinction between "identification" and "subjectification." Thus, identification is about taking up an identity that already exists, while subjectification is the production of a subject that is not previously identifiable within a given field of experience.
6. Another important distinction that needs to be made here is the one between the political and the moral. Drawing on Mouffe, both Biesta (2011) and Ruitenberg (2009, 2010) highlight that in many conflicts today, the opponent is viewed in moral (e.g., right vs. wrong) rather than in political (e.g., right vs. left) terms. Both Biesta and Ruitenberg agree with Mouffe that disagreements should be envisaged in political and not in moral terms, because it is the political that recognizes the role of power relations in constituting any social order. This distinction has important implications for the way we educate children and young people to analyze political conflicts and view others as adversaries rather than moral enemies (Ruitenberg, 2009). Thus, an important component of the notion of shared fate is not necessarily to erase completely the distinction between "us" and "them" (e.g., in the context of an ethnic conflict), but to imagine how a we/they relation can be established in different ways (e.g., on the basis of common objectives).
7. This is particularly evident in chapter 9.

12 RECLAIMING NOSTALGIA

One of the students from the international school discussed in chapters 7 and 8 said once in one of our conversations: "I wish we could go back in time when we were happy and there were no Turks in Cyprus. This is the Cyprus I dream of." This *nostalgia* involves a backward glance toward a place or time that no longer exists (or never existed), and often emerges after experiences of loss and change (Boym, 2001). On the one hand, nostalgic recollections of the past are often considered with skepticism, particularly by historians, because it is feared that nostalgia for the past may in fact distort the historical record (Shircliffe, 2001). Also, as it is argued, nostalgia may be fixed in a determinate backward-looking stance that valorizes a convenient version of the past and glosses over perceptions about one's self and identity, especially concerning issues of national memory and historical trauma (Pickering & Keightley, 2006). On the other hand, there are scholars who acknowledge that this desire for backward-looking may function as a mechanism to make sense out of experiences of loss, trauma, and change (Davis, 1979). In other words, nostalgia may serve as a survival mechanism or an existential way of finding meaning in loss and changing one's life. Both positions deserve further analysis, especially when one considers their implications in the context of educational politics and practice.

As Boym (2001) and Davis (1979) both assert, the experience of loss and change is endemic in modernity—whether it is through war, conflict, trauma, or mass (in)voluntary migration. To condemn, therefore, nostalgia solely on the position that it yearns for something which is now unattainable or that it functions as a false historical consciousness denies us the opportunity to explore further how the past may actively engage with the present and the future (Pickering & Keightley, 2006). Nostalgia, in other words, may not only work *against* but also *for* us, as a starting point for critical social commentary (Muller, 2007) or critical transformation in education (Zembylas, 2007a). Such an understanding of nostalgia cannot be subsumed entirely within a "negative" view, "not least because feelings of loss are at times commingled with a sense of social gain or liberation, or with efforts to regain what has been lost in new ways that actively engage with the process or consequences of change" (Pickering & Keightley, 2006, p. 921). But if we accept that there is indeed a "positive" view of nostalgia, then how does this view help educators and students develop critical perspectives on memory, change, trauma, and loss?

In this chapter I attempt to complicate the reading of nostalgia in the cultural politics of education, arguing that the blind rhetoric of nostalgia for an idealized past can and should be critiqued in productive ways. Despite some literature discussing nostalgia in the context of teaching (Goodson, Moore, & Hargreaves, 2006) or the analysis of nostalgic images of classroom in media culture (Otto, 2005), little has been done toward the direction of critically examining nostalgia in relation to the complex issues of national memory and historical trauma and how those influence educational politics and practice. Nostalgic claims for a "paradise lost" are often found in educational discourses and practices, especially in the context of conflicted societies, making dichotomies between the "good-us" and the "evil-them" (e.g. see Davies, 2004; McGlynn et al., 2009; Zembylas, 2008a). This sense of nostalgia has also been evident in several chapters of this book (e.g. chapters 3, 7, and 9), particularly through teacher and student discourses in which statements about what has been lost are invoked in conjunction with claims concerning historical trauma and victimhood. I argue here that nostalgia can be reconfigured through a theorizing that recognizes aspects of the past as the basis for renewal in interactions with those perceived as "evil-enemies." This opens up a positive dimension of nostalgia in the cultural politics of education, one that is grounded in the possibility of engaging with counter-memory practices in the classroom as well as with pedagogical practices that encourage aporetic mourning of loss. This effort is situated in the overall project of this book to develop pedagogies of critical emotional praxis that interrogate taken-for-granted ways of feeling, thinking, and being within a conflicted society.

Nostalgia and National Memory

The term *nostalgia* derives etymologically from the Greek words *nostos* (home) and *algia* (painful longing), that is, nostalgia is defined as the longing for home (Boym, 2001). A historicization of the concept itself is interesting in order to unpack its differentiated meanings over time and its intersection with "memory crisis" in modernity (Terdiman, 1993). Although the phenomenon of nostalgia goes back a long way—at least to Homer's *Odyssey*, as well as to ancient

Chinese texts (Walder, 2009)—the term is of relatively recent origin. As Davis (1979) informs us, it was coined in 1688 by the Swiss physician Johannes Hofer to describe the disease of Swiss mercenaries positioned outside their homeland. The apparent disease—with symptoms ranging from melancholia and weeping to anorexia and suicide—was related to a prolonged and usually involuntary stay away from home. Over the succeeding two centuries, nostalgia became de-pathologized and de-medicalized, coming to be associated to the incurably wistful modern condition of "unrepeatable and irreversible time" (Boym, 2001, p. 13) born out of "an anxiety about the vanishing past" (p. 19). Thus, there was a shift from spatial dislocation to temporal dislocation (Grainge, 2002) and a feeling of inability to make oneself "at home in a constantly changing world" (Berman, 1982, p. 6).

Although the meanings of nostalgia are linked to the sociocultural and political-economic conditions that change over time, the "home" that is yearned for need not be so real (Legg, 2005). As Stewart (1984) has pointed out, nostalgia is a form of mourning without object; it is longing for a utopian dwelling. However, Davis (1979) has argued that nostalgia is not simply an isolated mind trick that does not partake in lived experience; rather, nostalgia can be used to interrogate the articulation of the past in the present, and in particular "to investigate sentimentally inflected mediated representations of the past" (Pickering & Keightley, 2006, p. 922). Davis (1979) proposed three orders of nostalgia: the first, simple nostalgia, is the positive evocation of the past against negative feelings toward the present; the second, reflexive nostalgia, is the questioning of the accuracy and completeness of nostalgia itself; the third, interpreted nostalgia, is the questioning of the reaction to nostalgia, such as how one explains feelings of longing.

Similarly, Boym (2001) distinguishes two basic kinds of nostalgia: *restorative* and *reflective*. Restorative nostalgia emphasizes the reconstruction of the lost home, often in association with nationalist myths and revivals of conspiracy theories (Legg, 2005; Walder, 2009). For example, children in schools may be encouraged to remember the glorious past of their nation-state, before immigrants and other foreigners arrived to change the nation's demographics and its "purity" (see Ahmed, 2004). Reflective nostalgia, on the other hand, dwells on loss and trauma, driven by an awareness that the past cannot be restored not only because of the irreversibility of time but also as a result of "the imperfect process of remembrance" (Boym, 2001, p. 41). Boym points out: "If restorative nostalgia ends up reconstructing emblems and rituals of home and homeland in an attempt to conquer and spatialize time, reflective nostalgia cherishes shattered fragments of memory and temporalizes space" (2001, p. 49). Thus, an example of teaching about reflective nostalgia in schools would be to problematize how particular emblems and rituals from the past reinforce certain inclusions/exclusions on the basis of one's ethnic, religious, or other identity. Clearly, then, restorative and reflective nostalgias are not only personal but also social and political (Davis, 1979).

As Boym (2001) explains, much of twentieth century violence from Nazi and Soviet terror to recent nationalist revivals (e.g. in the former Yugoslavia) operated as a response to perceptions of threat for an imagined homeland. Manifestations of these nationalist revivals are the dichotomous us-and-them categorizations that are often perpetuated in schools within conflicted societies (Davies, 2004; McGlynn et al., 2009; Zembylas, 2008a). As national memory becomes envisaged as a representation of a particular version of a nation's past, it gradually becomes amenable to nostalgic desires (Lowenthal, 1993). What drives nostalgia—restorative nostalgia, in this case—is an attempt to homogenize the past; thus nostalgia contributes to creating images of an idealized yesterday. This idealization of the past—manifest both in school practices and the wider societal ethos (see Bar-Tal, 2000a)—ignores its less pleasant aspects (e.g. atrocities and violence against others) and promotes the development of a national identity that supposedly has historical continuity and unites everyone considered to belong to the same national group. Nationalists have attempted to use this form of nostalgia to promote ideological goals and to institutionalize it in monumental reconstructions of the past, school and public ceremonies, museums, and memorials (Lowenthal, 1993).

An interesting theoretical issue, therefore—one that has important implications for educational politics and practice—is the link between nostalgia and memory. In much of the more recent work in many fields of study (e.g. psychology, history, cultural studies) nostalgia is closely linked with a distorted public version of a particular historical period, that is, a distorted memory of the past. At the same time, memory is defined as something shared (Margalit, 2002); shared memories may involve remembrances, legacies, traditions, heritage, histories, and monuments. In other words, it is emphasized how memories—as well as particular nostalgias—are constructed, shared, and legitimated in the society (Pickering & Keightley, 2006). Needless to say, the (de)legitimating process of particular memories and nostalgias in society reflects processes similar to those that are followed in schools (see Cole, 2007; Simon, Rosenberg, & Eppert, 2000; Van Sledright, 2008). A particular challenge for educators, therefore, is how to unpack the complex entanglement between memory and nostalgia in schools in ways that encourage reflective rather than restorative nostalgia. But before doing so, one further clarification needs to be made concerning, this time, the distinction between memory and history.

In their monumental seven-volume work on *Realms of Memory* in France, Nora (1996) and his colleagues have made some important conceptual advances in clarifying memory and history. According to Nora, collective memory is the significant product of a society in which people live "inside" the past through long-existing traditions, shared values, and heritage. In contrast, a historical perception of the past is a product of a secular, analytical, and critically reflective society in which the past is viewed from the "outside." The only points at which history and memory meet, explains Nora, are *realms of memory* that contain both symbolic and functional meanings. These realms of memory are, for example, old history schoolbooks, annual meetings of war veterans, or statues of heroes. However, realms of memory can be used by "nostalgia-merchants" (Le Goff, 1992) to articulate a convenient remembrance of past events. Nostalgia, in this sense, is coupled with banality, functioning by covering up certain aspects of the past and highlighting others; as such, nostalgia fails historical knowledge (Boym, 2001). This is the version of nostalgia, I argue, that is more often promoted in schools of conflicted societies—through school textbooks, curricula, and everyday school practices (see Cole, 2007; McGlynn et al, 2009). This version of nostalgia essentially promotes an idealized version of the past and fails critical historical knowledge in teaching children about a nation's loss and trauma.

But there are alternative ways of teaching about nostalgia in schools and these ways do not have to be stuck to notions of restorative nostalgia. In fact, several scholars in various fields of study argue that nostalgia need not be viewed negatively but can be taken as a point of departure for a critical approach to understanding loss and trauma (Boym, 2001; Davis, 1979; Le Goff, 1992). A nostalgic relation to the past from this point of view could represent a refusal to accept dominant representations of the past by activating a reflective engagement with history and memory. Rather than dismissing altogether nostalgic recollections of the past as invariably negative and limiting, then, there is a valuable alternative; that is, there is the potential to derive from nostalgic recollections of the past a more complex understanding of relations between historical reconstructions and their trace through time, including the possibility of irony in rethinking and reflecting on history and our various relationships to it (Pickering & Keightley, 2006).

In Boym's (2001) words, "Re-flection suggests a new flexibility, not the re-establishment of stasis. The focus here is not on recovery of what is perceived to be an absolute truth but on the meditation on history and passage of time" (p. 49). So what is needed is recognition of the multiple ways—positive and negative—in which nostalgia is linked to critically negotiated representations of the past and their relations to collective memories. Recognition of the *politics of nostalgia*—that is, how nostalgia is politicized in political, social, educational, and other settings—can precisely emerge from these multiple conceptions of nostalgia and its links to loss, trauma, and memory (Grainge, 2002). Reclaiming, first of all, nostalgia as not only restorative but also as critical is an important step in engaging with the pedagogical openings that may be created.

Reclaiming Nostalgia

Boym correctly points out that restorative nostalgia and reflective nostalgia "are not absolute types, but rather tendencies, ways of giving shape and meaning to longing" (p. 2001, p. 41). Similarly, Pickering and Keightley (2006) argue that we should be careful not to assume that different types of nostalgia constitute "a fixed scaling of orientations to the past and to historical knowledge" (p. 926). These statements by Boym, and by Pickering and Keightley, suggest two important points for my analysis here: first, there are different versions of nostalgia which are not absolute or fixed types; and second, restorative nostalgic representations are not the only ones to constitute the content of collective memories. These points are central to my argument about how to approach nostalgia and its different manifestations: one-sided readings—for instance, the claim that nostalgia is inherently and utterly restorative—are simplistic and rather limiting versions of the concept of nostalgia. Importantly, what such readings miss is how nostalgic representations of the past may actually express feelings that are not always or not necessarily restorative; rather, these alternative manifestations of nostalgia may involve critical rather than static views of memory and loss.

What the above two points reveal, once again, is how nostalgia is *not* devoid of politics; on the contrary, any expression of nostalgic longing unfolds some form of ideological operation at work. This ideological operation needs to be fully investigated in educational settings so that all forms of nostalgic representations of the past—including those that are traditionally present in school textbooks or school ceremonies and practices—can be critically analyzed. In this way, the politics of nostalgia can be a valuable point of departure in assessing and critiquing any taken-for-granted representations of the past. Assessing and critiquing nostalgic representations of the past is always a difficult task (Pickering & Keightley, 2006), perhaps even more so in the context of education, in which certain hegemonies may prevent critical work (Giroux & McLaren, 1994). However, this struggle may be seen as part of critical pedagogues' ongoing efforts to open up interpretations and practices that have previously been neglected or suppressed. But where does one begin to reclaim nostalgia *politically* and *pedagogically*?

If nostalgia "works as a double-edged sword: [as] an emotional antidote to politics, and thus [. . . as] the best political tool" (Boym, 2001, p. 58), a recognition of the politicization of nostalgia can initially expose the invented nature of some "traditional" memories and narratives. For example, these traditional memories may be evident in public and educational discourses that represent the nation's past as "unpolluted" by the presence of immigrants (Ahmed, 2004) or the nation as "peaceful" and "just" until the "enemy" (another nation) violated peace and justice principles (e.g. see chapters 7, 8, and 9). What these accounts fail to critique, however, is the fixed categorizations they make about the "good-us" and the "evil-them." These categorizations flourish in the discourse of restorative nostalgia (Boym, 2001). A critical analysis of nostalgia would be truly reflective, then, if it questions the certainties that restorative nostalgia claims and dismisses the search for absolute truths and origins in favor of a Foucauldian genealogy (Foucault, 1977b) that historicizes nostalgia and reveals its multiple and heterogeneous backgrounds (Legg, 2005). Reflective nostalgia can act both as a political and a pedagogical tool that uses the disturbance of taken-for-granted categories, made available by a critique of mythologized pasts, to make feelings of loss (characteristic in many forms of nostalgia) politically and pedagogically meaningful. But before delineating further what possible formulations reflective nostalgia takes in educational settings, it is necessary to explain how politics (i.e. power relations) and nostalgia are connected.

Following Foucault, Abu-Lughod (1990) has theorized resistance as a "diagnostic of power." Resistance, according to Abu-Lughod, signals sites of struggle; thus looking at these sites may illuminate the workings of power in social structures and practices. I am making a similar argument here for exploring the oppositional modes of nostalgia. Focusing on the relationship between power and nostalgia raises important questions such as these: How does power work in the construction of hegemonic collective memories and idealized past representations in schools? Whose memories become hegemonic and in what ways? Which narratives that political regimes have struggled to suppress make it to the surface and threaten hegemonic memories? In other words, issues of power and nostalgia cannot be divorced from ways of representing the past in either national memory or historical knowledge, not only in wider society but also in schools. Foucault's (1977a, 1980, 1982/2001) work encourages us to ask what makes some resistances (im)possible, while problematizing the ways that certain educational discourses of nostalgia are sustained through technologies and practices of self and power.

A focus on oppositional forms of nostalgia in educational politics and practice not only offers possibilities for reconceptualizing the domains in which history and memory are constructed and deployed in schools, it can reveal the specific workings of hegemonic forms of nostalgia (see also Berdahl, 1999). In other words, there is no such thing as "mere" or "innocent" (see Herzfeld, 1997) nostalgia, because there are potentially disruptive practices that emanate from the margins to challenge hegemonic forms of nostalgia. A Foucauldian genealogy of the relationship between nostalgia and power, therefore, clarifies the interplay between hegemonic and oppositional nostalgias, with their different interpretations of memory and loss in school curricula and practices. Without its historicization, nostalgia remains stuck to calls for a simple reestablishment of an idealized past (Fritzsche, 2001), focused on the "recovery of what is perceived to be an absolute truth" (Boym, 2001, p. 49). The only way to avoid falling prey to ahistorical forms of nostalgia is to acknowledge the existence of multiple nostalgias—some productive and socially useful and others less so (Tannock, 1995).

Pickering and Keightley (2006) point out that the argument about multiple nostalgias may seem to entail such a broad definition of the concept of nostalgia that is in danger of losing any critical edge. In their view, however, the opposite is the case: "It is not so much its lack of specificity that is the problem as the tendency to see it in a singular and deterministic way. The problem is in not accepting and keeping in play its multiple senses and manifestations" (2006, p. 929). For example, the role of critical pedagogues becomes to interrogate the different manifestations of nostalgia (as they are taking place through social mechanisms, material structures, and school practices), and engage students with the specific ways in which nostalgia and power interact. In this way, it becomes visible how nostalgia cannot be merely thought of as an ideal space and time of perfect belonging that includes some individuals and excludes others, but nostalgia can also formulate a vision of multiperspectival understanding and openness.

Therefore, in reclaiming nostalgia, there are two possible ruptures through which we might begin to sketch its pedagogical traces. First, reflective nostalgia is suspicious of hegemonic narratives of memory and loss, and thus it is important for critical pedagogues to expose the practices of the body, social and individual, that harbor these narratives as well as analyze their consequences. Thus, for example, critical pedagogues need to explore how repression of some traumatic, negative, and difficult memories fit conceptually with representations of an idealized past. Second, the historicization of nostalgia helps also to reveal how "nostalgia-merchants" attempt to speak for, and therefore silence, other stories. To the extent that nostalgia destabilizes "traditional" memory, then its critical and subversive potential helps critical pedagogues keep in view the multiple ways with which nostalgia is politicized. In the final part of this chapter I discuss more explicitly the pedagogical implications of these two possible ruptures.

Toward a Critical Pedagogy of Nostalgia: Counter-memory and Aporetic Mourning

In spite of growing work, particularly in the fields of history education and peace education, that examines how to deal pedagogically with the controversial issues of national memory and historical trauma (e.g. see McGlynn et al., 2009; Simon et al., 2000; Van Sledright, 2008), there is surprisingly little investigation directed at understanding, theoretically and practically, the effects of the politicization of nostalgia in schools. The aim here is to begin theorizing what it means to problematize the politics of nostalgia in schools and, more importantly, to acknowledge how reclaiming nostalgia, as discussed earlier, can formulate a critical pedagogy that provides alternatives to hegemonic readings of nostalgia.

First, I argue that nostalgia—in the same way as "remembrance" (see Simon et al., 2000)—does not simply become *pedagogical* when past representations are situated and engaged in educational settings. Rather, nostalgia *can* potentially become a pedagogical practice when it is not confined to trivialized representations or sentimentalized expressions of regret and yearning for past times. Here I focus on two constructs that are well suited to support the formulation of a critical pedagogy of nostalgia: counter-memory and aporetic mourning. Both constructs are concerned with issues of memory and loss, yet both of them challenge the relentless use of memory and loss through monumentalization of the past. Grounded in critical scholarship, counter-memory (Foucault, 1977b) and aporetic mourning (Butler, 2004; Derrida, 1989, 2001) provide the theoretical lenses through which to begin sketching pedagogical openings that reclaim nostalgia in productive ways.

Counter-memory

Foucault (1977b) developed the concept of "counter-memory" to undermine the hegemonic history/memory pair—that is, the notion that historical narratives are connected with "traditional" memories and narratives focusing on claims about ancient bonds of blood, continuity, and fixed categorizations of "us" and "them." Foucault argued that counter-memories are moments of interrupting the perceived unbroken tradition of heritage from past to present. He called for a historicization of memory that uproots claims about traditional foundations and disrupts history's "pretended continuity" (1977b, pp. 153–154). As Burlein (1999) elaborates on the term, the prefix implies that *counter*-memories take shape within mainstream collective memories, and as pointed out earlier, these are not monolithic but heterogeneous. Counter-memories "are 'counter' not because they are foreign to the mainstream, but because they draw on mainstream currents in order to redirect the flow" (1999, p. 216).

The notion of counter-memories implies that domination is always partial and thus counter-memories denote resistance to mainstream discourses. However, Abu-Lughod (1990) has argued, looking for resistance is often helpful only to the extent that it discloses the role of power relations involved; it is possible, then, that counter-narratives, researched with a focus primarily on identifying resistances, might do very little to challenge the terms of dominant discourse other than to reveal its gaps. In relation to nostalgia, Boym (2001) stresses that counter-memory can provoke further challenge to dominant discourses in that it exists as an embryonic public—I would also add *pedagogical*—sphere that can use oral histories (anecdotes, photographs, films, stories) to challenge a nation's collective memory of a mythologized past. For example, Aboriginal memories challenge the memory of the mythic Australian adventure (Ahmed, 2004). Or, repressed memories of collaboration between the two conflicting communities in Cyprus challenge the hegemonic view that these communities have always been enemies (Zembylas, 2008a, 2009a). Counter-memories provide resources for contesting hegemonic interpretations of nostalgia in the classroom, as well as overly optimistic suggestions that nostalgia itself may exist as a resistant agency.

The use of counter-memories in the classroom directly challenges "traditional" memories and narratives about the past, and students learn how to approach nostalgia critically and openly. For example, some people's conceptualization of nostalgia in a manner unlike most other people, or the fact that these people's conceptualization of nostalgia highlights other and different things than those encouraged by restorative norms of nostalgia, creates a new set of pedagogical openings. One such opening is how to develop practices of critical learning that attend to counter-memories. As Gross (1990) has emphasized, "It takes effort, determination and self-initiation to search out and hold onto counter-memories at a time when most others are content with the memories that are already in circulation" (p. 134). What this signals is the pedagogical struggle to work through one's traditional narratives of nostalgia in schools, a working through that has to take into account the particularities of the space and time of one's engagement and, specifically, the politics of nostalgia and how it is manifested in this particular space and time context.

The idea of counter-memories as resources of a critical pedagogy of nostalgia brings into question in the classroom who is engaging in nostalgia, what is being desired in feeling nostalgia for the past, and to what degree does the school—as a major mechanism of the nation-state—work to promote (without ever being entirely successful) monopolized interpretations of memory? These questions help problematize how nostalgia may operate ideologically or carry convenient ideological meanings through schooling. Counter-memories may constitute, then, a means for critical transformative learning that impels students and teachers to confront the multiple meanings of nostalgia; through analysis of counter-memories students can understand first-hand that nostalgia is neither an absolute nor a singularly universal phenomenon. Furthermore, enriching classroom work with counter-memories provides a venue in which to examine the consequences of traumatic memories and nostalgic representations of the past.

A specific case that can be analyzed in the classroom, as an example of examining the consequences of traumatic memories, is the nostalgia of second-generation exiles and refugees (Hirsch & Spitzer, 2003), such as the postmemory of the children of those who survived historical trauma like the Holocaust (Hirsch, 1997). "Postmemory describes the relationship of the second generation to powerful, often traumatic experiences that preceded their birth but were nevertheless transmitted to them so deeply as to seem to constitute memories in their own right" (Hirsch, 2008, p. 103). Children in the classroom may have postmemories themselves (e.g. see chapters 3, 4, 9), and thus an analysis of their own nostalgia for places never visited (and which may never have existed) can move forward a critical yet undoubtedly risk-laden learning. In other words, nostalgia—as mediated through postmemories—can be engaged in the classroom to enact a possibility of transformative breaking with its restorative meanings. The pedagogical goal, again, is not to reject restorative interpretations but to problematize them and to show their consequences in understanding the past and its relation to the present.

Aporetic Mourning

"Reflective nostalgia," writes Boym, "is a form of deep mourning that performs a labor of grief both through pondering pain and through play that points to the future" (2001, p. 55). Nostalgia and mourning, in this view, are theoretically and practically linked. While nostalgia denotes a positive attachment to an ideal past, mourning denotes the struggle to deal effectively with a loss in the past. Both conditions represent difficult engagements with the past, but nostalgia highlights a time and place before or beyond loss and mourning (Legg, 2005).

Butler (2004) investigates loss and mourning as a social and political condition rather than as a psychological state. Genocide, slavery, war, and colonization are deep mourning events that should constitute points of departure for reflecting on loss. Although no nostalgic memories to an idealized past before these events can retrieve loss, what binds us together as humans, argues Butler, is precisely the experience of mourning, that is, the realization that we are all exposed and vulnerable, and are all engaged with bereavement. The denial of such vulnerability unleashes violence against others, whereas its acknowledgment creates openings for an ethical encounter with others. Therefore, it is important to ask "about the conditions under which a grievable life is established and maintained, and through what logic of exclusion, what practice of effacement and denominalization" (Butler, 2004, p. 39).

Furthermore, mourning remains essentially *aporetic*, as Derrida (1989, 2001) would have it—that is, as an impossible-to-resolve contradiction—because all effort to incorporate, in anyone's framework of understanding, the singular and unknowable differences embodied by "the other" is doomed to fail. No memory or mourning can retrieve what was lost. It is from this perspective that, Derrida argues, true mourning is impossible; if it succeeds, the otherness of the other is not respected. Perhaps to *truly* mourn, then, we must fail to mourn, being faithful to the indigestibility of the other. The notion of aporetic mourning suggests that social transformation can take place within a context in which sufferers endure pain but are ethically generous in wanting to build an inclusive society (Zembylas, 2009c). Without refusing to acknowledge the extent of past injustice, subsequent responsibilities are not locked into static identities of *oppressor* and *victim, repentant* and *forgiver*. This ethics of otherness constitutes an engagement with history that aims to interrupt all totalities (including political ones) through one's infinite ethical responsibility to the other. Such an ethical responsibility is not tied to restorative notions of nostalgia as the paradigm of understanding one's self and others but poses instead a reflective nostalgia that provides space for solidarity with others.

Butler's emphasis on common vulnerability joined with Derrida's notion of impossible or aporetic mourning constitutes the point of departure for a renewed politics of relationality and provides an important link between nostalgia and mourning.

The recognition of our vulnerability to loss opens up the potential for recognition of *all* humanity as vulnerable. In particular, the link between nostalgia and mourning helps us reconsider one's relation to the other as a source of transformation. According to Butler (2004), to mourn, is to make mourning a resource for politics grounded in a consideration of the vulnerability of others. What emerges through the irrecoverable is, paradoxically, the condition of a new political agency (Legg, 2005). Nostalgia, then, is a potential resource for political agency that may inspire affective solidarity with others who are also vulnerable and experience loss. While we may want to mourn the loss of a time and space that can never return, it does not mean what we should become "imprisoned" in an idealized past and the vilification of those perceived to be responsible for our loss.

Employing the notion of aporetic mourning in the classroom raises a number of important questions that can be explored with students. For example we might ask the following: When and from what locations and positions do "we" (i.e. teachers and students; the communities to which we belong) decide what counts as grievable? How do we negotiate these terms? In what ways are we to handle the dilemma of what counts as a loss and what does not, and how can common vulnerability be a catalyst for affective solidarity with others? (e.g. see chapter 9). These questions help to interrogate how mourning and nostalgia are entangled in ways that perpetuate or prevent dichotomies between grievable and ungrievable lives. Aporetic mourning, as described above, may provide pedagogical openings that recognize loss as irreconcilable yet without remaining stuck in restorative manifestations of nostalgia. The pedagogical struggle that utilizes the notion of aporetic mourning while promoting reflective nostalgia has two formidable adversaries that need to be "fought": national sentimentality and voyeurism. Navigating through the dangers that these two conditions pose is an important component of pedagogical efforts to use aporetic mourning as a resource of reflective nostalgia.

For one thing, learning/teaching about mourning and nostalgia, and/or how to mourn loss in the classroom, has the risk of leading to *national sentimentality* (Berlant, 2000). National sentimentality, according to Berlant, is a liberal rhetoric that makes it likely that mourning will translate into kitsch communitarianism grounded on the notion that the burden of others' loss can indeed be felt (e.g. in the classroom) through channels of affective identification, compassion, and empathy. As Berlant rightly warns us, not only is this alignment far from implying any identification with someone else (or someone else's loss), but also it may lead to mourning's being fetishized, which thereby condenses mourning in self-repetition and habituated banality (Zembylas, 2009c). Enriching classroom work with activities that promote aporetic mourning (e.g. organizing common mourning events with students coming from the "other" community) entails risks, yet it also provides a venue to minimize this sort of sentimentality, if it is organized in critical ways (Zembylas, 2013b).

Furthermore, a school curriculum that does not have a critical and multiperspectival grasp of loss can easily weaken the ethical force of mourning and nostalgia by treating them voyeuristically (Britzman, 2000). Britzman suggests that, in our desire to yearn for the past and therefore be loyal to the dead, there is the danger of making our own selves the focus of inquiry, thus leading to both voyeurism and the inability to listen and respond critically. Thus, the pedagogical goal of promoting aporetic mourning emphasizes how students must learn to encounter "the utter singularity of loss," and still "find a way to resume the obligations of learning to live, to risk new attachments in the world, and to demand something of the living" (2000, p. 33). Idealization or fetishization of mourning will inhibit the work of critical learning and instead make likely the incorporation of nostalgia narratives into predetermined categorizations. In contrast, reclaiming nostalgia through the pedagogical use of aporetic mourning expands the space of critical learning in which memory and mourning might be contested and reconstructed.

Rethinking Nostalgia in Education

In this chapter I have considered the discourse of nostalgia and its pedagogical implications. Central to my thinking is that nostalgia has multiple meanings, some of which promote nationalist agendas in both the wider society and schools. One way to begin the process of reclaiming nostalgia in schools is to shift the discourse of nostalgia from restorative nostalgia to reflective nostalgia. This idea may be translated to pedagogy as a consideration of how counter-memory and aporetic mourning intersect with reflective nostalgia and create pedagogical openings for alternative understandings of memory, loss, and the past.

Rethinking nostalgia in educational politics and practice may involve redesigning the pedagogical strategies of engaging students in representations of the past so that the dialectic between memory and history is taken into consideration. This task does not simply mean to overcome the opposition between history and memory, but also to refuse remaining stuck in monological interpretations of nostalgia. The pedagogical aim of problematizing nostalgia in the classroom is essentially to create spaces that enable new interpretations of nostalgia—interpretations that "break through routine cultural codes to express counter discourse that assaults and even perhaps undermines the taken-for-granted meanings of things as they are" (Das & Kleinman, 2001, p. 21). An important pedagogical condition, therefore, is that learning how to analyze and critique nostalgia has to take place in ways that neither undermine nor fetishize one's loss.

A critical pedagogy of nostalgia is an invaluable tool that encourages investigations into how schools of nation-states construct the past, often according to the imperatives of nationalism, fetishism, and voyeurism. Reclaiming the meaning of nostalgia in education, both theoretically and practically, enables students and teachers to conceive the relationship between past and present "as fragile and corruptible, inherently dependent on how the resources of the past are made available" (Pickering & Keightley, 2006, p. 938). Understanding how resources of the past are made available, students and teachers become able to trace the circulation of certain narratives, how they are used for political and other purposes, and what consequences they have in conceptualizations of the present and the past. A critical pedagogy of nostalgia provides an important point of departure from which to distinguish between productive uses of the past and those that are regressive. This point of departure can launch a radical critique of hegemonic educational discourses about loss, trauma, and memory, especially in conflicted societies; it also offers the critical ability to teachers and students to be keenly aware of the multiple efforts by various political forces to repackage an idealized past in a way that constantly promotes its omnipresence. However, students and teachers who, together, learn to recognize and challenge these efforts will contest narratives of nostalgia that aim to assimilate the present into the signs of the past.

13 EPILOGUE
AN AGONISTICS FOR HEALING

Sometimes I think the purpose of life is to reconcile us to its eventual loss by wearing us down, by proving, however long it takes, that life isn't all it's cracked up to be.

—JULIAN BARNES, *The Sense of an Ending*

You must go on, I can't go on, I'll go on.

—SAMUEL BECKETT, *The Unnamable*

The emotions of traumatic conflict are complex phenomena. As shown throughout this book, the emotional complexities of traumatic conflict are neither easily addressed nor always successfully tackled in education. Besides, as Kaplan (2005) has emphasized, trauma can never be "healed" in the sense of returning to how things were before a traumatic event took place, or before one witnessed such an event; but the impact of trauma can be worked through, individually and collectively. And here is exactly where the ideas of critical pedagogies in posttraumatic contexts, critical peace education, and critical emotional praxis—and their various manifestations documented or suggested in this book—have been put forward in our agonistics to seek pedagogical openings for individual and social transformation and healing.

This book has addressed a number of challenging issues: the complex emotional geographies of racism and nationalism in schools; the consequences of emotions of traumatic conflict in negotiating coexistence in educational settings in which children from conflicting communities come together; and critical responses to navigate through the emotional tensions and dilemmas identified. All in all, in this book I have argued that a peace education effort grounded in pedagogies of critical emotional praxis *can* constitute—under some circumstances—a productive form of engagement with the emotions of traumatic conflict in schools. This productive engagement is developed along two dimensions: First, pedagogical practices inspired by critical emotional praxis create spaces for destabilizing certain emotional boundaries and norms. Second, these spaces can help reframe trauma and inspire healing and reconciliation in constructive ways, that is, in ways that do not marginalize, ostracize, or exclude unpleasant emotions (e.g. fear, resentment, anger), but also render visible the implications of appropriating trauma, healing, or reconciliation for social and political purposes. A main argument in this book, then, has been that the impact of traumatic conflict can be usefully "translated" across pedagogical forms of critical emotional inquiry to encourage some sort of "healing." Yet, healing is not the end-point of this pedagogical "intervention," but rather an endless agonistics. The conjunction of emotion, praxis, and criticality within a viable theoretical and practical approach offers pedagogical opportunities for creating those spaces that might eventually transform hegemonic perceptions about "self" and the "other" and the normative values that accompany these categorizations.

A major challenge, though, that makes the work of pedagogues difficult in conflicted societies, as shown especially through the empirical evidence provided in this book, is the extent to which it is possible to nurture spaces of healing and reconciliation in schools, particularly in light of a conflicting emotional ethos that may become dominant in the society at large (Bar-Tal, 2004; Bar-Tal, Halperin, & de Rivera, 2007). On the one hand, these pedagogical spaces offer opportunities for the acknowledgment of empathy, compassion, common suffering, and vulnerability in schools; on the other hand, it has to be acknowledged that schools and education alone cannot do much for healing and reconciliation unless there are significant structural changes in the emotional orientation of the society at large (Bar-Tal & Bennink, 2004). Nevertheless, what pedagogues *can* do is to highlight the crucial linkages among emotion, trauma, healing, and reconciliation—through pedagogical interventions such as those described in several chapters of this book—that involve students in active learning, trauma healing, meaningful social interaction between adversary groups, intercommunity cooperation, critical peace education, and critical emotional praxis.

The ethical and political importance of critical emotional praxis, in particular, as an affective event and a pedagogical framework in conflicted societies is the degree to which, by cultivating a commitment to deal critically with emotions of trauma, it facilitates the emergence of pedagogical spaces of healing and reconciliation. The call for critical emotional praxis is affirmative and need not result in narcissistic, voyeuristic, or melancholic rhetoric; rather, the trauma can be worked through by reconfiguring "witnessing" in affective, pedagogical, and critical terms. My argument seeks to imagine openings, even relatively "small" ones, in enacting healing and reconciliatory forms of pedagogies and renewed affective relations grounded in compassion, solidarity, and social justice. Trauma and suffering educate emotion and often inculcate *violent* affective relations with one's self, others, and the world. Families, workplaces, and schools instill particular pedagogies of emotion. They are social and political mechanisms for educating emotion in public and school arenas; hence, we are "schooled" to express, talk about, and use emotion in certain ways that strengthen and perpetuate inclusion/exclusion and us/them binaries. A major assumption made here is that emotion both enables and disables transformation—of one's self, others, and the world. This is precisely why I argue, in agreement with Worsham (2001), that a fundamental political and pedagogical task for the work of decolonizing violent affective relations is essentially the *reeducation* of emotions in schools.

However, there are dangers associated with ambitions to reeducate the minds and hearts of students. For one thing, there is the ever-present peril of replacing one "tyranny" with another; that is, the reeducation of emotions might not always be in the students' best interest. The most we (educators) can do is open spaces of possibility for engaging students in critical dialogue, hoping that they will "unlearn" emotional violence, "undo" oppressive practices, and indeed reimagine their affective relations with themselves, others, and the world. Importantly, the agonistics for social transformation might involve some measure of *letting go,* not of our work and striving but of our emotional attachments to certain ideologies.

What constitutes this "letting go," and under what circumstances, is hugely complex, and is in part related to whether "critical hope" (Freire, 1994), rather than despair, offers a balance between a pedagogy that places emphasis on "mindful witnessing" (Eppert, 2009) and the remaking of the self, on the one hand, and the realization that we (teachers, students, etc.) are not really *in control*, on the other. Critical hope is what enables teachers and students to see patterns in their emotional, historical, and material lives, to realize how these patterns are made and what their consequences are for maintaining the status quo, and to motivate teachers and students to position themselves critically not only through reflection but also praxis (Zembylas, 2014b). In other words, critical hope entails a willingness to speak with and enact the "language of possibility" in the struggle for a transformed "lifeworld" that rises above injustice, oppression, and trauma. According to Boler (2004b), in contrast to naïve hope, critical hope recognizes the tensions that any attempt to re-educate the emotions entails in-depth critical inquiry about such beliefs along with an "emotional willingness to engage in the difficult work of possibly allowing one's worldviews to be shattered" (p. 128).

This "difficult" or "discomforting" work begins from mindful witnessing of one's own self and its remaking. This work, I further suggest, constitutes a renewed pedagogical relation with one's self and consequently with others and the world. The undoing of the self in/through witnessing trauma in education involves a radical disruption of the wars within and the dualistic identity schemes (e.g., the us-and-them binary). The act of mindful witnessing or bearing witness to trauma in the context of education facilitates this remaking of the self, if a number of emotional practices are integrated into our pedagogies, including the capacity to tolerate uncertainty and ambivalence and the realization that the self is fundamentally relational—"vulnerable enough to be undone by violence and yet resilient enough to be reconstructed with the help of others" (Brison, 1999, p. 40). But still, there is no assurance that our enactments of critical emotional praxis and critical peace education in conflicted settings will succeed, because institutional structures and practices might be oppositional.

This creates a paradoxical situation. As educators we may want to open and invite dialogue, support student inquiries into their own journeys, and let them find their own ways in the world, without imposing our own agendas on them. At the same time the zone of contact between teachers and students is heavily policed by social and political institutions and practices. So while we may offer pedagogies of emotion that undermine violence (in some respects), our efforts are essentially "re-territorialized"—to use Deleuze and Guattari's (1987) term—to abide the workings of the social norms. The issue concerning the tensions embedded in the hope that critical emotional praxis might make a difference is now rephrased into the following question: In what ways can (public and school) pedagogies of emotion that undermine (various forms of) violence contribute to decolonizing the institutional and material structures of subordination?

This question cannot be fully answered here, I am afraid; however, I want to push things a bit further. I have consistently argued throughout several chapters that critical emotional praxis—in its different manifestations and enactments—might make a difference in dealing with the tensions of witnessing trauma in education. However, what has not been adequately emphasized is how critical emotional praxis as a pedagogy cannot adequately resolve this tension and might even remystify pedagogies of emotion so that they extend dominant regimes of truth. A similar limitation occurs in the way that critical pedagogy and social justice scholarship understand the nature of resistance and empowerment (see, e.g., Pinar et al., 2002). In spite of its best intentions and the euphoria of some of its claims, a pedagogy of critical emotional praxis may operate ultimately as a strategy of condescension (see chapter 2).

The interesting issue, then, is not whether critical pedagogies of emotion might make a difference in inspiring some sort of healing and reconciliation; it is all too well known that even radical trajectories often become re-territorialized. Instead, educators and students must explore and pursue their own (singular) ethical responses to the contextual demands of each challenge. Following Rose (1999), I argue therefore that the role of critical pedagogies of emotion (such as critical emotional praxis) is to help maximize the capacity of educators and students (both individually and collectively) to reconfigure "the practices that govern them in the name of their nature, their freedom, and their identity . . . revealing the lies, falsehoods, deceptions, and self-deceptions which are inherent within these attempts to govern us for our own good" (p. 282). By not engaging in a dualistic thinking (e.g., "we-the-good" and "they-the-evil") that sets up hierarchies, oppression, inequality, and exclusion—as shown through some students' and teachers' discourses and practices in this book—a pedagogy of critical emotional praxis, for example, can only *hope* that it works to instigate different lines of flight, even if the small openings it creates have (momentarily) limited effect. But the difference now is that this "hope" is a critical hope, not a naïve hope, because it is grounded in the mobilization of those sensibilities toward new social imaginaries that are grounded in social praxis and solidarity. But let's go back for a moment to the macro-level context to remind ourselves how dualistic thinking is so strongly embedded in societal structures and what role education can play to "heal" this "scar" in our minds and our hearts.

Toward an Agonistic Framework of Healing and Reconciliation Pedagogies

Mouffe (2005) explains that when distinctions such as "we-the-good" and "they-the-evil" acquire hegemonic status in society on the basis of "fixed" meanings (e.g. fixed ethnic identities), then various sorts of exclusions come about. What is particularly problematic is that these us-and-them contradistinctions are not based on *political* arguments but on social, cultural, and other traits that are perceived as immutable. By "political" Mouffe refers to the dimension of antagonism that is constitutive of human societies, while by "politics" she means the practices and institutions through which an order is created. Mouffe's argument is that we must develop *agonistic* relations, that is, relations that do not lump others into categories "friends" and "enemies" on the basis of moralistic arguments or traits perceived as immutable (e.g. good/evil); rather, agonistic relations recognize opponents as legitimate adversaries on the basis of political terms and arguments. *Agonistic democracy*, in particular, emphasizes that "modern democracy's specificity lies in the recognition and legitimation of conflict and the refusal to suppress it by imposing an authoritarian order" (Mouffe, 1999, p. 756). Therefore, agonistic democracy for Mouffe is not something fixed, but it is a continually evolving political process in which conflict/dissensus and harmony/consensus are not permanent states but contingent political practices.

To return to a tension raised earlier concerning the emotional complexities of healing and reconciliation processes in schools while there are still unresolved personal or collective traumas (e.g. chapters 3, 6), an agonistic account asserts that only a critical perspective—e.g. of how a "we" and "they" comes to appear; who are included (friends), who are excluded (enemies) and why—would offer a political language (not grounded in fixed identities) for understanding conflict and peace (Mouffe, 2005). An agonistic account is important "to allow ambiguity to unsettle those oppositional terms by which we make sense of the world [. . .] and to call into question the terms of friend and enemy" (Schaap, 2004, p. 538). For example, when reconciliation is construed merely in terms of one side's collective memory (vs the other side's collective memory) or universal moral categories (we-the-good vs they-the-evil), the freedom of citizens to contest the terms of community in new terms is already overdetermined by the ethnic identities that are available; thus, the formation of political associations on the basis of compassion, humanity, and solidarity is undermined. Consequently, this effort fails to establish grounds for why members of a divided society might want to seek any terms of social and political cooperation in the first place (Schaap, 2006).

In other words, an agonistic framework of healing and reconciliation pedagogies—in the public arena, in schools, in the workplace—draws attention to the politics of healing and reconciliation in terms of the fragility and contingency of the processes and demands involved. What is distinctive about this agonistic account is not that it seeks to resolve traumatic conflict and bring about healing on the basis of competing identities, although the role of identities is clearly not undermined. Rather, it aims to mediate the conflict in such a way that the "other" is not perceived as an ethnic other-enemy to be destroyed (Schaap, 2006). Importantly, this agonistic account provides the framework on which to build an understanding of the community as a contingent achievement of political action; to do so, however, there seem to be two conditions that need to be present.

First, there needs to be a political account of plural belongings as having a profound importance in political life; that is, ethnic (or religious or other) affiliation is recognized as only one of those belongings, perhaps not always the most important one (see also Bekerman & Zembylas, 2012). As Fraser (1997) reminds us "people participate in more than one public, and . . . the membership of different publics may overlap" (p. 84). In fact, it is these multiple and overlapping belongings (e.g. on the basis of shared social, political, or work interests) that increase possibilities to reach common ground in struggles for healing and reconciliation. In this way, the political communities that are formulated are able to form all sorts of bonds, unities, and solidarities. It is important to emphasize that commonalities, however, are not presupposed in terms of a regulative moral consensus; rather, they are the contingent outcomes of political interactions that enable the development of healing and reconciliatory discourses and practices necessary for unity in new terms, with due recognition of traumatic conflict and its consequences. When reconciliation is construed in terms of a thin moral consensus (e.g. based on human rights only), asserts Humphrey (2000), it tends to replicate the divisions of the past—e.g. what counts as a human right and its violation by one side is contested by the other side (see chapter 11).

Second, an agonistic account is transformative insofar as it changes the distinction between "friend" and "enemy" (on the basis of an ethnic us-and-them monological divide) into a political struggle. In other words, it offers a political language in understanding healing and reconciliation as political undertakings—not only as social or emotional processes taking place in various corners of society. To the extent that they are political, healing and reconciliation are concerned "with the constitution of a plural "we" in terms of which former enemies might re-cognize past violence and ongoing conflict in the present" (Schaap, 2006, p. 271). Undoubtedly, the encounter with the other, as Schaap asserts, is always conditioned by the interpretive framework (or identity) we bring to it; however, this does not imply that certain ethnic or other identities should become hegemonic and reified. When conceived in these terms, healing and reconciliation remain unsettling processes, aware of their fragility, yet they constitute an agonistic endeavor that seeks a radical break with the social, political, and educational order of the past. Now that this macro-level context has been addressed to some degree, I will return—one last time—to the theorization of critical emotional praxis and critical peace education that was begun in chapter 2.

Critical Emotional Praxis and Critical Peace Education in Conflicted Societies

The main thesis of this book has emphasized that an exploration of "troubled knowledge" (Jansen, 2009) in conflicted societies should be integrated into critical pedagogy in ways that take into account the complexity of "difficult knowledge" (Britzman, 1998, 2000; Pitt & Britzman, 2003; Simon, 2011a, 2011b). In the remaining part of this Epilogue, I summarize a few ideas that offer the possibility to promote integration of critical emotional praxis and critical peace education, creating pedagogical spaces for healing and reconciliation. As it has been argued, the "traditional" means of enhancing criticality in students, stimulating argument-based, rationalist capacities, may unwittingly contribute to sustaining the dominant affective, social, and political regime (Amsler, 2011; Yoon, 2005;

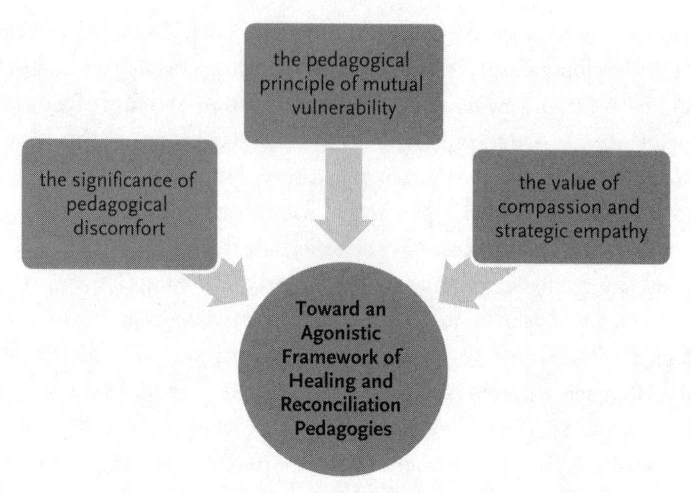

FIGURE 13.1 Three aspects of an "agonistic framework of healing and reconciliation pedagogies."

Worsham, 2001). However, if our analysis acknowledges the affective dimensions of critical pedagogy in new ways and takes into account the particularities of conflict and postconflict situations, it is possible to enhance pedagogical efforts to disrupt dominant affective investments and emotion-informed ideologies that underlie students' and teachers' troubled knowledge. To consider this issue more concretely, I discuss here three aspects of an agonistic framework of healing and reconciliation pedagogies—as they have emerged in various chapters—and how these aspects may inform critical emotional praxis and critical peace education in addressing troubled knowledge and its emotional complexities. These aspects are (1) the significance of pedagogic discomfort; (2) the pedagogical principle of mutual vulnerability; and (3) the value of compassion and strategic empathy (see Figure 13.1). Each of these aspects—along with its strengths and limitations—is discussed in terms of how it helps navigate troubled knowledge in ways that are sensitive and productive and that promote the prospects of healing and reconciliation.

The Significance of Pedagogic Discomfort

Research shows that challenging students and teachers beyond their "comfort zones" and pushing them to deconstruct the ways in which they have learned to see, feel, and act constitute a valuable pedagogic approach in social justice, citizenship, and anti-racist education (e.g. see Boler, 1999, 2004a; Boler & Zembylas, 2003; Zembylas & McGlynn, 2012; Zembylas, Charalambous, & Charalambous, 2012). In fact, it has been argued that if a major purpose of teaching is to unsettle taken-for-granted views and emotions, then a "pedagogy of discomfort" is not only unavoidable but may also be necessary (Berlak, 2004). "A pedagogy of discomfort begins," explains Boler, "by inviting educators and students to engage in critical inquiry regarding values and cherished beliefs, and to examine constructed self-images in relation to how one has learned to perceive others" (1999, pp. 176–177). For example, individuals who belong to the hegemonic culture experience discomfort when having to confront their privileges in relation to educational and social inequities (see e.g., Leibowitz et al., 2010). Leibowitz and her colleagues, who have studied and written in the context of post-apartheid South Africa, demonstrate how a pedagogy of discomfort is valuable in uncovering and questioning the deeply embedded emotional dimensions that shape some individual and group privileges (e.g. those of white students) through daily habits and routines. By closely problematizing these emotional habits and routines and their attachments to whiteness and structural injustices, it is shown that teachers and students in a posttraumatic context can begin to identify the invisible ways in which they comply with dominant ideologies.

Additionally, in a recent study Zembylas and McGlynn (2012) have discussed the emotional tensions, ethical dilemmas, and transformative possibilities of using pedagogy of discomfort in the context of Belfast, Northern Ireland. It is suggested that discomforting pedagogies require considerable vulnerability and thus the ethical responsibility of the teacher becomes a complex issue. Similarly, Bauer (2001) has considered the institutional restrictions of using critical pedagogies in the classroom and suggested that there is less and less room there to negotiate the ethics or politics proposed by critical pedagogies. These observations about the ethical, political, and institutional restrictions reiterate once again the complexity of handling difficult emotional knowledge in posttraumatic societies and why it is not always ethical or productive to address difficult knowledge on the basis of a predetermined collectivity that reiterates "we" and "they" distinctions.

When examined through the lens of a conflict and post-conflict setting, then, it becomes clearer how and why certain features of pedagogic discomfort concern students and teachers beyond divisions of the world into rival camps (e.g. "oppressors" and "victims"). Students and teachers come into the classroom carrying their troubled knowledge about "conquest and humiliation, struggle and survival, suffering and resilience, poverty and recovery, black and white" (Jansen, 2009, p. 361). Unsettling this troubled knowledge demands emotional effort, careful listening to each other's traumatic experiences, and explicit discussion of the potential and the harm that troubled knowledge stimulates. The value of pedagogic discomfort in conflicted societies cannot be overstated. This process should not be assumed to be always already transformative, and beyond question. In other words, there are no guarantees for change in the social and political status quo; a pedagogy of discomfort, especially in light of the tensions identified in this book (e.g. see chapter 6), demands time and realistic decisions about what can and what cannot be achieved. Also, concerns about the ethical implications of pedagogic discomfort must be foremost on the agenda. That involves asking these questions: Is pedagogic discomfort concerning troubled knowledge always appropriate and effective? How far can critical peace education and critical emotional praxis engage students' discomfort without violating some ethical sensibilities? Needless to say, not all students will respond in the same way or benefit from pedagogic discomfort in the same manner; some may adopt some sort of change, others may resist, and still others may experience distress (Kumashiro, 2002). Therefore, the concern here is not simply about overcoming resistance or motivating students who express apathy or hostility; "it is, rather, a pedagogical commitment to locate, interrogate, and engage troubled knowledge ... in ways that permit disruption of received authority" (Jansen, 2009, p. 267).

The Pedagogical Principle of Mutual Vulnerability

The second aspect that enriches the task of critical peace education and critical emotional praxis in conflicted societies concerns the pedagogical principle of "mutual vulnerability" (e.g. see Keet, Zinn, & Porteus, 2009; Zembylas, 2009a). The notion of mutual vulnerability is grounded in the idea that there is interdependence between human beings and that the recognition of all people as "vulnerable" has important pedagogical consequences concerning the possibility of assuming critical responsibility toward one's own life and the lives of others in a community. The argument that is developed here is grounded theoretically in the work of Butler (2004), in particular her essay "Violence, Mourning, Politics" (see also chapters 11 and 12).

Butler (2004) presents a number of examples to show that "each of us is constituted politically in part by virtue of the social vulnerability of our bodies. . . . Loss and vulnerability seem to follow from our being socially constituted bodies, attached to others, at risk of losing those attachments, exposed to others, at risk of violence by virtue of that exposure" (p. 20). This is evident, for instance, in the experience of losing someone to whom one is attached; thus each of us is mutually obliged to others because of this common vulnerability. The denial of such vulnerability unleashes violence against others, whereas its acknowledgment creates openings for an ethical encounter with others. Consequently, "we might critically evaluate and oppose," Butler emphasizes, "the conditions under which certain human lives are more vulnerable than others, and thus certain human lives are more grievable than others" (p. 30). Once we consider how hegemonic power relations determine "who will be a grievable human" and what "acts are permissible for public grieving" (p. 37), then we may begin to realize how a prohibition of grieving others' lives extends the aims of violence and conflict.

The notion of vulnerability has important pedagogical consequences because the mutual experience of loss and mourning reveals the possibility of an alternative moral responsibility and sense of community (Vlieghe, 2010). Butler's theorization of common vulnerability constitutes the point of departure for a renewed pedagogical politics of recognition in posttraumatic contexts—a politics that is not founded in a rationalist or individualistic morality but in the experience of vulnerability as such (Zembylas, 2009c). The notion of mutual vulnerability, then, enriches critical peace education because it disrupts normative frames of community on the basis of rationality and self-advancement and puts forward the notion of community on the basis of loss. This idea does not imply, however, an equalization of vulnerability, but the recognition that there are different forms of vulnerabilities in posttraumatic contexts.

Furthermore, "mutual vulnerability" provides "a new grammar" for critical emotional praxis in conflicted societies because the experiences of "the traumatized and the distressed and the micro-politics of peoples' struggles for survival become its central pre-occupation" (Keet et al., 2009, p. 116). As Keet and his colleagues point out, writing in the context of post-apartheid South Africa, the notion of mutual vulnerability enhances the emancipatory interests of education "because the frames of its interlocutor are made vulnerable and therefore hospitable to moderation" (p. 116.). In this sense, there is more exchange of troubled knowledge between different sets of meaning-making frames; thus, in pedagogic terms, the notion of mutual vulnerability can be the starting point for acknowledging the burden of troubled knowledge carried more or less by all participants in posttraumatic settings.

The Value of Compassion and Strategic Empathy

Finally, the third aspect for consideration here concerns the value of compassion and strategic empathy for critical peace education and critical emotional praxis in conflicted societies (e.g. Zembylas, 2012a, 2013b). In light of the empirical data provided in many chapters, it is evident that troubled knowledge provokes strong emotional reactions in classrooms of conflicted societies—reactions that could be quite discomforting for teachers and students alike. Teachers have to find ways to handle constructively these reactions as well as the discourses that put too much focus on one's own traumatic experiences and ignore the other's sufferings. A constructive relationship with difficult knowledge, suggest Bonnell and Simon (2007), is based on the process of confronting and dismantling any assumptions taken for granted upon encountering such unfamiliar knowledge. Importantly, then, teachers need to establish trust in the classroom, develop strong relationships and enacting compassionate understanding in every possible manner. Critical peace education and critical emotional praxis in conflicted societies require the strategic use of those pedagogical resources to enable the formation of new affective alliances among members of traumatized communities.

As noted earlier, attentiveness to mutual vulnerability is an important component of critical pedagogies and critical emotional praxis in conflicted societies. Students are enabled to establish and maintain this attentiveness, when they begin to question and challenge arguments based on binaries like us/them, perpetrators/victims, friends/enemies, and good/evil, a stereotyping of groups considered being *more* or *less* grievable (Butler, 2004). Jansen (2009) highlights two pedagogical tactics that I find particularly useful in teaching students how to learn compassion by challenging these binaries: first, the acknowledgment of brokenness by all sides—that is, the idea that humans are prone to failure and incompleteness and as such we constantly seek a higher order of living that cannot be accomplished without being in communion with others. Second, a pedagogical reciprocity is also required; that is, everyone carrying the burden of troubled knowledge has to move toward every other. As Jansen puts it in the context of post-apartheid South Africa: "the white person has to move across the allegorical bridge toward the black person; the black person has to move in the direction of the white person. Critical theory demands the former; a postconflict pedagogy requires both" (2009, p. 268).

To promote the prospects of compassion in classrooms of conflicted societies, I also argue that one of those pedagogical resources that will be needed is strategic empathy. Strategic empathy is essentially the use of empathetic emotions in both critical and strategic ways (Lindquist, 2004); that is, it refers to the willingness of the critical pedagogue to make herself strategically skeptical (working sometimes against her own emotions) in order to empathize with the troubled knowledge students carry with them, even when this troubled knowledge is disturbing to other students or to the teacher. The use of strategic empathy can function as a valuable pedagogical tool that opens up affective spaces that might eventually disrupt the emotional roots of troubled knowledge—an admittedly long and difficult task (Zembylas, 2012a). Undermining the emotional roots of troubled knowledge through strategic empathy ultimately aims at helping students integrate their troubled views into compassionate and socially just perspectives.

Compassion is further cultivated if students begin to understand the conditions (structural inequalities, poverty, globalization, for example) that give rise to troubled knowledge and suffering and acknowledge some sort of human connection (e.g. mutual vulnerability) between themselves and others (see chapter 11). But mere understanding is clearly not enough; students will become more susceptible to affective transformation, when they enact compassionate action early on in their lives, starting with simple things, such as learning to be more patient and tolerant with peers who do not grasp a "difficult" concept in language or mathematics. As they grow up, children are offered opportunities to enact more complex manifestations of compassion that include action to alleviate the suffering of people who experience difficult times, no matter which community they come from. What needs to follow the acknowledgment of mutual vulnerability is taking action that dismisses essentialized categories of "victims" and "oppressors" and highlights instead the impact of solidarity on reducing everyday inequalities.

Final Thoughts

In this Epilogue I have reiterated the argument about the importance of enriching critical emotional praxis and critical peace education in conflicted societies with considerations about troubled knowledge and its consequences. This argument entails making pedagogical spaces for understanding troubled knowledge in more nuanced terms, a process enabled by "a pedagogy of strategic performance, in which teachers work to tactically position themselves as conduits of students' affective responses" (Lindquist, 2004, p. 189). What this means for the practice of critical emotional praxis and critical peace education more generally is that pedagogies of emotions are inevitably implicated in the way that troubled knowledge operates both as a provocation of critical pedagogy *and* as a way of structuring affect in a conflicted situation. Without a fundamental revision of our thinking about troubled knowledge and its consequences, in spite of our best intentions the radical potential of critical emotional praxis and critical peace education to reconstitute the emotional connections of traumatized students and teachers may be compromised (see Worsham, 2001). This task requires a constant reconsideration of new pedagogical resources to enhance the potential of critical emotional praxis and critical peace education such as some of the ideas discussed in various chapters; undoubtedly, there are many more ideas that can contribute toward this effort.

At the same time, the limits and restrictions of using critical emotional praxis and critical peace education in conflicted societies need to be kept in mind. There are important unanswered questions in the effort to make the emotional complexities of troubled knowledge explicit and constructive: How can critical pedagogues and peace educators avoid becoming some sort of therapists for their students, when there is pressure in current times to provide therapeutic education? What are the limits of discomfort, mutual vulnerability, and compassion in different conflicted settings so that critical emotional praxis and critical peace education retain their radical, realistic possibility? How far can critical pedagogues and peace educators push their students to problematize their emotional responses toward troubled knowledge and to critique self and otherness in light of open wounds within a traumatized community?

These and other important questions offer the potential to broaden the ways that incorporate the emotional complexities of troubled knowledge into our understanding of critical emotional praxis and critical peace education in conflicted societies. Pondering these questions and reading through some of the empirical evidence shared in this book, it can gradually become apparent that pedagogies of troubled knowledge in conflicted societies encompass a set of difficult issues that are beginning to be adequately acknowledged, understood, and analyzed with the purpose of advancing healing and reconciliation practices in schools.

REFERENCES

Abu-Lughod, L. (1990). The romance of resistance: Tracing transformations of power through Bedouin women. *American Ethnologist, 17*(1), 41–55.

Abu-Lughod, L., & Lutz, C. A. (1990). Introduction: Emotion, discourse, and the politics of everyday life. In C. Lutz & L. Abu-Lughod (Eds.), *Language and the politics of emotion* (pp. 1–23). Cambridge: Cambridge University Press.

Abu-Nimer, M. (2004). Education for coexistence and Arab-Jewish encounters in Israel: Potential and challenges. *Journal of Social Issues, 60*(2), 405–422.

Ahluwalia, P., Atkinson, S., Bishop, P., Christie, P., Hattam, R., & Matthews, J. (Eds.). (2012). *Reconciliation and pedagogy*. London: Routledge

Ahmed, S. (2004). *The cultural politics of emotion*. Edinburgh, UK: Edinburgh University Press.

Ahmed, S. (2005). The skin of the community: Affect and boundary formation. In T. Chanter & E. Zaire (Eds.), *Revolt, affect, collectivity: The unstable boundaries of Kristeva's polis* (pp. 95–111). Albany, NY: State University of New York Press.

Alexander, J., Eyerman, R., Giesen, B., Smelser, N., & Sztompka, P. (2004). *Cultural trauma and collective identity*. Berkeley, CA: University of California Press.

Al-Haj, M. (2003). Jewish-Arab relations and the education system in Israel. In Y. Iram (Ed.), *Education of minorities and peace education in pluralistic societies* (pp. 213–227). Bar Ilan University, Israel.

Al-Haj, M. (2004). The political culture of the 1990s immigrants from the former Soviet Union in Israel and their views toward the indigenous Arab minority: A case of ethnocratic multiculturalism. *Journal of Ethnic and Migration Studies, 30*(4), 681–696.

Al-Haj, M. (2005). National ethos, multicultural education, and the new history textbooks in Israel. *Curriculum Inquiry, 35*(1), 47–71.

Allport, G. W. (1954). *The nature of prejudice*. Reading, MA: Addison-Wesley.

Amsler, S. (2011). From 'therapeutic' to political education: The centrality of affective sensibility in critical pedagogy. *Critical Studies in Education, 52*(1), 47–63.

Anderson, K., & Smith, S. (2001). Editorial: Emotional geographies. *Transactions of the Institute of British Geographers, 26*, 7–10.

Anthias, F., & Yuval-Davis, N. (1992). *Racialized boundaries: Race, nation, gender, color and class and the anti-racist struggle*. London: Routledge.

Archer, L. (2003). *Race, masculinity and schooling: Muslim boys and education*. Buckingham: Open University Press.

Archer, L., & Francis, B. (2005). "They never go off the rails like other ethnic groups": Teachers' constructions of British Chinese pupils' gender identities and approaches to learning. *British Journal of Sociology of Education, 26*(2), 165–182.

Arnot, M., & Dillabough, J. A. (Eds.). (2000). *Challenging democracy: International perspectives on gender, education and citizenship*. New York, NY: Routledge.

Arslan, Z. (1999). Taking rights less seriously: Postmodernism and human rights. *Res Publica, 5*(2), 195–215.

Attalides, M. (1979). *Cyprus, nationalism, and international politics*. New York, NY: St. Martin's Press.

Auerbach, Y. (2009). The reconciliation pyramid—A narrative-based framework for analyzing identity conflicts. *Political Psychology, 30*(2), 291–318.

Bajaj, M. (2008). "Critical" peace education. In M. Bajaj (Ed.), *The encyclopaedia of peace education* (pp. 135–146). Charlotte, NC: Information Age Publishing.

Bajaj, M. (2011). Human rights education: Ideology, location, and approaches. *Human Rights Quarterly, 33*, 481–508.

Bajaj, M., & Brantmeier, E. J. (2011). The politics, praxis, and possibilities of critical peace education. *Journal of Peace Education, 8*(3), 221–224.

Balibar, E., & Wallerstein, I. (1991). *Race, nation, class: Ambiguous identities*. London: Verso.

Banks, J. (Ed.). (2004). *Diversity and citizenship education: Global perspectives*. San Francisco, CA: Jossey-Bass.

Bar-Siman-Tov, Y. (Ed.). (2004). *From conflict resolution to reconciliation*. Oxford: Oxford University Press.

Barajas, H., & Ronnkvist, A. (2007). Racialized space: Framing Latino and Latina experience in public schools. *Teachers College Record, 109*(6), 1517–1538.

Barbalet, J. M. (1998). *Emotion, social theory, and social structure: A macrosociological approach*. Cambridge: Cambridge University Press.

Barrett, L. (2006). Solving the emotion paradox: Categorization and the experience of emotion. *Personality and Social Psychology Review, 10*, 20–46.

Bar-Tal, D. (2000a). *Shared beliefs in a society: Social psychological analysis*. Thousands Oaks, CA: Sage.

Bar-Tal, D. (2000b). From intractable conflict through conflict resolution to reconciliation: Psychological analysis. *Political Psychology, 21*, 351–365.

Bar-Tal, D. (2003). Collective memory of physical violence: Its contribution to the culture of violence. In E. Cairns & M. D. Roe (Eds.), *The role of memory in ethnic conflict* (pp. 77–93). London: Palgrave Macmillan.

Bar-Tal, D. (2004). Nature, rationale, and effectiveness of education for coexistence. *Journal of Social Issues, 60*(2), 253–271.

Bar-Tal, D., & Bennink, G. (2004). The nature of reconciliation as an outcome and as a process. In Y. Bar-Siman-Tov (Ed.), *From conflict resolution to reconciliation* (pp. 11–38). Oxford: Oxford University Press.

Bar-Tal, D., Halperin, E., & de Rivera, J. (2007). Collective emotions in conflict situations: Societal implications. *Journal of Social Issues, 63*, 441–460.

Bauer, D. (2001). Classroom spaces and the corporate university. *Pedagogy*, 1(3), 554–559.

Bekerman, Z. (2004). Potential and limitations of multicultural education in conflict-ridden areas: Bilingual Palestinian-Jewish schools in Israel. *Teachers College Record, 106*(3), 574–610.

Bekerman, Z. (2005). Complex contexts and ideologies: Bilingual education in conflict-ridden areas. *Journal of Language, Identity, and Education, 4*(1), 1–20.

Bekerman, Z. (2007). Rethinking intergroup encounters: Rescuing praxis from theory, activity from education, and peace/co-existence from identity and culture. *Journal of Peace Education, 4*(1), 21–37.

Bekerman, Z. (2009). "Yeah, it is important to know Arabic—I just don't like learning it": Can Jews become bilingual in the Palestinian Jewish integrated bilingual schools? In C. McGlynn, M. Zembylas, Z. Bekerman, & T. Gallagher (Eds.), *Peace education in conflict and post-conflict societies: Comparative perspectives* (pp. 231–246). New York, NY: Palgrave Macmillan.

Bekerman, Z., & Maoz, I. (2005). Troubles with identity: Obstacles to coexistence education in conflict ridden societies. *Identity: An International Journal of Theory and Research, 5*(4), 341–357.

Bekerman, Z., & McGlynn, C. (Eds.). (2007). *Addressing ethnic conflict through peace education*. New York, NY: Palgrave Macmillan.

Bekerman, Z., & Zembylas, M. (2012). *Teaching contested narratives: Identity, memory and reconciliation in peace education and beyond*. Cambridge: Cambridge University Press.

Bekerman, Z., Zembylas, M., & McGlynn, C. (2009). Working towards the de-essentialization of identity categories in conflict and post-conflict societies: Israel, Cyprus, and Northern Ireland. *Comparative Education Review, 53*(2), 213–234.

Bénéï, V. (Ed.). (2005). *Manufacturing citizenship: Education and nationalism in Europe, South Asia, and China*. London: Routledge.

Ben-Eliezer, U. (2008). Multicultural society and everyday cultural racism: Second generation of Ethiopian Jews in Israel's 'crisis of modernization.' *Ethnic and Racial Studies, 31*(5), 935–961.

Bennett, J. (2005). *Empathic vision: Affect, trauma, and contemporary art*. Stanford, CA: Stanford University Press.

Ben-Porath, S. (2006). *Citizenship under fire: Democratic education in times of conflict*. Princeton, NJ: Princeton University Press.

Ben-Porath, S. (2011). Wartime citizenship: An argument for shared fate. *Ethnicities, 11*(3), 313–325.

Berdahl, D. (1999). '(N)Ostalgie' for the present: Memory, longing and East German things. *Ethnos, 64*(2), 192–211.

Berezin, M. (2001). Emotions and political identity: Mobilizing affection for the polity. In J. Goodwin, J. Jasper, & F. Polletta (Eds.), *Passionate politics: Emotions and social movements* (pp. 83–98). Chicago, IL: The University of Chicago Press.

Berlak, A. (2004). Confrontation and pedagogy: Cultural secrets and emotion in antioppressive pedagogies. In M. Boler (Ed.), *Democratic dialogue in education: Troubling speech, disturbing silence* (pp. 123–144). New York, NY: Peter Lang.

Berlant, L. (2000). The subject of true feeling: Pain, privacy, and politics. In S. Ahmed, J. Kilby, C. Lury, M. McNeil, & B. Skeggs (Eds.), *Transformations: Thinking through feminism* (pp. 33–47). London: Routledge.

Berman, M. (1982). *All that is solid melts into air: The experience of modernity.* New York, NY: Penguin Books.

Biesta, G. (2007). Education and the democratic person: Towards a political conception of democratic education. *Teachers College Record, 109*(3), 740–769.

Biesta, G. (2009). What kind of citizenship for European higher education? Beyond the competent active citizen. *European Educational Research Journal, 8*(2), 146–158.

Biesta, G. (2010). How to exist politically and learn from it: Hannah Arendt and the problem of democratic education. *Teachers College Record, 112*(2), 556–575.

Biesta, G. (2011). The ignorant citizen: Mouffe, Rancière, and the subject of democratic education. *Studies in Philosophy and Education, 30,* 141–153.

Billig, M. (1995). *Banal nationalism.* London: Sage.

Bishop, B. (2006). Walking on and off line: Reconciliation, public protest, and media. *Australian Journal of Communication, 33*(2/3), 109–126.

Blumer, M., & Solomos, J. (Eds.). (1999). *Racism.* Oxford: Oxford University Press.

Boler, M. (1999). *Feeling power: Emotions and education.* New York, NY: Routledge.

Boler, M. (Ed.). (2004a). *Democratic dialogue in education: Troubling speech, disturbing silence.* New York, NY: Peter Lang

Boler, M. (2004b). Teaching for hope: The ethics of shattering world views. In D. Liston & J. Garrison (Eds.), *Teaching, learning and loving: Reclaiming passion in educational practice* (pp. 117–131). New York, NY: RoutledgeFalmer.

Boler, M., & Zembylas, M. (2003). Discomforting truths: The emotional terrain of understanding differences. In P. Tryfonas (Ed.), *Pedagogies of difference: Rethinking education for social justice* (pp. 110–136). New York, NY: Routledge.

Bondi, L., Davidson, J., & Smith, M. (2005). Introduction: Geography's "emotional turn." In J. Davidson, L. Bondi, & M. Smith (Eds.), *Emotional geographies* (pp. 1–16). Aldershot: Ashgate.

Bonnell, J., & Simon, R. (2007). "Difficult" exhibitions and intimate encounters. *Museum and Society, 5*(2), 65–85.

Bourdieu, P. (1990). *The logic of practice.* Cambridge: Polity.

Bourdieu, P. (2000). *Pascalian meditations* (Trans. R. Nice). Stanford, CA: Stanford University Press.

Bourdieu, P., & Wacquant, L. (1992). *An invitation to reflexive sociology*. Cambridge: Polity.

Bourke, J. (2006). *Fear: A cultural history*. Emeryville, CA: Shoemaker Hoard.

Boym, S. (2001). *The future of nostalgia*. New York, NY: Basic Books.

Bowman, J. (2006). Seeing what's missing in memories of Cyprus. *Peace Review: A Journal of Social Justice, 18*, 119–127.

Bracken, P. (2002). *Trauma, culture, meaning and philosophy*. London: Whurr Publishers Ltd.

Brah, A., & Phoenix, A. (2004). "Ain't I a woman?" Revisiting intersectionality, *Journal of International Women's Studies, 5*, 75–86.

Brantmeier, E. J. (2011). Toward mainstreaming critical peace education in US teacher education. In C. S. Malott & B. Portfilio (Eds.), *Critical pedagogy in the 21st century: A new generation of scholars* (pp. 349–375). Greenwich, CT: Information Age Publishing.

Brewer, M. B., & Miller, N. (1984). Beyond the contact hypothesis: theoretical perspectives on desegregation. In N. Miller & M. B. Brewer (Eds.), *Groups in contact: The psychology of desegregation* (pp. 213–227). New York, NY: Academic Press.

Brison, S. (1999). Trauma narratives and the remaking of the self. In M. Bal, J. Crewe, & L. Spitzer (Eds.), *Acts of memory: Cultural recall in the present* (pp. 37–54). Hanover, NH: University Press of New England.

Britzman, D. (1998). *Lost subjects, contested objects: Toward a psychoanalytic inquiry of learning*. Albany, NY: State University of New York Press.

Britzman, D. (2000). If the story cannot end: Deferred action, ambivalence, and difficult knowledge. In R. Simon, S. Rosenberg, & C. Eppert (Eds.), *Between hope and despair: Pedagogy and the remembrance of historical trauma* (pp. 27–57). Lanham, MD: Rowman & Littlefield.

Brown, R., & Hewstone, M. (2005). An integrative theory of intergroup contact. In M. P. Zanna (Ed.), *Advances in experimental social psychology: Volume 37* (pp. 256–343). San Diego, CA: Elsevier Academic Press.

Bryant, R. (2004). *Imagining the modern: The cultures of nationalism in Cyprus*. London: I. B. Tauris.

Burbules, N. (1997). A grammar of difference: Some ways of rethinking difference and diversity as educational topic. *The Australian Educational Researcher, 24*(1), 97–116.

Burkitt, I. (1997). Social relationships and emotions. *Sociology, 25*(1), 1–29.

Burkitt, I. (2005). Powerful emotions: Power, government and opposition in the "war on terror." *Sociology, 39*(4), 679–695.

Burlein, A. (1999). Countermemory on the right: The case of focus on the family. In M. Bal, J. Crewe, & L. Spitzer (Eds.) *Acts of memory: Cultural recall in the present* (pp. 208–217). Hanover, NH: University Press of New England.

Burns, R., & Aspeslagh, R. (1996). *Three decades of peace education around the world: An anthology*. New York, NY: Garland.

Bush, K. D., & Saltarelli, D. (2000). *The two faces of education in ethnic conflict: Towards a peace-building education for children*. Florence, Italy: Innocenti Research Centre, UNICEF.

Butler, J. (1997). *Psychic life of power*. Stanford, CA: Stanford University Press.

Butler, J. (2004). *Precarious life: The powers of mourning and violence*. London: Verso.

Callahan, J. (2004). Breaking the cult of rationality: Mindful awareness of emotion in the critical theory classroom. *New Directions for Adult and Continuing Education, 102*, 75–83.

Calotychos, V. (Ed.). (1998) *Cyprus and its people: Nation, identity and experience in an unimaginable community, 1955–1997*. Boulder, CO: Westview Press.

Card, C. (2002). *The atrocity paradigm: A theory of evil*. New York, NY: Oxford University Press.

Carspecken, P., & Walford, G. (Eds). (2001). *Critical ethnography and education*. New York, NY: Routledge.

Caruth, C. (1996). *Unclaimed experience: Trauma, narrative, and history*. Baltimore, MD: Johns Hopkins University Press.

Christou, M. (2006). A double imagination: Memory and education in Cyprus. *Journal of Modern Greek Studies, 24*, 285–306.

Christou, M. (2007). The language of patriotism: Sacred history and dangerous memories. *British Journal of Sociology of Education, 28*(6), 709–722.

Chubbuck, S., & Zembylas, M. (2008). The emotional ambivalence of socially just teaching: A case study of a novice urban schoolteacher. *American Educational Research Journal, 45*(2), 274–318.

Clarke, S., Hoggett, P., & Thompson, S. (Eds.). (2006). *Emotion, politics and society*. New York, NY: Palgrave Macmillan.

Cole, E. (Ed.) (2007). *Teaching the violent past: History education and reconciliation*. Lanham, MD: Rowman & Littlefield.

Connolly, P. (1998). *Racism, gender identities and young children*. London: Routledge.

Connolly, W. (2002). *Neuropolitics: Thinking, culture, speed*. Minneapolis, MN: University of Minnesota Press.

Constantinou, C. M., & Papadakis, Y. (2001). The Cypriot state(s) in situ: Crossethnic contact and the discourse of recognition. *Global Society, 15*, 125–148.

Crenshaw, K., Gotanda, N., Peller, G., & Kendall, T. (1995). *Critical race theory: The key writings that formed the movement*. New York, NY: The New Press.

Darder, A., Baltodano, M., & Torres, R. D. (2003). *The critical pedagogy reader*. New York, NY: Routledge.

Das, V., & Kleinman, A. (2001). Introduction. In V. Das, A. Kleinman, M. Lock, M. Ramphele, & P. Reynolds (Eds.), *Remaking a world: Violence, social suffering and recovery* (pp. 1–31). Berkeley, CA: University of California Press.

Das, V., Kleinman, A., Ramphele, M., & Reynolds, P. (Eds). (2000). *Violence and subjectivity*. Berkeley, CA: University of California Press.

Davidson, J., & Milligan, C. (2004). Editorial: Embodying emotion sensing space: Introducing emotional geographies. *Social & Cultural Geography, 5*, 523–532.

Davidson, J., Bondi, L, & Smith, M. (2005). *Emotional geographies*. Aldershot: Ashgate.

Davies, L. (2004). *Education and conflict: Complexity and chaos*. London: RoutledgeFalmer.

Davies, L. (2008). *Educating against extremism*. Stoke on Trent: Trentham.

Davis, F. (1979). *Yearning for yesterday: A sociology of nostalgia*. New York, NY: The Free Press.

De Haan, M., & Elbers, E. (2004). Minority status and culture: Local constructions of diversity in a classroom in the Netherlands. *Intercultural Education, 15*(4), 441–453.

DeJaeghere, J. (2009). Critical citizenship education for multicultural societies. *Interamerican Journal of Education for Democracy, 2*(2), 223–236.

DeJaeghere, J., & Tudball, L. (2007). Looking back, looking forward: Critical citizenship as a way ahead for civics and citizenship education in Australia. *Citizenship Teaching and Learning, 3*(2), 40–57.

Deleuze, G., & Guattari, F. (1987). *A thousand plateaus: Capitalism and schizophrenia*. Minneapolis, MN: University of Minnesota Press.

Deleuze, G., & Guattari, F. (1994). *What is philosophy*. New York, NY: Columbia University Press.

Delgado, R., & Stefancic, J. (2001). *Critical race theory*, New York, NY: New York University Press.

Denzin, N. K. (1984). *On understanding emotion*. San Francisco, CA: Jossey-Bass Publishers.

Denzin, N. K. (1997). *Interpretive ethnography: Ethnographic practices for the 21st century*. Thousand Oaks, CA: Sage.

Derrida, J. (1989). *Mémoires: For Paul de Man* (Trans. C. Lindsay, E. Cadava, J. Culler, & P. Kamuf). New York, NY: Columbia University Press.

Derrida. J. (2001). *The work of mourning*. Chicago and London: The University of Chicago Press.

Des Forges, A. (1999). *Leave none to tell the story: Genocide in Rwanda*. New York, NY: Human Rights Watch.

Devine, D., Kenny, M., & Macneela, E. (2008). Naming the "other": Children's construction and experience of racisms in Irish primary schools. *Race Ethnicity and Education, 11*(4), 369–385.

Diaz-Soto, L. (2005). How can we teach peace when we are so outraged? A call for critical peace education. *Taboo: The Journal of Culture and Education*, Fall-Winter, 91–96.

Dikomitis, L. (2005). Three readings of a border: Greek Cypriots crossing the Green Line in Cyprus. *Anthropology Today, 21*(5), 7–12.

Donnelly, C. (2004a). Constructing the ethos of tolerance and respect in an integrated school: The role of teachers. *British Educational Research Journal, 30*, 263–278.

Donnelly, C. (2004b). What price harmony? Teachers' methods of delivering an ethos of tolerance and respect for diversity in an integrated school in Northern Ireland. *Educational Research, 46*, 3–16.

Dovidio, J. F., & Gaertner, S. L. (1998). On the nature of contemporary prejudice: The cause, consequences and challenges of aversive racism. In J. L. Eberhardt & S. T. Fiske (Eds.), *Confronting racism: The problem and the response* (pp. 3–33). Thousand Oaks, CA: Sage.

Dovidio, J. F., Gaertner, S. L.,& Kawakami, K. (2003). Intergroup contact: The past, present, and the future. *Group Processes & Intergroup Relations, 6*(1), 5–21.

Ecclestone, K., & Hayes, D. (2009). *The dangerous rise of therapeutic education.* Abingdon, UK: Routledge.

Eckmann, M. (2010). Exploring the relevance of Holocaust education for human rights education. *Prospects, 40*, 7–16.

Eisenstein, Z. (1996). *Hatreds: Racialized and sexualized conflicts in the 21st century.* New York, NY: Routledge.

Eisner, E. (1991). *The enlightened eye: Qualitative inquiry and the enhancement of educational practice.* New York, NY: Maxwell Macmillan International Publishing Group.

Ellsworth, E. (1989). Why doesn't this feel empowering? Working through the repressive myths of critical pedagogy. *Harvard Educational Review, 59*, 297–324.

Emirbayer, M., & Goldberg, C. A. (2005) Pragmatism, Bourdieu, and collective emotions in contentious politics. *Theory and Society, 34*(5-6), 469–518.

Eppert, C. (2009). Review of Michalinos Zembylas: *The Politics of Trauma in Education. Studies in Philosophy and Education, 28*(5), 473–480.

Erickson, F. (1986). Qualitative methods in research on teaching. In M. Wittrock (Ed.), *Handbook of research on teaching* (pp. 119–161). New York, NY: Macmillan Publishing Company.

Evdokas, T. (1978). *A psychopolitical approach to the Cyprus problem: The symbiosis of the two communities and the emotional factors used to promote partition.* Nicosia, Cyprus: Socio-Psychological Research Group.

Essed, P. (1991). *Understanding everyday racism.* London: Sage.

Eyerman, R., Alexander, J., & Breese, E. (Eds.). (2011). *Narrating trauma: On the impact of collective suffering.* Boulder, CO: Paradigm Publishers.

Ferreira, A., Janks, H., Barnsley, I., Marriot, C., Rudman, M., Ludlow, H., & Nussey, R. (2012). Reconciliation pedagogy in South African classrooms: From the personal to the political. In P. Ahluwalia, S. Atkinson, P. Bishop, P. Christie, R. Hattam, & J. Matthews (Eds.), *Reconciliation and pedagogy* (pp. 173–193) London: Routledge.

Festinger, L. (1957). *A theory of cognitive dissonance*. Stanford, CA: Stanford University Press.

Fisher, R. M. (2006). Invoking "fear" studies. *Journal of Curriculum Theorizing, 22*, 39–71.

Foucault, M. (1977a). *Discipline and punish* (Trans. A. Sheridan). New York, NY: Vintage Books.

Foucault, M. (1977b). Nietzsche, genealogy, history. In D. F. Bouchard (Ed.), *Language, counter-memory, practice: Selected essays and interviews by Michel Foucault* (pp. 139–164). Ithaca, NY: Cornell University Press.

Foucault, M. (1980). *Power/knowledge: Selected interviews and other writings, 1972–1977.* Hemel Hemstead, Herts: Harvester Wheatsheaf.

Foucault, M. (1982/2001). The subject and power. In J. D. Faubion (Ed.), *Essential works of Foucault, 1954–1984: Power Vol. 3* (pp. 326–329). Harmondsworth, Middlesex: Penguin Books.

Foucault, M. (1988). Technologies of the self. In L. H. Martin, H. Gutman & P. H. Hutton (Eds.), *Technologies of the self* (pp. 16–49). Amherst: University of Massachusetts Press.

Foucault, M. (1994). For an ethic of discomfort. In J. D. Faubion (Ed.), *Essential works of Foucault, 1954–1984, volume three* (pp. 443–448). New York, NY: The New Press.

Fountain, S. (1999). *Peace education in UNICEF.* New York, NY: Programme Division UNICEF.

Fraser, N. (1997). *Justice interruptus*. New York, NY: Routledge.

Freire, P. (1994). *Pedagogy of hope: Reliving pedagogy of the* oppressed. New York, NY: Continuum.

Freire, P. (2000). *Pedagogy of the* oppressed. New York, NY: Continuum.

Freire, P. (2001). *Pedagogy of freedom: Ethics, democracy and civic courage*. Lanham, MD: Rowman & Littlefield.

Freire, P. (2005). *Education for critical consciousness*. New York, NY: Continuum.

Fritzsche, P. (2001). Specters of history: On nostalgia, exiles, and modernity. *American Historical Review, 106*(5), 1587–1618.

Furedi, F. (2006). *The politics of fear: Beyond left and right*. London: Continuum Press.

Gaertner, S., J. F. Dovidio, P. A. Anastasio, B. A. Bachevan, & Rust, M. C. (1993). The common ingroup identity model: Recategorization and the reduction of intergroup bias. In W. Stroewe & M. Hewstone (Eds.), *European Review of Social Psychology* (Vol 4, pp. 1–26). Chichester: Wiley.

Gallagher, T. (2004). *Education in divided societies*. London: Palgrave Macmillan.

Gandhi, L. (2006). *Affective communities: Anticolonial thought, fin-de-siècle radicalism, and the politics of friendship*. Durham, NC: Duke University Press.

Geertz, C. (1984/1974). From the native's point of view: On the nature of anthropological understanding. In R. A. Shweder & R. A. LeVine (Eds.), *Culture theory: Essays on mind, self, and emotion* (pp. 123–136). Cambridge: Cambridge University Press.

Gellner, E. (1983). *Nations and nationalism*. Oxford: Blackwell.

Georgis, D., & Kennedy, R. M. (2009). Touched by injury: Toward an educational theory of anti-racist humanism. *Ethics and Education*, *4*, 19–30.

Gillborn, D. (1992). Citizenship, 'race' and the hidden curriculum. *International Studies in Sociology of Education*, *2*(1), 57–73.

Gillborn, D. (2005). Education policy as an act of white supremacy: Whiteness, critical race theory and education reform. *Journal of Education Policy*, *20*(4), 484–505.

Gillborn, D. (2008). *Racism and education: Coincidence or conspiracy*. London: Routledge.

Gillborn, D., & Mirza, H. (2000). *Educational inequality: Mapping race, class and gender: A synthesis of research evidence*. London: Office of Standards in Education.

Giroux, H. (Ed.). (1991). *Postmodernism, feminism and cultural politics*. Albany, NY: State University of New York Press.

Giroux, H. (1993). *Living dangerously: Multiculturalism and the politics of difference*. New York, NY: Peter Lang.

Giroux, H. (2003). *The abandoned generation: Democracy beyond the culture of fear*. New York, NY: Palgrave Macmillan.

Giroux, H. A. (2004). Critical pedagogy and the postmodern/modern divide: Towards pedagogy of democratization. *Teacher Education Quarterly*, *31*(1), 132–153.

Giroux, H. A., & McLaren, P. (1989). *Critical pedagogy, the state, and cultural struggle: Teacher empowerment and school reform*. Albany, NY: State University of New York Press.

Giroux, H., & McLaren, P. (1994). *Between borders: Pedagogy and politics in cultural studies*. New York, NY: Routledge.

Gobodo-Madikizela, P. (2008). Empathetic repair after mass trauma: When vengeance is arrested. *European Journal of Social Theory*, *11*(3), 331–350.

Gobodo-Madikizela, P. & Van Der Merwe, C. (Eds.). (2009). *Memory, narrative and forgiveness: Perspectives on the unfinished journeys of the past*. Newcastle, UK: Cambridge Scholars Publishing.

González, N., Moll, L., & Amanti, C. (Eds). (2005). *Funds of knowledge: Theorizing practices in households, communities and classrooms*. New York, NY: New Press.

Good, B. (2004). Rethinking 'emotions' in Southeast Asia. *Ethnos, 69*, 529–533.

Goodson, I., Moore, S., & Hargreaves, A. (2006). Teacher nostalgia and the sustainability of reform: The generation and degeneration of teachers' missions, memory, and meaning. *Educational Administration Quarterly*, *42*(1), 42–61.

Goodwin, J., Jasper, J., & Poletta, F. (2001). Introduction: Why emotions matter. In J. Goodwin, J. Jasper, & F. Poletta (Eds.), *Passionate politics: Emotions and social movements* (pp. 1–24). Chicago and London: The University of Chicago Press.

Grainge, P. (2002). *Monochrome memories: Nostalgia and style in retro America*. Westport, CT: Praeger.

Green, P. (2009). The pivotal role of acknowledgment in social healing. In Gobodo-Madikizela & Van Der Merwe (Eds.), *Memory, narrative and forgiveness: Perspectives on the unfinished journeys of the past* (pp. 74–97). Newcastle, UK: Cambridge Scholars Publishing.

Gross, D. (1990). Critical synthesis on urban knowledge: Remembering and forgetting in the modern city. *Social Epistemology, 4*(1), 3–22.

Gutmann, A. (2004). Unity and diversity in democratic multicultural education. In J. Banks (Ed.), *Diversity and citizenship education: Global perspectives* (pp. 71–96). San Francisco, CA: Jossey-Bass.

Hadjipavlou, M. (1993). Unofficial Inter-communal contacts and their contribution to peace-building in conflict societies: The case of Cyprus. *Cyprus Review,* 5, 68–87.

Hadjipavlou, M. (2007a). The Cyprus conflict: Root causes and implications for peacebuilding. *Journal of Peace Research, 44*, 349–365.

Hadjipavlou, M. (2007b). Multiple realities and the role of peace education in deep-rooted conflicts: The case of Cyprus. In Z. Bekerman & C. McGlynn (Eds.), *Addressing ethnic conflict through peace education: International perspectives* (pp. 35–48). New York, NY: Palgrave Macmillan.

Hadjiyanni, T. (2002). *The making of a refugee. Children adopting refugee identity in Cyprus.* Westport, CT: Praeger.

Halpern, J. (2001). *From detached concern to empathy: Humanizing medical practice.* New York, NY: Oxford University Press.

Halpern, J., & Weinstein, H. M. (2004). Rehumanizing the other: Empathy and reconciliation. *Human Rights Quarterly, 26*, 561–583.

Hammack, P. (2011). *Narrative and the politics of identity: The cultural psychology of Israeli and Palestinian youth.* New York, NY: Oxford University Press.

Harding, J., & Pribram, D. (2004). Losing our cool? Following Williams and Grossberg on emotions. *Cultural Studies, 18*, 863–883.

Harré, R. (1986). An outline of the social constructionist viewpoint. In R. Harré (Ed.), *The social construction of emotions* (pp. 2–14). New York, NY: Basil Blackwell.

Harry, B., & Klingner, J. (2006). *Why are so many minority students in special education? Understanding race and disability in schools.* New York, NY: Teachers College Press.

Harvey, D. (1989). *The condition of postmodernity.* Cambridge, MA & Oxford, UK: Blackwell.

Hattam, R., & Matthews, J. (2012). Reconciliation as a resource for critical pedagogy. In P. Ahluwalia, S. Atkinson, P. Bishop, P. Christie, R. Hattam, & J. Matthews (Eds.), *Reconciliation and pedagogy* (pp. 10–28) London: Routledge.

Hattam, R., Atkinson, S., & Bishop, P. (2012). Rethinking reconciliation and pedagogy in unsettling times. In P. Ahluwalia, S. Atkinson, P. Bishop, P. Christie, R. Hattam, & J. Matthews (Eds.), *Reconciliation and pedagogy* (pp. 1–9) London: Routledge.

Herman, J. (1997). *Trauma and recovery: The aftermath of violence from domestic abuse to political terror* (2nd ed.). New York: Basic Books.

Herzfeld, M. (1997). *Cultural intimacy: Social poetics in the nation state*. New York, NY: Routledge.

Hewstone, M. (1996). Contact and categorization: Social psychological interventions to change intergroup relations. In C. N. Macrae, C. Stangor, & M. Hewstone (Eds.), *Foundations of stereotypes and stereotyping* (pp. 323–368). New York, NY: Guilford.

Hirsch, M. (1997). *Family frames. Photography, narrative and postmemory*. Cambridge, MA: Harvard University Press.

Hirsch, M. (2008). The generation of postmemory. *Poetics Today*, *29*(1), 103–128.

Hirsch, M., & Spitzer, L. (2003). We would never have come without you: Generations of nostalgia. In K. Hodgkin & S. Radstone (Eds.), *Contested pasts: The politics of memory* (pp. 79–95). London: Routledge.

Hitchens, C. (1984). *Cyprus*. London: Quartet Books.

Hodgkin, M. (2006). Reconciliation in Rwanda: Education, history and the state. *Journal of International Affairs*, *60*(1), 199–210.

Hoggett, P. (2006). Pity, compassion, solidarity. In S. Clarke, P. Hoggett, & S. Thompson (Eds.), *Emotion, politics and society* (pp. 145–161). New York, NY: Palgrave Macmillan.

Hollan, D. (2008). Being there: On the imaginative aspects of understanding others and being understood. *Ethos*, *36*(4), 475–489.

Hollan, D., & Throop, C. J. (2008). Whatever happened to empathy? Introduction. *Ethos*, *36*(4), 385–401.

Holmes, M. (2010). The emotionalization of reflexivity. *Sociology*, *44*(1), 139–154.

Holstein, J., & Gubrium, J. (2000). *The self that we live by: Narrative identity in the postmodern world*. New York, NY: Oxford University Press.

Hook, D. (2005). Affecting whiteness: Racism as technology of affect. *International Journal of Critical Psychology*, *16*(1), 74–99.

Hook, D. (2007). *Foucault, psychology and the analytics of power*. New York, NY: Palgrave Macmillan.

Hoy, D. (2004). *Critical resistance: From poststructuralism to post-critique*. Cambridge, MA: The MIT Press.

Humphrey, M. (2000). From terror to trauma: Commissioning truth for national reconciliation. *Social Identities*, *6*(1), 7–27.

Husserl, E. (1970). *The crisis of European sciences and transcendental phenomenology*. Evanston, IL: Northwestern University Press.

Hutchison, E., & Bleiker, R. (2008). Emotional reconciliation: Reconstituting identity and community after trauma. *European Journal of Social Theory*, *11*, 385–403.

Ignatieff, M. (2001). *Human rights as politics and idolatry*. Princeton, NJ: Princeton University Press.

Jansen, J. (2009). *Knowledge in the blood: Confronting race and the apartheid past*. Stanford, CA: Stanford University Press.

Jenkins, R. (1996). *Social identity*. London, Routledge.

Johnson, L. (2001). *The practice of integrated education in Northern Ireland: The teachers' perspective on what is working and what is not*. Belfast, Northern Ireland: Northern Ireland Council for Integrated Education.

Johnson, L. (2007). From piecemeal to systemic approaches to peace education in divided societies: Comparative efforts in Northern Ireland and Cyprus. In Z. Bekerman & C. McGlynn (Eds.), *Addressing ethnic conflict through peace education: International perspectives* (pp. 21–33). New York, NY: Palgrave Macmillan.

Johnson, L., & Morris, P. (2010). Towards a framework for critical citizenship education. *The Curriculum Journal*, *21*(1), 77–90.

Kalantzis, M., & B. Cope (2001). *Reconciliation, multiculturalism, identities: Difficult dialogues, sensible solutions*. Melbourne: Common Ground.

Kansteiner, W. (2004). Genealogy of a category mistake: A critical intellectual history of the cultural trauma metaphor. *Rethinking History*, *8*, 193–221.

Kaplan, A. (2005). *Trauma culture: The politics of terror and loss in media and literature*. New Brunswick, NJ: Rutgers University Press.

Keet, A. (2010). *Human rights education: A conceptual analysis*. Saarbrücken, Germany: Lambert Academic Publishing.

Keet, A., Zinn, D., & Porteus, K. (2009). Mutual vulnerability: A key principle in a humanising pedagogy in post-conflict societies. *Perspectives in Education*, *27*(2), 109–119.

Kelly, P. (2002). *Multiculturalism reconsidered*. Cambridge: Polity.

Kincheloe, J. L. (2005). *Critical pedagogy*. New York, NY: Peter Lang.

Kincheloe, J. L., & Steinberg, S. R. (1997). *Changing multiculturalism*. Buckingham, UK, Philadelphia, PA: Open University Press.

Kirmayer, L. (2008). Empathy and alterity in cultural psychiatry. *Ethos*, *36*(4), 457–474.

Kiwan, D. (2005). Human rights and citizenship: An unjustifiable conflation? *Journal of Philosophy of Education*, *39*(1), 37–50.

Kizilyürek, N. (1999a). *Cyprus: The impasse of nationalisms*. Athens: Mauri Lista [in Greek].

Kizilyürek, N. (1999b). National memory and Turkish-Cypriot textbooks. *Internationale Schulbuchforschung*, *21*(4), 387–396.

Kizilyürek, N. (2001). History textbooks and nationalism. In C. Koulouri (Ed.), *Teaching the history of Southeastern Europe* (pp. 431–442). Thessaloniki: Centre for Democracy and Reconciliation in Southeast Europe.

Knight Abowitz, K., & Harnish, J. (2006). Contemporary discourses of citizenship. *Review of Educational Research*, *76*, 653–690.

Kreuzer, P. (2002). *Applying theories of ethno-cultural conflict and conflict resolution to collective violence in Indonesia*. Frankfurt: Peace Research Institute of Frankfurt.

Kriesberg, L. (1998). Coexistence and the reconciliation of communal conflicts. In E. Weiner (Ed.), *The handbook of interethnic coexistence* (pp. 182–198). New York, NY: Continuum.

Kristeva, J. (1993). *Nations without nationalism* (trans. L. S. Roudiez). New York, NY: Columbia University Press.

Kristeva, J. (2000). *The sense and nonsense of revolt: The power and limits of psychoanalysis* (trans. J. Herman). New York, NY: Columbia University Press.

Kumashiro, K. K. (2002). Against repetition: Addressing resistance to anti-oppressive change in the practices of learning, teaching, supervising, and researching, *Harvard Educational Review*, *72*(1), 67–92.

Kymlicka, W. (2001). *Politics in the vernacular: Nationalism, multiculturalism, and citizenship*. Oxford: Oxford University Press.

Laclau, E. (1995). Universalism, particularism and the question of identity. In R. Rajchman (Ed.), *The identity in question* (pp. 93–100). New York, NY: Routledge.

Laclau, E., & Mouffe, C. (1985). *Hegemony and socialist strategy: Towards a radical democratic politics*. London, UK, and New York, NY: Verso.

Ladson-Billings, G. (2005). The evolving role of critical race theory in educational scholarship. *Race Ethnicity & Education*, *8*(1), 115–119.

Ladson-Billings, G., & Tate, W. F. (1995). Toward a critical race theory of education. *Teachers College Record*, *97*(1), 47–68.

Lederach, J. P. (1997). *Building peace: Sustainable reconciliation in divided societies*. Washington, DC: U.S. Institute of Peace.

Leep, M. C. (2010). The affective production of others: United States policy towards the Israeli- Palestinian conflict. *Cooperation and Conflict*, *45*(3), 331–352.

Legg, S. (2005). Contenting and surviving memory: Space, nation, and nostalgia in *Les Lieux de Mémoire*. *Environment and Planning D: Society and Space*, *23*(4), 481–504.

Le Goff, J. (1992). *History and memory*. New York, NY: Columbia University Press.

Leibowitz, B., Bozalek, V., Rohleder, P., Carolissen, R., & Swartz, L. (2010). "Ah, but the whiteys love to talk about themselves": Discomfort as a pedagogy for change. *Race Ethnicity and Education*, *13*(1), 83–100.

Liechty, J., & Clegg C. (2001). *Moving beyond sectarianism: Religion, conflict and reconciliation in Northern Ireland*. Blackrock, Dublin: Columbia Press.

Lindner, E. (2009a). *Emotion and conflict: How human rights can dignify emotion and help us wage good conflict*. Westport, CT: Praeger.

Lindner, E. G. (2009b). Why there can be no conflict resolution as long as people are being humiliated. *International Review of Education*, *55*(2–3), 157–181.

Lindquist, J. (2004). Class affects, classroom affectations: Working through the paradoxes of strategic empathy. *College English*, *67*(2), 187–209.

Liston, D. (2008). Critical pedagogy and attentive love. *Studies in Philosophy and Education*, *27*, 387–392.

Loizos, P. (1981). *The heart grown bitter: A chronicle of Cypriot war refugees*. Cambridge: Cambridge University Press.

Loizos, P. (1998). How might Turkish and Greek Cypriots see each other more clearly?. In V. Calotychos (Ed.), *Cyprus and its people: Nation, identity, and experience in an unimaginable community, 1955–1997* (pp. 35–52). Boulder, CO: Westview Press.

Loizos, P. (2008). *Iron in the soul: Displacement, livelihood and health in Cyprus.* Oxford, UK, and New York, NY: Berghahn.

Long, W., & Brecke, P. (Eds.). (2003). *War and reconciliation: Reason and emotion in conflict resolution.* Cambridge, MA: MIT Press.

Lopez, C. (2011). The struggle for wholeness: Addressing individual and collective trauma in violence-ridden societies. *Explore, 7*(5), 300–313.

Lowenthal, D. (1993). Memory and oblivion. *Museum Management and Curatorship, 12*(2), 171–182.

Ludvig, A. (2006). Differences between women? Intersecting voices in a female narrative. *European Journal of Women's Studies, 13*, 245–258.

Lupton, D. (1998). *The emotional self: A sociocultural exploration.* London: Sage.

Lutz, C., & Abu-Lughod, L. (Eds). (1990). *Language and the politics of emotion.* Cambridge: Cambridge University Press.

Lynn, M., & Parker, L. (2006). Critical race studies in education: Examining a decade of research on U.S. schools. *The Urban Review, 38*(4), 257–290.

Lyotard, J-F. (1984). *The postmodern condition: A report on knowledge.* Minneapolis, MN: University of Minnesota Press.

Madison, D. S. (2005). *Critical ethnography: Method, ethics, performance.* Thousand Oaks, CA: Sage.

Mahalingham, R., & McCarthy, C. (2000). *Multicultural curriculum: New directions for social theory, practice and policy.* New York, NY: Routledge.

Mallinson, W. (2005). *Cyprus: A modern history.* London: I. B. Tauris.

Margalit, A. (2002). *The ethics of memory.* Cambridge, MA: Harvard University Press.

Matsuda, M. (1991). Beside my sister, facing the enemy: Legal theory out of coalition. *Stanford Law Review, 43*(6), 1183–1196.

Mavratsas, C. (1998). *Facets of Greek nationalism in Cyprus: Ideological contest and the social construction of Greek-Cypriot identity 1974–1996.* Athens: Katarti.

May, S. (1999). *Critical multiculturalism: Rethinking multicultural and antiracist education.* London: RoutledgeFalmer.

McCall, L. (2005). The complexity of intersectionality. *SIGNS: Journal of Women in Culture and Society, 30*(3), 1771–1800.

McCarthy, C., & Dimitriadis, G. (2000). Governmentality and the sociology of education: Media, educational policy and the politics of resentment. *British Journal of Sociology of Education, 21*(2), 169–185.

McCormack, D. P. (2003). An event of geographical ethics in spaces of affect. *Transactions of the Institute of British Geographers, 28*, 488–507.

McGlynn, C. (2009). Negotiating cultural difference in divided societies: An analysis of approaches to integrated education in Northern Ireland. In C. McGlynn, M. Zembylas, Z. Bekerman, & T. Gallagher (Eds.), *Peace education in conflict and post-conflict societies: Comparative perspectives* (pp. 9–26). New York, NY: Palgrave Macmillan.

McGlynn, C., & Bekerman, Z. (Eds.). (2007a). *Addressing ethnic conflict through peace education: International perspectives.* New York, NY: Palgrave Macmillan.

McGlynn, C., & Bekerman, Z. (2007b). The management of pupil difference in Catholic Protestant and Palestinian-Jewish integrated education in Northern Ireland and Israel. *Compare, 37*(5), 689–705.

McGlynn, C., U. Niens, E. Cairns, & Hewstone, M. (2004). Moving out of conflict: The contribution of integrated schools in Northern Ireland to identity, attitudes, forgiveness and reconciliation. *Journal of Peace Education, 1*(2), 147–163.

McGlynn, C., Zembylas, M., & Bekerman, Z. (Eds.). (2013). *Integrated education in conflicted societies*. New York, NY: Palgrave Macmillan.

McGlynn, C., Zembylas, M., Bekerman, Z., & Gallagher, T. (Eds.). (2009). *Peace education in conflict and post-conflict societies: comparative perspectives*. New York, NY: Palgrave Macmillan.

McKenzie, J. (2003). *Perform or else: From Discipline to performance*. New York, NY: Routledge.

McLaren, P. (1994). Multiculturalism and the postmodern critique: Towards a pedagogy of resistance and transformation. In H. Giroux & P. McLaren (Eds.), *Between borders: Pedagogy and the politics of cultural studies* (pp. 192–222). New York, NY: Routledge.

McLaren, P. (2003). *Life in schools: An introduction to critical pedagogy in the foundations of education*, 4th ed. Boston, MA: Allyn and Bacon.

McNay, L. (1999). Gender, habitus and the field: Pierre Bourdieu and the limits of reflexivity. *Theory, Culture & Society, 16*(1), 95–117.

Merriam, S. (1998). *Qualitative research and case study applications in education*. San Francisco, CA: Jossey-Bass.

Miles, M. B., & Huberman, A. M. (1994). *Qualitative data analysis: An expanded sourcebook*. Newbury Park, CA: Sage.

Miles, R. (1989). *Racism*. London: Routledge.

Milikowski, M. (2000). Exploring a model of de-ethnicization: the case of Turkish television in the Netherlands. *European Journal of Communication*, *15*(4), 443–468.

Ministry of Education and Culture. (1996). *Curriculum for the primary education in the frame of the nine-year education*. Nicosia, Cyprus: Department of Primary Education, Curriculum Development Unit (in Greek).

Ministry of Education and Culture. (2008). *F:7.1.05.21, Objectives of the school year 2008–2009*. Nicosia: Ministry of Education and Culture of the Republic of Cyprus (in Greek).

Ministry of Education and Culture. (2011). *Annual report on education*. Nicosia, Ministry of Education and Culture (in Greek).

Mirza, H. S. (1992). *Young, female and black*. London: Routledge.

Mohanty, C. (1994). On race and voice: Challenges for liberal education in the 1990s. In H. A. Giroux & P. McLaren (Eds.), *Between borders: Pedagogy and the politics of cultural studies* (pp. 145–166). New York, NY: Routledge.

Mohanty, C. (2003). *Feminism without borders: Decolonizing theory, practicing solidarity*. Durham, NC: Duke University Press.

Morag, N. (2004). Cyprus and the clash of Greek and Turkish nationalisms. *Nationalism and Ethnic Politics, 10,* 595–624.

Moreno Figueroa, M. (2008). Historically rooted translationalism: Slightedness and the experience of racism in Mexican families. *Journal of Intercultural Studies, 29,* 283–297.

Moscovici, S. (1980). Toward a theory of conversion behavior. In L. Berkowitz (Ed.), *Advances in experimental social psychology.* (vol. 13, pp. 209–239). San Diego, CA: Academic Press.

Moscovici, S., & Facheux, C. (1972). Social influence, conformity bias, and the study of active minorities. In L. Berkowitz (Ed.), *Advances in experimental social psychology.* (vol. 6, pp. 150–202). San Diego, CA: Academic Press.

Mouffe, C. (1999). Deliberative democracy or agonistic pluralism. *Social Research, 66*(3), 745–759.

Mouffe, C. (2005). *On the political: Thinking in action.* New York, NY: Routledge.

Muller, A. (2007). Notes toward a theory of nostalgia: Childhood and the evocation of the past in two European "heritage" films. *New Literary History, 37*(4), 739–760.

Mutua, M, (2002). *Human rights: A political and cultural critique.* Philadelphia: University of Pennsylvania Press.

Nash, J. (2008). Re-thinking intersectionality. *Feminist Review, 89,* 1–15.

Niens, U. (2009). Towards the development of a theoretical framework for peace education using the contact hypothesis and multiculturalism. In C. McGlynn, M. Zembylas, Z. Bekerman, & T. Gallagher (Eds.), *Peace education in conflict and post-conflict societies: comparative perspectives* (pp. 145–160). New York, NY: Palgrave Macmillan.

Niens, U., & Cairns, E. (2008). Peace education in Northern Ireland: A review. In D. Berliner & H. Kupermintz (Eds.), *Contributions of educational psychology to fostering change in institutions, environments, and people: A festschrift in honor of Gavriel Salomon* (pp. 193–210). Mahwah, NJ: Lawrence Erlbaum.

Nieto, S. (2000). *Affirming diversity: The sociopolitical context of multicultural Education.* New York, NY: Longman.

Nora, P. (1996). General introduction: Between memory and history. In P. Nora (Ed.), *Realms of memory, volume 1* (pp. 1–20). New York, NY: Columbia University Press.

Novelli, M., & Lopes Cardozo, M. T. A. (2008). Conflict, education and the global south: New critical directions. *International Journal of Educational Development, 28,* 473–488.

Oliver, K. (2001). *Witnessing: Beyond recognition.* Minneapolis, MN: University of Minnesota Press.

Oliver, K. (2004). *The colonization of psychic space: Toward a psychoanalytic social theory of* oppression. Minneapolis,MN: University of Minnesota Press.

Oliver, K. (2005). Revolt and forgiveness. In T. Chanter & E. Ziarek (Eds.), *Revolt, affect, collectivity: The unstable boundaries of Kristeva's polis* (pp. 77–92). Albany, NY: State University of New York Press.

Osler, A., & Starkey, H. (2005). *Changing citizenship: Democracy and inclusion in education*. New York, NY: Open University Press.

Otto, S. (2005). Nostalgic of what? The epidemic of images of the mid-20th century classroom in American media culture and what it means. *Discourse: Studies in the Cultural Politics of Education, 26*(4), 459–475.

Panayiotopoulos, C., & M. Nicolaidou. (2007). At a crossroads of civilizations: Multicultural education provision in Cyprus through the lens of a case study. *Intercultural Education, 18*(1), 65–79.

Papadakis, Y. (1998). Greek Cypriot narratives of history and collective identity: Nationalism as a contested process. *American Ethnologist, 25*(2), 149–165.

Papadakis, Y. (2005). *Echoes from the dead zone: Across the Cyprus divide*. London: I. B. Tauris.

Papadakis, Y. (2008). Narrative, memory and history education in divided Cyprus. *History & Memory, 20*, 128–148.

Papastephanou, M. (2003). Forgiving and requesting forgiveness. *Journal of Philosophy of Education, 37*(3), 503–524.

Parent, G. (2011). Peacebuilding, healing, reconciliation: An analysis of unseen connections for peace. *International Peacekeeping, 18*(4), 379–395.

Penninx, R. (1988). *Minderheidsvorming en emancipatie*. Balans van kennisverwerving ten aanzien van immigranten en woonwagenbewoners 1967–1987 (Minority Formation and Emancipation). Alphen aan den Rijn: Samsom.

Persianis, P. (2006). *Comparative history of education in Cyprus (1800–2004)*. Athens: Gutenberg.

Pettigrew, T. F. (1998). Intergroup contact theory. *Annual Review of Psychology, 49*, 65–85.

Pettigrew, T. F., & Meertens, R. W. (1995). Subtle and blatant prejudice in Western Europe. *European Journal of Social Psychology, 25*, 57–75.

Pettigrew, T. F., & Tropp, L. R. (2006). A meta-analytic test of intergroup contact theory. *Journal of Personality and Social Psychology, 90*(5), 751–783.

Phoenix, A. (1998). Dealing with difference: The recursive and the new. *Ethnic and Racial Studies, 21*(5), 859–880.

Phoenix, A. (2002). Mapping present inequalities to navigate future success: Racialisation and education. *British Journal of Sociology of Education, 23*, 505–515.

Phoenix, A. (2006). Editorial: Intersectionality. *European Journal of Women's Studies, 13*(3), 187–192.

Pickering, M., & Keightley, E. (2006). The modalities of nostalgia. *Current Sociology, 54*(6), 919–941.

Pinar, W. F., Reynolds, W. M., Slattery, P., & Taubman, P. M. (2002). *Understanding curriculum,* 4th ed. New York, NY: Peter Lang.

Pinson, H., Arnot, M., & Candappa, M. (2010). *Education, asylum and the "non-citizen" child: The politics of compassion and belonging*. New York, NY: Palgrave Macmillan.

Pitt, A., & Britzman, D. (2003). Speculations on qualities of difficult knowledge in teaching and learning: An experiment in psychoanalytic research. *International Journal of Qualitative Studies in Education, 16*(6), 755–776.

POED (Pangypria Organosi Ellinon Didaskalon). (2009). *Objectives under emphasis*. Nicosia: POED (in Greek).

Porter, E. (2007). *Peacebuilding: Women in international perspective*. London: Routledge.

Prins, B. (2006). Narrative accounts of origins: A blind spot in the intersectional approach. *European Journal of Women's Studies, 13*(3), 277–290.

Probyn, E. (2004). Shame in the habitus. *Sociological Review, 52*(2), 224–248.

Rabinow, P., & Rose, N. (2003). Introduction: Foucault today. In P. Rabinow & N. Rose, (Eds.), *The essential Foucault: Selections from essential works of Foucault, 1954–1984* (pp. vii–xxxv). New York, NY: The New Press.

Ramanathapillai, R. (2006). The politicizing of trauma: A case study of Sri Lanka. *Peace and Conflict: Journal of Peace Psychology, 12*, 1–18.

Rattansi, A., & Phoenix, A. (2005). Rethinking youth identities: Modernist and postmodernist frameworks. *Identity: An International Journal of Theory and Research, 5*(2), 97–123.

Reddy, W. M. (1997). Against constructionism. *Current Anthropology, 38*, 327–340.

Retzinger, S. M. (1991). *Violent emotions*. Newbury Park, CA: Sage.

Retzinger, S., & Scheff, T. (2000). Emotion, alienation, and narratives: Resolving intractable conflict. *Mediation Quarterly, 18*, 71–85.

Riggs, D., & Augoustinos, M. (2005). The psychic life of colonial power: Racialized subjectivities, bodies, and methods. *Journal of Community and Applied Social Psychology, 15*, 461–477.

Robin, C. (2004). *Fear: The history of a political idea*. New York, NY: Oxford University Press.

Roginsky, D. (2006). Nationalism and ambivalence: Ethnicity, gender and folklore as categories of otherness. *Patterns of Prejudice, 40*(3), 237–258.

Rosaldo, R. (1989/1984). Grief and a headhunter's rage. In *Culture and truth: The remaking of social analysis* (pp. 1–21). Boston, MA: Beacon.

Rose, G. (1993). *Feminism and geography: The limits of geographical knowledge*. Minneapolis, MN: University of Minnesota Press.

Rose, N. (1998). *Inventing ourselves: Psychology, power, and personhood*. Cambridge: Cambridge University Press.

Rose, N. (1999). *Powers of freedom: Reframing political thought*. Cambridge: Cambridge University Press.

Rosenblum, P. (2002). Teaching human rights: Ambivalent activism, multiple discourses and lingering dilemmas. *Harvard Human Rights Journal, 15*, 301–315.

Ross, A. (2007). Multiple identities and education for active citizenship. *British Journal of Educational Studies, 55*(3), 286–303.

Ruitenberg, C. W. (2009). Educating political adversaries: Chantal Mouffe and radical democratic citizenship education. *Studies in Philosophy and Education, 28*, 269–281.

Ruitenberg, C. W. (2010). Conflict, affect and the political: On disagreement as democratic capacity. *In Factis Pax, 4*(1), 40–55.

Salomon, G. (2002). The nature of peace education: Not all programs are created equal. In G. Salomon & B. Nevo (Eds.), *Peace education: The concept, principles, and practices around the world* (pp. 3–36). Mahwah, NJ: Lawrence Erlbaum.

Salomon, G., & Nevo, B. (Eds.). (2002). *Peace education: The concept, principles, and practices around the world*. Mahwah, NJ: Lawrence Erlbaum.

Sant Cassia, P. (2005). *Bodies of evidence: Burial, memory and the recovery of missing persons in Cyprus*. New York, NY: Berghahn.

Schaap, A. (2004). Political reconciliation through a struggle for recognition. *Social and Legal Studies, 13*(4), 523–540.

Schaap, A. (2006). Agonism in divided societies. *Philosophy & Social Criticism, 32*(2), 255–277.

Scheff, T. J. (1992). Emotions and identity: A theory of ethnic nationalism. In C. Calhoun (Ed.), *Social theory and the politics of identity* (pp. 277–303). Oxford:Blackwell.

Scheff, T. J. (1994). *Bloody revenge: Emotions, nationalism and war*. Boulder, CO: Westview Press.

Scheff, T. J., & Retzinger, S. (1991). *Emotions and violence: Shame and rage in destructive conflicts*. Lexington, MA: Lexington Books.

Schutz, P., & Zembylas, M. (Eds.). (2009). *Advances in teacher emotion research: The impact on teachers' lives*. Dordrecht, The Netherlands: Springer.

Seibel Trainor, J. (2002). Critical pedagogy's "other": Constructions of whiteness in education for social change. *College Composition and Communication, 53*(4), 631–650.

Sharoni, S. (2006). Compassionate resistance: A personal/political journey to Israel/Palestine. *International Feminist Journal of Politics, 8*(2), 288–299.

Shircliffe, B. (2001). "We got the best of that world": A case for the study of nostalgia in the oral history of school segregation. *Oral History Review, 28*(2), 59–84.

Sibley, D. (1995). *Geographies of exclusion*. London, UK, and New York, NY: Routledge.

Simon, R. (2011a). Afterword: The turn to pedagogy: A needed conversation on the practice of curating difficult knowledge. In E. Lehrer & C. Milton (Eds.), *Curating difficult knowledge* (pp. 193–209). London: Palgrave Macmillan.

Simon, R. (2011b). A shock to thought: Curatorial judgment and the public exhibition of "difficult knowledge." *Memory Studies, 49*(4), 432–449.

Simon, R., Rosenberg, S., & Eppert, C. (Eds.). (2000). *Beyond hope and despair: Pedagogy and the representation of historical trauma*. Totowa, NJ: Rowman and Littlefield.

Smith, A. (2004). *The antiquity of nations*. Cambridge: Polity.

Smith, A. (2005). Education in the twenty-first century: conflict, reconstruction and reconciliation. *Compare, 35*(4), 373–391.
Smith, D. (2006). *Globalization: The hidden agenda*. Cambridge: Polity.
Soja, E. (1989). *Postmodern geographies: The reassertion of space in critical social theory*. New York, NY: Verso.
Soja, E. (1996). *Thirdspace: Journeys to Los Angeles and other real and imagined places*. Cambridge: Blackwell.
Solomon, R. (1990). *A passion for justice*. Reading, MA: Addison-Wesley.
Soysal, Y. N. (1994). *Limits of citizenship: Migrants and postnational membership in Europe*. Chicago, IL: The University of Chicago Press.
Spyrou, S. (2002). Images of "the other": The Turk in Greek Cypriot children's imaginations. *Race, Ethnicity and Education, 5*, 255–272.
Spyrou, S. (2006). Constructing "the Turk" as an enemy: The complexity of stereotypes in children's everyday worlds. *South European Society and Politics, 11*, 95–110.
Spyrou, S. (2009). Between intimacy and intolerance: Greek-Cypriot children's encounters with Asian domestic workers. *Childhood, 16*(2), 155–173.
Srivastava, S. (2005). "You're calling me a racist?" The moral and emotional regulation of antiracism and feminism. *Signs: Journal of Women in Culture and Society, 31*, 29–62.
Srivastava, S. (2006). Tears, fears and careers: Anti-racism and emotion in social movement organizations. *Canadian Journal of Sociology, 31*, 55–90.
Statistical Service of the Republic of Cyprus. (2011). *Demographic report*. Nicosia, Cyprus Statistical Services.
Stake, R. E. (1995). *The art of case study research*. Thousand Oaks, CA: Sage.
Staub, E. (2000). Genocide and mass killing: Origins, prevention, healing and reconciliation. *Political Psychology, 21*(2), 367–382.
Staub, E. (2003). Notes on cultures of violence, cultures of caring and peace, and the fulfilment of basic human needs. *Political Psychology, 24*(1), 1–21.
Steiner-Khamsi, G. (2003). Cultural recognition or social redistribution: Predicaments of minority education. In Y. Iram (Ed.), *Education of minorities and peace education in pluralistic societies* (pp. 15–28). Ramat-Gan, Israel: Bar Ilan University.
Stenberg, S. (2011). Teaching and (re)learning the rhetoric of emotion. *Pedagogy: Critical Approaches to Teaching Literature, Composition and Culture, 11*(2), 349–369.
Stevens, P. (2007). Researching race/ethnicity and educational inequality in English secondary schools: A critical review of the research literature between 1980 and 2005. *Review of Educational Research, 77*(2), 147–185.
Stevens, P. (2008). Exploring pupils' perceptions of teacher racism in their context: A case study of Turkish and Belgian vocational education pupils in a Belgian school. *British Journal of Sociology of Education, 29*(2), 175–187.
Stewart, S. (1984). *On longing: Narratives of the miniature, the gigantic, the souvenir, the collection*. Baltimore, MD: Johns Hopkins University Press.

Stoler, A. (1995). *Race and the education of desire: Foucault's history of sexuality and the colonial order of things*. Durham, NC: Duke University Press.

St. Pierre, E., & Pillow, W. (Eds.). (2000). *Working the ruins: Feminist poststructural theory and methods in education*. London: Routledge.

Strauss, A., & Corbin, J. (1994). Grounded theory methodology: An overview. In N. K. Denzin & Y. S. Lincoln (Eds.), *Handbook of qualitative research* (pp. 273–285). Thousand Oaks, CA: Sage.

Sturdy, A. (2003). Knowing the unknowable? A discussion of methodological and theoretical issues in emotion research and organizational studies. *Organization, 10*, 81–105.

Suga, K. (2006). *Echos-Monde* and abrasions: Translation as a form of dialogue. *Social Identities, 12*, 17–28.

Svašek, M. (Ed.). (2008). *Postsocialism: Politics and emotions in central and eastern Europe*. New York, NY: Berghahn.

Svašek, M. (2010). On the move: Emotions and human mobility. *Journal of Ethnic and Migration Studies, 36*(6), 865–880.

Tajfel, H. (1978). *Differentiation between social groups: Studies in the social psychology of intergroup relations*. London: Academic Press.

Tajfel, H., & Turner, J. (1979). An integrative theory of intergroup conflict. In W. G. Austin & S. Worchel (Eds.), *The social psychology of intergroup relations* (pp. 33–47). Monterey, CA: Brooks/Cole.

Tajfel, H., & Turner, J. (1986). The social identity theory of intergroup behavior. In S. Worchel & L. W. Austin (Eds.), *Psychology of intergroup relations* (pp. 2–24). Chicago, IL: Nelson-Hall.

Tannock, S. (1995). Nostalgia critique. *Cultural Studies, 9*(3), 453–464.

Tate, W. F. (1997). Critical race theory and education: History, theory and implications. In M. W. Apple (Ed.), *Review of research in education* (vol. 22, pp. 195–247). Washington, DC: American Educational Research Association.

Taylor, E., Gillborn, D., & Ladson-Billings, G. (Eds.). (2009). *Foundations of critical race theory in education*. London: Routledge.

Tedeshi, R., & Calhoun, L. (1995). *Trauma and transformation: Growing in the aftermath of suffering.* Thousand Oaks, CA: Sage.

Tedeshi, R., & Calhoun, L. (2004). Posttraumatic growth: Conceptual foundations and empirical evidence. *Psychological Inquiry, 15*(1), 1–18.

Terdiman, R. (1993). *Present past: Modernity and the memory crisis.* Ithaca, NY: Cornell University Press.

Tibbitts, F. (2002). Understanding what we do: Emerging models for human rights education. *International Review of Education, 48*(3), 159–171.

Throop, J. C. (2008). On the problem of empathy: The case of Yap, Federated States of Micronesia. *Ethos, 36*(4), 402–426.

Throop, J. C. (2010). Latitudes of loss: On the vicissitudes of empathy. *American Ethnologist, 37*(4), 771–782.

Trifonas, P., & Wright, B. (Eds.). (2013). *Critical peace education: Difficult dialogues*. Dordrecht, The Netherlands: Springer.

Trimikliniotis, N. (2004). Mapping discriminatory landscapes in Cyprus: Ethnic discrimination in a divided education system. *The Cyprus Review, 16*(1), 53–86.

Trimikliniotis, N., & Demetriou, C. (2006). *The primary education of the Roma/Gypsies: Anti-discrimination and multiculturalism as a post-accession challenge for Cyprus*. Nicosia: Reconciliation Research and Policy Paper.

Trimikliniotis, N., & Demetriou, C. (2009). The Cypriot Roma and the failure of education: Anti-discrimination and multiculturalism as a post-accession challenge. In N. Coureas, & A. Varnava, (Eds.), *The minorities of Cyprus: Development patterns and the identity of the internal-exclusion* (pp. 241–264). Cambridge: Cambridge Scholars Publishing.

Troyna, B., & Hatcher, R. (1992). *Racism in children's lives: A study of mainly-white primary schools*. London: Routledge.

Troyna, B., & Williams, J. (1986). *Racism, education and the state*. Beckenham, UK: Croom Helm.

Turner, J. (1991). *Social influence*. Milton Keynes, UK: Open University Press.

Turner, V. (1978). Foreword. In B. Mayerhoff, *Number our days* (pp. xiii–xvii). New York, NY: Touchstone.

Valentine, G. (2007). Theorizing and researching intersectionality: A challenge for feminist geography. *The Professional Geographer, 59*(1), 10–21.

Van Ausdale, D., & Feagin, J. (2001). *The first R: How children learn race and racism*. Lanham, MD: Rowman and Littlefield.

Vandeyar, S., & Esakov, H. (2007). Color coded: How well do students of different race groups interact in South African schools? In Z. Bekerman & C. McGlynn (Eds.), *Addressing ethnic conflict through peace education: International perspectives* (pp. 63–76). New York, NY: Palgrave Macmillan.

Van Sledright, B. (2008). Narratives of nation-state, historical knowledge, and school history education. *Review of Research in Education, 32*(1), 109–146.

Varnava. A., & Faustman, H. (Eds.). (2009). Reunifying Cyprus: The Annan Plan and beyond. London: I. B. Tauris.

Vaught, S. E., & Castagno, A. E. (2008). "I don't think I'm racist": Critical race theory, teacher attitudes, and structural racism. *Race Ethnicity and Education, 11*(2), 95–113.

Venn, C. (2005). The repetition of violence: Dialogue, the exchange of memory, and the question of convivial socialities. *Social Identities, 11*, 283–298.

Venn, C. (2010). Individuation, relationality, affect: Rethinking the human in relation to the living. *Body & Society, 16*(1), 129–161.

Vlieghe, J. (2010). Judith Butler and the public dimension of the body: Education, critique and corporeal vulnerability. *Journal of Philosophy of Education, 44*(1), 153–170.

Volkan, V. (1979). *Cyprus: War and adaptation*. Charlottesville, VA: University Press of Virginia.

Volkan, V. D., & Itzkowitz, N. (1994). *Turks and Greeks: Neighbors in conflict.* Huntingdon, UK: Eothen Press.

Walder, D. (2009). Writing, representation and postcolonial nostalgia. *Textual Practice, 23*(6), 935–946.

White, P. (2002). What should we teach children about forgiveness? *Journal of Philosophy of Education, 36*(1), 57–67.

Wikan, U. (1992). Beyond the worlds: The power of resonance. *American Ethnologist, 19*(3), 460–482.

Williams, R. (1977). *Marxism and literature.* Oxford and New York: Oxford University Press.

Williams, M. S. (2003). Citizenship as identity, citizenship as shared fate, and the functions of multicultural education. In K. McDonough & W. Feinberg (Eds.), *Citizenship and education in liberal-democratic societies* (pp. 208–247). Oxford: Oxford University Press.

Williams, M. S. (2009). Citizenship as agency within communities of shared fate. In S. Bernstein & W. Coleman (Ed.), *Political community, power, and authority in a global age: Unsettled legitimacy* (pp. 33–52). Vancouver, BC: University of British Columbia Press.

Woodward, K. (2002). *Understanding identity.* London: Arnold.

Woodward, K. (2004). Calculating compassion. In L. Berlant (Ed.), *Compassion: The culture and politics of an emotion* (pp. 59–86). New York, NY: Routledge.

Worsham, L. (2001). Going postal: Pedagogic violence and the schooling of emotion. In H. Giroux & K. Myrisides (Eds.), *Beyond the corporate university* (pp. 229–265). New York, NY: Rowman & Littlefield.

Worsham, L. (2006). Composing (identity) in a posttraumatic age. In B. T. Williams (Ed.), *Identity papers: Literacy and power in higher education* (pp. 170–181). Logan: UT, State University Press.

Wulf, C. (1974). *Handbook of peace education.* Frankfurt: Internal Peace Research Association.

Yoon, K. H. (2005). Affecting the transformative intellectual: Questioning “noble” sentiments in critical pedagogy and composition. *JAC: A Journal of Rhetoric, Culture & Politics, 25*(4), 717–759.

Youdell, D. (2006). *Impossible bodies, impossible selves: Exclusions and student subjectivities.* Dordrecht, The Netherlands: Springer.

Zembylas, M. (2005). *Teaching with emotion: A postmodern enactment.* Greenwich, CT: Information Age Publishing.

Zembylas, M. (2007a). *Five pedagogies, a thousand possibilities: Struggling for hope and transformation in education.* Rotterdam, The Netherlands: SensePublishers.

Zembylas, M. (2007b). Theory and methodology in researching emotions in education. *International Journal of Research & Method in Education, 30,* 57–72.

Zembylas, M. (2008a). *The politics of trauma in education.* New York, NY: Palgrave Macmillan.

Zembylas, M. (2008b). Trauma, justice and the politics of emotion: The violence of sentimentality in education. *Discourse: Studies in the Cultural Politics of Education, 29*(1), 1–17.

Zembylas, M. (2009a). Counter-narratives of mourning the missing persons in Cyprus: Pedagogical limits and openings for reconciliation education in conflict-ridden societies. *Perspectives in Education, 29*(2), 120–132.

Zembylas, M. (2009b). Global economies of fear: Affect, politics and pedagogical implications. *Critical Studies in Education, 50*(2), 187–199.

Zembylas, M. (2009c). Making sense of traumatic events. Towards a politics of aporetic mourning in educational theory and pedagogy. *Educational Theory, 59*(1), 85–104.

Zembylas, M. (2010a). Critical discourse analysis of multiculturalism and intercultural education policies in the Republic of Cyprus. *The Cyprus Review, 22*(1), 39–59.

Zembylas, M. (2010b). Pedagogic struggles to enhance inclusion and reconciliation in a divided community. *Ethnography and Education, 5*, 277–292.

Zembylas, M. (2011). Mourning and forgiveness as sites of reconciliation pedagogies. *Journal of Bioethical Inquiry, 8*(3), 257–265.

Zembylas, M. (2012a). Pedagogies of strategic empathy: Navigating through the emotional complexities of antiracism in higher education. *Teaching in Higher Education, 17*(2), 113–125.

Zembylas, M. (2012b). The politics of fear and empathy: Emotional ambivalence in "host" children and youth's discourses about migrants in Cyprus. *Intercultural Education, 23*(3), 195–208.

Zembylas, M. (2012c). Suffering, memory and forgiveness: Derrida, Levinas and the pedagogical challenges of reconciliation in Cyprus. In P. Ahluwalia, S. Atkinson, P. Bishop, P. Christie, R. Hattam, & J. Matthews (Eds.), *Reconciliation and pedagogy* (pp. 45–64). New York, NY: Routledge.

Zembylas, M. (2013a). Integrated schooling in divided Cyprus: Impossible or indispensible? *Studies in Ethnicity and Nationalism, 13*(3), 442–454.

Zembylas, M. (2013b). The "crisis of pity" and the radicalization of solidarity: Towards critical pedagogies of compassion. *Educational Studies: A Journal of the American Educational Studies Association, 49*, 504–521.

Zembylas, M. (2013c). Memorial ceremonies in schools: analyzing the entanglement of emotions and power. *Journal of Political Power, 6*(3), 477–493.

Zembylas, M. (2014a). Affective citizenship in multicultural societies: Implications for critical citizenship education. *Citizenship Teaching & Learning, 9*(1), 5–18.

Zembylas, M. (2014b). Affective, political and ethical sensibilities in pedagogies of critical hope: Exploring the notion of "critical emotional praxis." In V. Bozalek, B. Leibowitz, R. Carolissen, & M. Boler (Eds.), *Discerning critical hope in educational practices* (pp. 11–25). New York, NY: Routledge.

Zembylas, M., & Bekerman, Z. (2013). Peace education in the present: Dismantling and reconstructing some fundamental theoretical premises. *Journal of Peace Education, 10*(2), 197–214.

Zembylas, M., & Chubbuck, S. (2012). Growing immigration and multiculturalism in Europe: Teachers' emotions and the prospects of social justice education. In C. Day (Ed.), The Routledge *international handbook of teacher and school development* (pp. 139–148). New York, NY: Routledge.

Zembylas, M., & Iasonos, S. (2010). Leadership styles and multicultural education approaches: An exploration of their relationship. *International Journal of Leadership in Education, 13*(2), 163–183.

Zembylas, M., & McGlynn, C. (2012). Discomforting pedagogies: Emotional tensions, ethical dilemmas and transformative possibilities. *British Educational Research Journal, 38*(1), 41–60.

Zembylas, M., Charalambous, P., & Charalambous, C. (2012). Manifestations of Greek-Cypriot teachers' discomfort toward a peace education initiative: Engaging with discomfort pedagogically. *Teaching & Teacher Education, 28*, 1071–1082.

Zembylas, M., & Michaelidou, A. (2011). Teachers' understandings of forgiveness in a troubled society: An empirical exploration and implications for forgiveness pedagogies. *Pedagogies, 6*(3), 250–264.

Zembylas, M., Charalambous, C., Charalambous, P., & Kendeou, P. (2011). Promoting peaceful coexistence in conflict-ridden Cyprus: Teachers' difficulties and emotions towards a new policy initiative. *Teaching & Teacher Education, 27*(2), 332–341.

Zetter, R. (1991). Labeling refugees: Forming and transforming a bureaucratic identity. *Journal of Refugee Studies, 4*(1), 39–62.

Zetter, R. (1994). The Greek-Cypriot refugees: Perceptions of return under conditions of protracted exile. *International Migration Review, 28*(2), 307–322.

Zetter, R. (1999). Reconceptualizing the myth of return: Continuity and transition amongst the Greek-Cypriot refugees of 1974. *Journal of Refugee Studies, 12*(1), 1–22.

Zinner, E. S., & Williams, M. B. (1999). *When a community weeps: Case studies in group survivorship.* London: Brunner/Mazel.

INDEX